THE COMPLETE ENCYCLOPEDIA OF
TRACTORS

THE COMPLETE ENCYCLOPEDIA OF

TRACTORS

MIRCO DE CET

REBO
PUBLISHERS

© 2006 Rebo Productions, Lisse, The Netherlands

This edition printed in 2011.

www.rebo-publishers.com
info@rebo-publishers.com

Text: Mirco De Cet
Cover design: Minkowsky Graphics, Enkhuizen, The Netherlands
Layout: Richard Saunders, Bacroom Design, Birmingham, Great Britain
Pre-press services: www.christinelee.cz

ISBN: 978 90 366 1893 9

Contents

Tractors –
An Introduction

The first plows were drawn or pushed by men. Later, bullocks and horses were harnessed for their 'brute force,' and for centuries these animals proved the

With the onset of the First World War, and short-handedness on many farms, the demand for farm machinery increased. Enter Henry Ford, who employed production line methods to manufacture his Fordson tractor on a huge scale, as he did with his Model T. The Fordson was the first tractor available to farmers of average means. Its introduction in 1917 would help to provide food for millions of people,

Laborers take time out from harvesting for a photograph–no mechanization here, note the real horse power.

mainstay of working life on the farm. But by the late nineteenth century, the days of animal power were numbered: the first crude machines–harvesters and balers–had made their appearance, revolutionizing farm work and changing country life forever. These steam-driven contraptions were used to power stationary machines via connecting belts. However it wasn't long before such engines were mounted on wheels or tracks and became self-propelled. The ancestors of the modern tractor were born.

The first gasoline-powered farm vehicle was built in the USA. In 1892 John Froelich constructed a machine mounted with a gasoline engine made by the Van Duzen Gas and Gasoline Engine Co. of Cincinnati. (Froelich's Waterloo Gasoline Traction Engine Company would later become the John Deere Tractor Company–one of today's biggest tractor suppliers.) Although this model and the ones that followed were not exactly popular, the development of the tractor had begun in earnest. Engines improved, and the tractor (a name coined in 1906 by a salesman for the Hart-Parr company) began to be seen with increasing frequency on the farm.

A large belt from a steam traction engine could be used to work all the parts of the threshing machine as shown here.

Fordson model F, a real success when launched in 1917. It became the machine to be copied but was rarely bettered.

which in turn improved standards of living beyond anything imaginable before.

By 1930, in spite of the growing Depression, more than 900,000 tractors were in use on US farms–nearly double the number of five years before! These machines were now in use across Europe and communist Russia, but the main innovations continued to be made in the USA. In 1930 the Case Company presented its innovatory Model DD. This had three wheels instead of four–making the cultivation of row-crops easier–and was adaptable enough to take on the role of general-purpose agricultural machine. Soon afterwards came another improvement to farm vehicles: rubber tires, which gave farmers a smoother ride whilst increasing both speed and productivity.

The basic three-wheeled form of 1930s' tractors was to persist for another 30 years, despite oddities like the Minneapolis-Moline 'Comfortractor.' This boasted a streamlined motorcar-style body and bonnet, the idea being that the farmer could not only use it for work, but could take his family in it for jaunts to town!

Several companies contributed machinery to the war effort during World War II, and afterwards the industry continued to improve its products. Lighting was fitted, ignition was introduced, and transmission became more sophisticated. Power steering and many other modern requirements were supplied, even down

One of the most successful tractors in the International Harvester range was the Farmall–a totally new design, ideal for rowcrop duties.

The Massey-Ferguson 7480 of 2005. It uses a six- cylinder, Perkins diesel engine and has all the latest techno-goodies.

to padding of the driver's seat. It wasn't long before turbo-charged diesel engines began to replace the now aging petrol-powered units, and designers started looking at further ways of making farm labor more efficient and economical.

Today's machines, and the implements that go with them, are so sophisticated and full of gadgets that it might seem you need a degree in mechanical science even to step into a tractor cab. Computers now control most of the functions. Equipment such as the HydraMaxx front-axle suspension and the AirMaxx pneumatic cab suspension make tractors more stable and comfortable both on and off the field. Insulation ensures that interior sound levels can be as low as

71 decibels, while the modern cab also has features such as climate control and power-adjustable mirrors. As with all computer-reliant machinery, modern tractors come at a hefty price. Today a mid-range model can cost anything between $59,895 and $118,934, depending on specification. But for the modern farmer, a good tractor is an absolute necessity. In developed countries, competition is such that the farmer would be lost without this sophisticated mechanical 'workhorse.' Tractors, which once transformed the nature of farming itself, are now an essential aid in the constant struggle to bring food to the world's tables.

The Caterpillar company gained its name from the type of vehicle it produced and the way it moved.

One of the most modern cabs around, the Caterpillar operators workspace is stacked with hi-tech instrumentation.

A

Advance-Rumely

1853-1931

Meinrad Rumely was born in Baden, Germany, in 1823. He left for the USA in 1848, having been pistol-whipped in the German army because he was standing out of line during inspection. He and his brother Jacob first set up a blacksmith's shop and foundry in LaPorte, Indiana. In 1853 they formed the M&J Rumely Company, and in 1859 the Rumely separator won First Prize at the US Fair in Chicago. The company then produced steel threshers until the introduction of its first portable steam engine in 1872.

Meinrad bought his brother out in 1882, and the company made its first name change, becoming simply the M. Rumely Company. A few years later in 1886, the company produced its first traction engine. This engine burned straw, the heat turning water into steam to produce steam power. The company grew rapidly and by 1896 it was producing an extensive line of steam tractors, portable steam engines and separators.When Meinrad died in 1904 at the age of 79, new management took over at Rumely. Meinrad's sons Joseph and William were the most active of Meinrad's nine children, and Joseph's eldest son Edward, who was born in 1882, also took a great interest in the family business. After several years of college in the USA, England and Germany, he returned to LaPorte and took an active role in management. Strongly influenced by Rudolf Diesel, he came up with the idea of producing reliable farm tractors using the internal combustion engine.

He knew of a man named John Secor in New York City, who had been experimenting with the internal combustion engine since 1885. Secor subjected the engines to tests that determined how to get maximum power out of minimal fuel. Edward managed to get him to move to LaPorte, and in 1908 they began to build the OilPull tractor.

'Kerosene Annie,' which would later become the 25-45 Model B, was built as a prototype. By October 1909, testing of the tractor was complete. The new tractor plant in LaPorte opened on February 21,

Made through to the 1920s, this is the OilPull from Advance-Rumely. The chimney at the front sat over an oil-cooled radiator.

An advertisement of the period. These machines would get smaller and more manageable as time went on.

Only in production for three years, the DoAll was made to compete in the small tractor market.

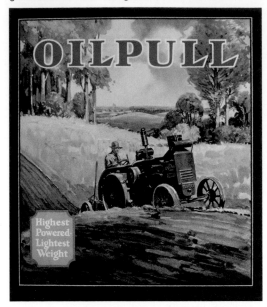

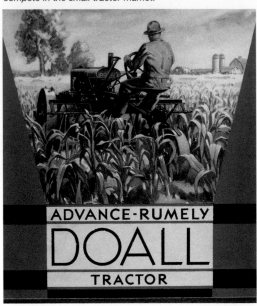

1910, and by November that year the first 100 OilPull tractors had been built. The Model B was followed by the bigger Model E 30-60, and later by the Model F 15-30 single-cylinder tractor. (This was Rumely's only single-cylinder model, all the others having two cylinders.) The company still made steam tractors, though gas was now becoming more popular.

Rumely merged with the Advance Thresher Company in 1911, although it wasn't until 1915 that the name of the firm changed to Advance-Rumely. Advance-Rumely made tractors of three main types: heavyweights, lightweights and super-lightweights. The company attempted to enter the market for smaller tractors with the DoAll and the 6A, but by now the market had moved on and competition was stiff. On 1 June 1931, Allis-Chalmers bought out Advance-Rumely and tractor production was discontinued.

These huge Oil Pull machines were soon seen as large and clumsy and were replaced by smaller models.

AGCO

1990-present

Able to carry large loads, this AGCO Allis 8630 was built for the company by the Italian SLH group.

Although AGCO has roots that can be traced back to the mid-nineteenth century, it is relatively new to tractor production. Its history in this sector can be traced through the acquisition of major companies that played a significant part in the evolution of farming machinery.

In 1985 Allis-Chalmers was purchased by the German company Deutz. Deutz closed down the

Although painted in the Allis Chalmers orange color, this is the AGCO 6690 front loader.

Allis-Chalmers factory and started exporting its own tractors to the USA under the Deutz-Allis name. At first intent on building its own tractors in the USA, Deutz changed its mind and contracted the White company to build for it, using Deutz air-cooled diesel engines. This project was short-lived: within a year the US Deutz-Allis management bought itself out and AGCO was born (Allis-Gleaner Co.). The company continued the relationship with White, fitting the Deutz engine to the American chassis, though now the tractors were named AGCO-Allis and painted Allis orange rather than Deutz green.

The following years saw a frenzy of purchases. In 1991 AGCO purchased the Hesston Corporation, a leading American brand of hay tools, along with a 50

This is the two-wheel-drive 5670. AGCO Allis also offered more powerful four-wheel-drive models.

Made between 1994 and 1995, the AGCO Allis 9650 used a six-cylinder, Deutz, turbo-diesel engine.

At over US$100,000 when new in 1994, the AGCO Allis 9690 used the Deutz, six-cylinder turbo engine.

The AGCOSTAR 8425 features the N14 Cummins engine, and has 18 forward and 2 reverse speed transmission.

percent stake in a manufacturing joint venture with Case International, known as Hay and Forage Industries (HFI). This year it also purchased the White tractor business from Allied Products, an important step which gave the company its first tractor-making facility.

In 1992, the company presented a range of 15 tractors of which 12 were painted orange, having been made for AGCO by SLH in Italy. These machines had AGCO-Allis badges, while the remainder were painted silver and bore the White badge. The range consisted of the 4650 and 4660 utility tractors, the mid-range 6670 and 6680 models, the bigger 7600 series, and the 8600 range.

The following year the company offered half its stock to be listed on the NASDAQ exchange, and in 1994, under the symbol 'AG', it was listed on the New York stock exchange. In 1993 AGCO purchased the White-New Idea business of planters, hay tools and spreaders along with the Coldwater, Ohio, manufacturing facility. It also purchased the US distribution rights to Massey-Ferguson products, expanding the AGCO US dealer network by over a thousand.

The remainder of the Massey-Ferguson world-wide holdings was snapped up in 1994, ensuring AGCO global status. McConnell Tractors was also bought, leading to the development of the AGCOSTAR articulated tractor line and Black Machine which gave the company a unique planter-frame line. In 1995 AGCO purchased the AgEquipment Group, makers of Glencoe tire and farmhand agricultural implements and tillage equipment.

By now the Deutz air-cooled engines were being slowly phased out as the company turned to the Detroit Diesel 40 series engines, which would power the top-end machines. In 1996 the Deutz diesel era came to an end.

This was an extremely busy year with the acquisition of the Iochpe-Mexion agricultural equipment company in Brazil, Deutz in Argentina, and the Western Combine Corporation and Portage Manufacturing Inc. in Canada. The following year AGCO acquired Fendt GmbH, a leading German tractor business, while in 1998 a joint venture was created with Deutz AG to produce engines in Argentina. Spra-Coupe and Willmar, leading companies in the agricultural sprayer market, were also purchased and merged in one manufacturing plant in Willmar, Minnesota.

By the year 2000, AGCO had completed its purchase of HFI, solidifying its planned strategy to achieve efficient manufacturing by consolidating its major operations in the USA. The following year the Ag-Chem Equipment company, a leading manufacturer and distributor of

AGCO took White over in the early 1990s. This is a product of that take-over, a six-cylinder Cummins, turbo-diesel.

specialized off-road, heavy equipment for agricultural and industrial applications, was purchased. This made AGCO the leader in the self-propelled sprayer market. In 2002 the company purchased Caterpillar's agricultural equipment business–primarily the design, assembly and marketing of its Challenger tractors. Later that year the acquisition of the Sunflower Manufacturing Company Inc., a leading producer of tillage, seeding and speciality harvesting equipment, was completed.

By 2003, AGCO could boast sales of tractors in 140 countries and under 18 different brand names. Now there was a tractor with just the AGCO name on it too, even though many of the machines look very similar and are basically just re-badged. Fendt Vario

The Spra-Coupe is a high clearance, high performance, rowcrop sprayer.

With tracks, the load is spread over a bigger area than with conventional tires. The Challenger MT765 uses rubber tracks.

produced three models of the company's fully automatic transmission line: the 400, 700 and 900.

In 2004 the Valtra Corporation, a global tractor and off-road engine manufacturer with market leadership in the Nordic region of Europe and South America, was purchased. This acquisition included SISU Diesel, which produces off-road diesel engines.

Despite AGCO's amazing history of purchases, not everything was well on the farm. Two US plants were shut down at the beginning of 2000, and the capacity of the Massey-Ferguson plant in Coventry, UK, was severely reduced in 2003. No company, however big, is entirely immune to the effects of an economic downturn.

Albaugh-Dover

1917-1925

In 1916 the American mailing house Albaugh-Dover took over the Kenny-Colwell Company from Norfolk, Nebraska, USA. Kenny-Colwell had previously announced a new tractor under its brand name. In 1917 the Square Turn Tractor Company was formed out of the Kenny-Colwell Company. One of the major complaints against the large steam and Oilpull tractors was their wide turning radius. The Square Turn 18-35 model, on the other hand, could turn around within its own length. It was powered by a four-cylinder Climax engine, while a

The Albaugh-Dover company produced the Square Turn Tractor, notorious for its very tight turning circle.

three-bottom Oliver plow came as standard equipment. However, despite its innovatory design, it seems the tractor never really became popular. The Square Turn Tractor company, which was still under the corporate umbrella of Albaugh-Dover, was sold at a sheriff's sale in 1925.

Allgaier-Porsche

1937-1963

PORSCHE DIESEL In 1937, Ferdinand Porsche received word from Adolf Hitler to design not only the 'people's car' (Volkswagen) but also a 'people's tractor' (Volk-schlepper). By 1938 he had designed model type 110 and a further model 111 followed. These used Porsche air-cooled gasoline engines. There were plans now for a factory for the construction of the tractors in Waldbroel. During 1940/41 the next model was designed, the type 112, which came in several different versions. For 1943 yet another new type, the 113, which had a larger engine and four gears instead of the three used in the previous models.

The war intervened but design continued post-war and a new model 312, with a 20hp engine was on the drawing board.

Small, reliable agricultural machinery was produced prior to taking on the manufacturing of the Porsche product.

By 1948 a type 313, with two-cylinder engine had been designed and by the end of 1949 an agreement was struck up with the Allgaier family business from Swabia, to produce these tractors. Allgaier had started building small but durable agricultural machinery after the war.

By 1950 the new type 313 Porsche tractor was ready for production by the Allgaier company. It would be designated the AP17 (Allgaier Porsche). This machine produced 18hp and had ultra-modern features such as lightweight metal construction and

The familiar Allgaier machine became very popular and production moved to Friedrichshafen in southern Germany.

an air-cooled, two-cylinder diesel engine and sold for about 4,500 Deutchmarks. The demand was so great for this model that Erwin Allgaier, with assistance from the State, acquired the old Dornier works in Friedrichshafen to extend the production facilities. In 1951 the 5000th tractor of this version rolled off the production line and in 1952 the model

AP22 was presented, which produced 22hp. The AP17 was also given the bigger engine. For 1953 a new series of models were presented, the A111, A122, A133 and A144, all using interchangeable engine units such as the pistons, cylinders and cylinder heads. Export sales at this time were good too, with a special narrow wheel tractor, based on the AP17/AP22S, with diesel engine, which was a special export to Brazil. Times were hard though and the Friedrichshafen factory was given up by Allgaier due to low sales. The factory was taken over by Mannesmann, who continued to make two of the models, but soon the badging was also changed to Porsche Diesel. The AP16 was replaced by the AP18 and production started to pick up once again. New premises were acquired and the Porsche Diesel started to be manufactured in large numbers. The marketing structure was changed and engines were made more powerful, all of which went to increase sales both in Germany and abroad. 1957 saw new machines, Junior, Standard and Super come onto the market, with the Masters model to follow. The year 1959 saw a drastic reduction in the pricing of the Junior and Standard models, now designated Junior V and Standard V. For 1960 there were changes in bore from 95mm to 98mm, the injection system was

This is the single-cylinder Junior model and the smallest of the Porsche range, now taken over by Mannesmann.

modified slightly and a general increase of engine performance was achieved. An extra model, the Standard T, was added to the line-up but in 1961 the production of tractors was moved to the Porsche Diesel Engines GmbH factory. Production came to an end and a new company was formed with Renault to supply spare parts for the new models. Some 12,000 tractors with the Porsche name on them were sold, with the factories finally being sold to Daimler-Benz.

The Porsche-Diesel model came with a choice of engines ranging from one to three cylinders.

The tractors now bore the Porsche-Diesel name. Seen here is the engine of the Junior model.

Allis-Chalmers

1901-1985

By 1979, Allis-Chalmers had grown into a corporation worth two billion US dollars and become one of the most important machinery manufacturers in the USA. But its origins were humble. Its roots lie in Edward P. Allis & Company, which was founded by E. P. Allis of New York following his acquisition of Reliance Works. This had collapsed during the financial panic of 1857. The Reliance Works' list of products included millstones, portable mills, water wheels, shafting, and hoisting screws.

In 1869 the new company expanded into steam power, and it wasn't long before the first Allis steam engine made its debut. The line-up grew to include steam pumps (one of which was the largest centrifugal pump in the USA), and the first triple expansion pumping engine. By now the company had moved into the West Allis works, where tractors were made until 1985.

Edward Allis died in 1889, but the company continued to manufacture machinery under the supervision of Edwin Reynolds, a steam expert who joined the firm in 1877. A chance meeting in 1900 between Reynolds and William Chalmers, of Fraser and Chalmers Company, led to the formation of Allis-Chalmers in 1901.

The new company continued to concentrate on heavy engineering. But as the US economy hit hard times so did the company, and in 1913 receivers were brought in to carry out re-organisation. One of these was General Otto Falk, who became President of Allis-Chalmers and its savior. With a personal interest in farming he decided to diversify into tractors. With World War I making heavy demands on agriculture, this sector was experiencing a period of sustained growth.

A couple of machines were tested and put up for sale prior to the 10-18 making its appearance. Small-scale production of the 10-18 three-wheeler was started in 1914. It used a horizontally-opposed, twin-cylinder engine that started on gasoline and then switched to paraffin when the running temperature was reached.

Demand for the 10-18 remained limited, however. By this time other manufacturers had improved their machines and signed contracts for the war effort. The 10-18 carried on being made for some years and was eventually replaced by the 12-20 in 1921. Allis-Chalmers managed to see the war through, and in 1918 it produced a smaller machine, the 6-12. This was not a complete tractor as such but a motor plough designed to be hooked up to existing horse-drawn ploughs or binders. It had its four-cylinder engine mounted over the front two wheels to give maximum traction.

Allis-Chalmers set up a new tractor division in 1918 and the company now produced the 15-30, a conventional tractor with four wheels and a four-cylinder engine. Though it produced plenty of power, it was still a heavy machine and had a large price tag compared to Henry Ford's current tractors. In an attempt to compete in the mid-range tractor market, Allis-Chalmers produced the smaller 12-20 machine, which was soon to be renamed the 15-25. With low sales figures and machines that were too expensive and too heavy, Allis-Chalmers found itself in trouble. General Falk now promoted Harry Merritt as head of the tractor division. Merritt instigated huge price reductions. The 20-35, for example, would soon be offered at half its original selling price. The machines started to sell in large numbers and the 20-35, or Model E as it was now known, sold over 19,000 units in 20 years.

When Henry Ford decided to pull out of tractor manufacturing in the USA, a group of Fordson dealers decided to get together and form an association. Allis-Chalmers was invited to join them and so the United Tractor and Equipment Company of Chicago came into being. Besides other farm machinery, it wanted to produce a medium-sized tractor that Allis-Chalmers would make for it. When introduced in 1929, the tractor was marketed as the United and used a Continental engine. But before long the consortium ran into difficulties, so Allis-Chalmers took on the marketing as well as the production of the tractor, which now became known as the Model U. After a while it was fitted with an Allis-Chalmers paraffin engine rather than the Continental gasoline one.

Allis-Chalmers continued to expand. In 1931 the company bought out the ailing Advance-Rumely concern.

Much work was being done at this time to improve tractor wheels, which were still made of steel with lugs or cleats. These were fine for working in the field, but on roads and pastureland they caused untold damage. Truck-type rubber tires were tested, and although more comfortable they didn't give the grip needed for fieldwork. A breakthrough came in 1932, however, when aircraft tires were tested. These were used with a low internal pressure, which

Allis-Chalmers was best known for its tractors, they also produced crawlers like this Model K.

Beneficial to the farmer were rubber tires, which gave the operator more comfort and better grip.

Early Model U's had a Continental, L-head, side-valve engine. Later they used a 34 hp engine.

An advertisement for the Model U, showing it could pull a three-plow unit with ease.

Allis-Chalmers were so keen to promote the power of the U, they organised tractor racing events.

helped them to mold round uneven surfaces and gave them better grip. Later in the year, the first tractor with rubber tires went on sale. There was some reluctance to accept the change. The threat of punctures was just one of the concerns. So Allis-Chalmers created a publicity campaign, deciding to race the tractors. The steel-wheel Model U had a top speed of about 3.5 mph (6 kph). When an extra gear was added to the rubber-tired model, it could reach 10 mph (16 kph). In the meantime the Model U was also modified for racing, not only creating a new Tractor World record but also becoming the fastest

A well restored Allis-Chalmers WC from 1940. This model was made between 1934 and 1947.

tractor in the world! It caused a sensation during 1933, being demonstrated at many a state fair and by 1937 almost 50 percent of tractors sold were fitted with rubber tires.

The Model WC followed the Model U. Launched in 1933, the WC was to become one of the company's best-selling machines. It was sold with either steel wheels or rubber tires. As yet there was no competitor

for rubber tires and the 'technology' was improving all the time. The tractor had a water-cooled, four-stroke engine and four-speed transmission, and could reach just over 9 mph (14 kph) on rubber tires. So popular was the machine that it went on selling through to the late 1940s, final sales reaching some 178,000 units.

Two tractors were added to the line-up for the 1930s. The Model A was effectively a replacement for the heavy 18-30 machine, but now that powered combine harvesters were making their mark, it was left somewhat redundant. Better though was the Model B of 1937, an ultra-lightweight machine

This is the big Model A. Powered by a four-cylinder gasoline engine, it replaced the Model E.

using unit construction and a four-cylinder engine. Designed by industrial designer Brooks Stevens, it came with a low price tag, which made it an affordable tractor for many of the smaller capacity farms. It remained in production until 1957, by which time it had sold some 100,000 units. This was followed by an up-rated version, the Model C, which also sold well. By now Allis-Chalmers had established itself as a major player in the tractor market.

A view from the operator's seat of the Model B. This is a 1948 version, which produced 15.6 hp at the drawbar.

The four-cylinder, 125.3 cubic inch Model B engine. The transmission was sliding gear.

Like International Harvester, Allis-Chalmers decided to open a factory in the UK, and from 1947 the Model B was made in a plant at Totton, near Southampton. Initially the tractor was assembled from components shipped over from the USA, but later the company used locally sourced parts, finally becoming completely UK-built at Essendine in Leicestershire. There was a Perkins P3 diesel option with four-speed transmission and hydraulics, which made a distinct improvement. However, by 1955 the Ferguson TE 20 was setting the standard. The Model B was no longer competitive and production ceased.

Engine unit of the Model D270. This tractor was a British built model and was an update of the Model B.

It was replaced by the D270, and later by the D272. The last Allis-Chalmers model to appear in the UK was the ED40 in 1960. It used a Standard-Riccardo 2.3 litre engine and featured an eight-speed gearbox, 'live hydraulics,' and the option of live PTO. Improved or 'Depth-O-Matic' hydraulics were introduced in 1963, as was an engine power increase from 37 to 41hp.

A view of the Allis Chalmers, WF model, gasoline engine, built between 1930 to 1958.

Just before World War II, the WF model, a standard tread version of the company's row-crop WC model, was presented. It used the same reliable, water-cooled, four-cylinder engine but unfortunately production was stopped due to material shortages caused by the on-going conflict. Production re-started

Ideal for the small farmer or market gardener, the Model G had its engine at the rear.

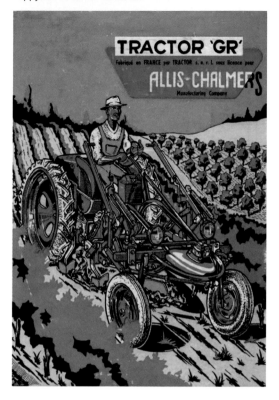

Made under license in France, this poster depicts a very happy farmer on his Model GR.

at the end of the war and by 1948 most of the pre-war features, which included electric lights and starter, were back on the market. That year the Model G, reminiscent of the early Allis-Chalmers motor plow model, made its appearance. Practically stripped of bodywork, the engine was positioned at the rear of the machine while the driver sat at the front. The machine was aimed at the farmer who couldn't afford even a basic tractor, and catered very much for the market gardener. It used a small four-cylinder Continental engine, as Allis-Chalmers itself didn't make a unit small enough to suit.

In 1948 the company also introduced the WD45, which had the same general look as the WD tractor but was much more powerful, having the new four-cylinder 'Power Crater' gasoline engine. In 1954 the WD45 was offered with the 'Snap-Coupler' system for hooking up implements. Mounted under the rear of the tractor, this was basically a funnel shape that guided the implement tongue into the spring-loaded latch. The operator simply backed up to the implement tongue, listened for the 'snap' of the coupler, attached the lift links and was off to the field without ever having to dismount from his tractor. The WD45 became the first in the Allis-Chalmers line-up to have power steering, a feature well received by both dealers and farmers. The last WD45 was made in 1957, by which time a total of 90,382 gasoline and diesel units had been made.

The WC Model was replaced by the WD, which was notorious for its two-clutch power control system.

The WD 45 used a powerful new 4-cylinder 'Power Crater' petrol engine.

The end of production for the B and G models saw Allis-Chalmers create a new designation, the 'D' series. The first to appear were the D14 and D17, which became replacements for the WD model, and were three-plow and four- or five- plow models respectively. The D17 was one of the company's most popular tractors and was built until 1967. It featured a power-director hand clutch, power-adjustable rear wheels, traction-booster system, and was powered by diesel or LPG engines.

In 1959 the D14 and D17 were joined by the D10 and D12, the smallest of the new models. The D10 was a single-row machine and the D12 was set up as a two-row tractor. Both used a water-cooled, four-cylinder engine. But these machines were never fitted with diesel engines and sales weren't spectacular.

The late 1950s was also a period of experimentation, and Allis-Chalmers toyed with the idea of a fuel-cell tractor. This tractor used a Model D12 chassis fitted with 1008 individual cells fuelled by a mixture of gases, mostly propane, which in turn created a current flow. This was channelled through to an Allis-Chalmers 20hp direct-current electric motor. Each fuel cell produced approximately one volt of output, and all together the 1008 fuel cells gave an output of about 15kw. The tractor was put into action by using the controller situated at the driver's left

A fine line-up of D15 tractors. These used the same engine as the D14 but with a higher compression ratio.

This is the four-cylinder, 138.7 cubic inch, gas engine of the D10.

(the four banks of fuel cells could be connected in series or in parallel) thus varying the voltage reaching the motor and acting in a way similar to a throttle. Reverse was simply a matter of reversing the polarity of the current through the controller with the crank-like handle. Allis-Chalmers was quick to point out that its tractor was twice as efficient as others of the period, that the power was derived from no moving parts, that it produced no emissions, and that it 'ran without a whisper.' Unfortunately, like many of the experiments being undertaken by other companies, it never really caught on.

Over the next decade, companies looked to produce more power from their machines and Allis-Chalmers was no exception. Its models were once again falling behind the competition, and so attempts were made to increase the power of current machines. The D18, for instance, was up-graded to the D19 with a 17hp gasoline engine, and there was also a turbo-charged diesel engine version–a first for the farming world. These machines were followed by the company's first 100hp model, the D21, which used a large capacity, direct-injection, six-cylinder diesel engine. This tractor was so powerful that not only did it need a completely new eight-speed transmission, but also new implements

designed to suit, such as a seven-bottom plow. The model stayed in production for the next six years, and ended up being turbo-charged.

The D21 was the last of that series, and a new '100' series was produced for the mid-to-late 1960s. The 100 continued with the rather squared-off styling of the D21, its replacement being the One-Ninety. Engines now available were diesel, gas and LPG. After its powerful predecessors, the One-Ninety was found lacking and Allis-Chalmers decided to add a turbocharger, then changed the designation to One-NinetyXT. The D17 was replaced by the One-Seventy, while the One-Eighty had the option of a cab for the driver. They were similar machines and benefited from a new family of six- and four-cylinder engines, with the One-Seventy also having a Perkins diesel option.

A One-Sixty machine was imported from Renault of France, but for machines with smaller engines the company turned to Fiat of Italy. Having already established links with the company, Allis-Chalmers produced the 5040 with a Fiat three-cylinder, diesel engine. Bigger versions followed in the shape of the 5045 and 5050, and shortly these were replaced by the 6000 series, all using Fiat engines.

The early 1970s saw the introduction of the big 7000

The Allis One-Ninety was under-powered. The One-Ninety XT had a turbocharger.

Allis had a long relationship with the Fiat concern of Italy. The 6080, seen here, used Fiat components.

With its Toyosha, three-cylinder, diesel engine, this is the Allis model 6140.

The 8030 was also a big machine using the Allis-Chalmers, six-cylinder, turbo-diesel engine.

The model 8050 was easily distinguished by their sloping front grille.

Austin

1919-1931

The Austin company had factories in both the UK and France. The English side of the business was based in Birmingham, and its first model appeared in 1919. Available in gas or gas/paraffin versions, this tractor had a four-cylinder engine that developed a maximum 27hp. But the Depression hit Austin hard: production in Birmingham was suspended in the mid-1920s, though it continued in the French factory. As well as other technical improvements, the French-made Austin had a three-speed gear-box rather than the two-speed gear-box of its British counterpart. In 1930 the French version was re-launched in the UK, but it was not a great success. The following year production stopped for good in the UK, and a short time afterwards it also ceased in France.

The Birmingham based Austin tractor was more popular and sold better in France.

Power Squadron machines, which used Allis-Chalmers seven-litre diesel engines. These produced 130hp when turbo-charged and 156hp when turbo-intercooled. The lower-powered 7000 series followed, including the 7080 four-wheel drive model, which in turn was replaced by the larger 8550.

By the early 1980s the company was finding the economic situation difficult. There was a huge downturn of sales both in the USA and Europe. The 7000 series was replaced in 1982 by the 8000 series. The 8000s could be distinguished by their sloping fronts. Meanwhile, at the big end of the market, the 8550 super tractor was superseded in turn by the 4W220 and the 4W305.

The last tractors bearing the Allis-Chalmers name were produced in the USA in December 1985, the farm equipment division being sold that year to K. H. Deutz AG of Germany. Deutz were more interested in selling tractors in the USA than actually making them there. The remaining stock of machines were re-badged Deutz-Allis, but this arm of the company was bought out by its US management. The Allis name survived into the twenty-first century under the AGCO flag, but Allis-Chalmers was no more.

Avery (Peoria, USA)

1874-1931

The two Avery brothers, Robert and Cyrus, set up a business in 1874 to manufacture planters and cultivators. In 1891 they moved to Peoria in Illinois, and here they started building steam tractors. Their first model, the 'Farm and City', was made in 1909. The machine resembled a truck more than a tractor, and was introduced for road as well as farm work. The following year, however, the Avery Company introduced a more conventional tractor–though it wasn't until 1911 that it achieved real success with the 20-35. This was followed in 1912 by the 12-25. The 40-80, weighing in at 9,900 kg, came in 1913, and there were two new models for 1914, the small 8-16 and the popular 25-50. Two- and four-cylinder engines were used and there was a distinctive gear-change system on the 25-50, the engine sliding forwards or backwards on a frame to select the required forward or reverse ratio.

Hard times hit the company in the 1920s. Although revived twice for short periods, and despite the production of the two-plow 'Ro-Track' tractor, Avery eventually fell victim to the Depression.

This is the huge Avery model 40-80, the biggest machine they made, it weighed around 9980 kg.

B.F. Avery & Sons

B.F. Avery & Sons (not to be confused with Avery of Peoria, Illinois), was founded as a plow-producing company by Benjamin Franklin Avery in 1825. In 1845 the factory moved from Clarkesville, Virginia to Louisville, Kentucky. Avery plows were widely exported, and by the late nineteenth century the company was the largest plow manufacturer in the world.

Avery made its first motorized tractor, the Louisville Motor Plow, in 1915. However, this was only made for a short time before the company again concentrated on farm implements.

The B F Avery machines were eventually sold off to the Minneapolis Moline company.

In 1941 Cletrac sold the manufacturing rights for its Model GG to B.F. Avery–a sensible move as Avery produced all the attachments for the machine. After B.F. Avery took over the line, it used the 'GG' designation but changed it to Model A. The Avery A was red with a yellow hood. It used Hercules flat-head, four-cylinder engines, the engine increasing in size from the model IXK3 to the IXB3 version. The company also made other tractors, including the V and R models. It continued until the early 1950s, when the manufacturing rights to the line-up were purchased by Minneapolis Moline.

Belarus

1946-present

The Production Association of Minsk Tractor Works (P/A MTW), the main tractor plant of the former Soviet region of Belarus (now a republic), was founded on May 29, 1946. It was a true association on the communist model. It consisted of a Special Tools and Production Equipment Plant, the Vitebsk Tractor Spare Parts Plant, the Bobruisk Tractor Parts and Units Plant, and the Specialized Engineering Bureau for Versatile Row-Crop Tractors! It became one of the world's largest manufacturers of agricultural equipment, employing nearly 20,000 workers, producing over three million tractors, and exporting some 500,000 of these to more than 100 countries.

Production started with the KD-35 tracked model. This was followed in 1953 by the MTZ-2 tractors, which used pneumatic tires, then by the odd-looking KT-12 tracked model. By 1958 MTW had made its 100,000th machine. Production of the MTZ-50 versatile wheeled tractor was launched in 1961, and the MTZ-52 was introduced shortly afterwards. In 1974, MTW started bulk production of the more powerful MTZ-80 model, which was to become the biggest selling tractor in the world.

MTW started to develop mini-tractors in 1978, creating and producing motoblocks (walk-behind type tractors), the MTZ-05, MTZ-06, MTZ-08BS and MTZ-12, along with the MTZ-082, a four-wheeled mini-tractor that used a 12hp engine. The association continued to improve its products and 1984 saw the introduction of the MTZ-102 100hp machine.

The late 1990s brought the 401M, a tractor that could handle a multitude of tasks.

Two advertisements for Belarus tractors showing the old models along with new ones.

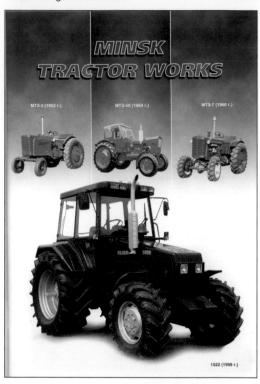

The new generation of Belarus tractors look good and have a good model coverage.

The 952.3, with its rounded style and extensive cab area, is very comfortable too.

By March 1984 the 2,000,000th tractor left the main assembly line, while the first examples of the MTZ-142, 150hp tractor was made the following year. Several versions of the MTZ-220 tractor, which used a 220hp unit, were designed and put into mass production.

The 1990s were almost as busy. MTW started production of a new tractor, the MTZ-1221, which used a 130hp unit, in 1994, and by 1995 the 3,000,000th tractor had rolled off the production line. In 1999, MTW presented a new development, the MTZ-2522, 250hp versatile tractor. The Belarus 1802 tracked vehicle was quickly designed and presented in time for the anniversary of the Minsk Tractor Works in 2000

Today the customer can choose from 62 vehicle models and more than 100 assembly options for all climates and operating conditions. New models give the possibility of mounting agricultural machinery from various producers, while all tractors for sale have international certificates that confirm their compliance with European Union standards.

Big Bud

1961-1992

Big Bud Tractors Inc was established in Havre, Montana, USA in 1961. In 1969 Northern Manufacturing Company, a subsidiary of Big Bud, was formed with the objective of meeting demand for sophisticated, high-horsepower, heavy-duty, four-wheel drive tractors.

A number of innovations were incorporated into the original Big Bud design. A patented tilt-cab and hood for easy access to the engine, transmission and hydraulics, plus a simple skid system for engine removal, were devised. Big Bud performance was backed by easy maintenance and ready access to major overhaul points.

In 1974 the 300 and 350hp units were marketed, with virtually all tractors going to farmers in Montana. But the company had greater ambitions and by 1977, following expansion by Northern Manufacturing into a new production plant, sales areas included California, Hawaii and other states, as well as Canada, Australia and Iran.

In 1978 Northern Manufacturing built the 'Biggest Big Bud' ever, the 16v-747. This tractor was powered by a Detroit Diesel 16-cylinder engine and featured Twin Disc power-shift transmission.

The early 1980s were financially difficult for many manufacturers, and Big Bud suffered with the rest. In 1985 the Meissner Brothers of Chester, Montana, bought the assets of Northern Manufacturing, Big

The Big Bud 525, a monster machine, comes into its own on vast farms.

The Big Bud 525 engine, a 250 hp, six-cylinder, diesel unit, with nine-speed transmission.

Big Bull

1913-1920

In 1913 the Bull Tractor Company of Minneapolis made a prototype, the production model appearing in 1914. It was a three-wheeler powered by an opposed twin-cylinder 12hp engine, and the company named it Little Bull. However, this tractor was somewhat unreliable, and the company set about making a new model. The Big Bull of 1916 also used an opposed twin engine of 25hp and, like the Little Bull, it had a front wheel positioned on the right-hand side. Initially the drive came through one rear wheel, but this was later installed on both rear wheels. The success of this tractor attracted the attention of the Massey-Harris Company, which offered to distribute the tractor in Canada. Bull, however, could not deliver the quantity required and the agreement was dissolved. The arrival of the Fordson in 1917 effectively sealed the fate of the Bull Tractor Company.

Bud Tractors Inc. and Big Bud Industries Inc. Although they built another large Big Bud, the 740, powered by a 740 Komatsu diesel engine and also boasting Twin Disc power-shift transmission, the writing was on the wall for this very individual brand. The last Big Bud rolled off the production line in 1992.

The Bull Pull 45-90 with its engine cover removed and showing off its four-cylinder engine.

When launched in 1968, the Big Bud was classed as the biggest tractor in the world.

B.M.B President

1950-1956

The B.M.B. President was the largest tractor in its range and manufactured by Brockhouse Engineering, Southport, UK, between 1950 and 1956. It used the four-cylinder Morris 8 side-valve engine, which was essentially the same as that used in the Morris Minor up to 1952.

Brockhouse Engineering also produced the two-wheeled B.M.B Cult-Mate, the Hoe-Mate, and the Plow-Mate garden tractors. These were powered by a JAP engine and originally made by British Motor Boats of London.

This was the largest of the model range and it used a four-cylinder, Morris car engine.

In 1954 a vineyard version of the B.M.B. President was introduced, but by that time the company was in decline. Production ceased in 1956.

A later version of the B.M.B. President, made by H. J. Stockton of London, was exhibited at the 1957 Smithfield Show.

Bolinder-Munktell

1932-1950

The two companies, Bolinder and Munktell, had a manufacturing history together before amalgamating in 1932. Founded in 1832, Munktell was an established engineering concern in Sweden, producing locomotives and portable steam engines. In 1913 the company turned to making tractors with internal combustion engines. Many of the engines for these machines were supplied by Bolinder, which had been making engines since 1893.

The first Bolinder-Munktell, the 25, used a twin-cylinder unit and was produced in 1934.

During World War II, many of the tractors in Sweden were converted to run on wood gas, due to the shortage of oil.

In 1950 Volvo merged with Bolinder-Munktell, and the first four-stroke diesel engine, a three-cylinder

Munktell was a long-established Swedish concern which used Bolinder power units.

These machines were powered by a hot-bulb engine. Heating the bulb with a blow-torch would ignite the engine.

An extravagant gesture for a tractor, a chrome radiator makes it look more like the front end of a car.

unit, was unveiled. These were fitted to the 35 and 36 models. During the 1950s the tractor range was updated and new two- and four-cylinder diesel engines were introduced.

A new tractor, the T350 Boxer, was introduced in 1959. This had 10 forward and two reverse gears, independent PTO and differential lock. The T470 Bison was the bigger brother, and the smaller T320 Buster produced 40hp from a bought-in three-cylinder Perkins engine.

By 1966 Volvo started to fit its own engines, and US-influenced design could be seen in the new T800 and T600. The T810 and T814 were among the first tractors to use a turbo engine, the Volvo D50, six-cylinder unit. A new four-cylinder diesel model was announced in 1970, the mid-range T650.

The company, having changed its name to Bolinder-Munktell-Volvo, changed it again in 1973, placing the name Volvo at the beginning. Bolinder-Munktell was now truly integrated into the Volvo fold.

By 1970, Bolinder-Munktell were part of Volvo, hence the Volvo BM badge. This is the T650 turbo.

Bristol

1930s-1970s

Bristol of England made miniature crawlers. These were largely designed by Walter Hill, who was well known in the tractor design field. Made for use on small farms and in market gardens, the crawlers were produced at Douglas Motorcycles, which also supplied the horizontally-opposed twin-cylinder engines.

The Bristol model 20 crawler. Early models even used Douglas motorcycle engines.

In 1933 Walter Hill moved Bristol production to Jowett Cars in Yorkshire. Here the tractors were fitted with Jowett two- and four-cylinder gasoline engines, although a Victor Cub diesel was also an option. After the World War II, Austin gasoline engines and Perkins three-cylinder engines were used. The new Bristol 'D' series appeared in 1960, though the Power Diesel crawler (PD) continued to use the Perkins P3. Not long afterwards the Marshall company, which also made crawlers, took over at Bristol. The last Bristol model, the Track Marshall 1100, was produced in the early 1970s.

Buhrer

1929-1978

Buhrer was a Swiss tractor company, and was based in the town of Hinwil near Zurich. It made its first tractor in 1930, just a year after it began producing self-propelled mowers. Initially these machines used gasoline engines, but in 1941 diesel units began to be fitted. Although the company used its own four-cylinder 4.33 litre engines, it also bought in engines such as the Chevrolet six-cylinder unit. As for gear-boxes, from 1954 three-range units were installed, though this changed in 1964 when the company adopted the 15-ratio, shift-on-the-move Tractospeed gear-box. The 1970s were to prove a tough period for Buhrer.

An example of a working model 455. Today Buhrer restores and services existing machines.

Due to escalating costs and poor sales, the company finally ceased production in 1978. However, it continued to service and supply parts for its own machines.

Bukh

1956-1968

The Bukh company of Denmark is a long-established maker of fine quality marine diesel engines. However, Bukh was fairly active in tractor production for 12 years. The company's first tractor model was the DZ30, launched in 1956. This used a two-cylinder, two litre, 30hp engine. The next model, the DZ45, was more powerful, having a three-cylinder, 45hp engine. Between 1961 and 1962 the company made the D30, the D45 and the 452, while between 1962 and 1966 the 302, 403, 554 and 452 models were launched. In 1967 Bukh brought out the three-cylinder Juno, the four-cylinder Jupiter, and the massive six-cylinder Herkules. In 1968 the company ceased tractor production.

Bukh, better known for their diesel marine engines, also made tractors, of which this poster depicts their 554.

Bungartz

1934-1974

Based in Munich, Germany, Bungartz & Co built its first tractors in the 1930s. These were walk-behind types powered by DKW, Ilo, or Bungartz engines. After the war, the company replaced its F90 machine with the U1 tractor. The U1's successor was the L5, presented in 1953. This used a Sachs two-stroke or a Hatz four-stroke diesel engine. The smaller H3, the F55 FR, the medium FK, and even four-wheel tractors such as the T3 and T5, were all capable of using gasoline or paraffin engines.

A fine example of a post-war German tractor is this Bungartz. The company used a variety of diesel engines.

In 1958 the company expanded into a new factory. Seven years later, Bungartz and Karl Peschke agreed to form a joint engineering works, and by mid-1966 the entire Bungartz production was marketed as Bungartz & Peschke. New models, such as the T8DA and T9, helped to produce the company's best sales year in 1969. The Kommutrac was the last machine made before the company was taken over by Gutbrod in 1974.

C

Case

1842-present

Jerome Increase Case founded the J. I. Case Company in 1842 and soon gained recognition as the first builder of a steam engine for agricultural use. During his tenure as president of the company, the Case company manufactured more threshing machines and steam engines than any other manufacturer in history.

In addition to his talents as an inventor and manufacturer, Case also took an interest in politics and finance. He was three times mayor of Racine, Wisconsin, USA, and was state senator for the Racine area for two terms. He was President of the

Manufacturer's National Bank of Racine and founder of the First National Bank of Burlington (Wisconsin). Case also founded the Wisconsin Academy of Science, Arts and Letters. He was President of the Racine County Agricultural Society and President of the Wisconsin Agricultural Society.

Known in manufacturing circles as the 'Threshing Machine King,' Case received more popular recognition as the owner of 'Jay-Eye-See,' a black gelding racehorse acknowledged as the world's all-time champion trotter-pacer.

'Father, come look at this!' With these words, or others like them, was born a great industrial empire. For what young Jerome Increase Case wanted his father, Caleb, to see was an article in the Genesee Farmer about a new machine that would thresh wheat. The farmer since biblical times had cut wheat with scythes, threshed it by hand with flails, and winnowed the grain from the chaff by tossing it in the air. It was back-breaking work. One person could thresh only six or seven bushels a day.

Manpower in early nineteenth-century America was scarce. In 1820, the year after Jerome's birth, the US population was about five and a half million, not including slaves. The further west one travelled, the fewer people there were. Farmers on America's frontiers could count on little more than their own families for labor (one reason farm families tended to be large).

Case was born into a pivotal period in American agriculture. During his lifetime the Industrial Revolution and expansion of the United States combined to produce one of the most powerful nations on Earth. Case was to become a part of this process, alongside Cyrus McCormick, Major Leonard Andrus, Eli Whitney and other individuals who used the fruits of the Industrial Revolution to transform American agriculture. By applying technology to farming, these men so raised production levels that the United States was to become the breadbasket of the world.

In 1842, Case took a crude 'Ground Hog' threshing machine with him from Williamstown, New York, to Rochester, Wisconsin. Here he worked on the machine, improving its design and establishing his company. Just a year later Case relocated to the shores of Lake Michigan at Racine, Wisconsin. His need of water for power made him choose this spot for his factory, and here he further improved his old machine and designed and made new ones.

By the start of the American Civil War, the number of reapers and mowers being used on farms had grown from 90,000 to 250,000. The war itself stimulated a huge expansion in farm mechanization.

Above, the famous Case eagle and globe emblem. Jerome Increase Case is depicted below.

A very early Case steam engine is being used by farmers to work a threshing machine.

In 1863 Case took on three partners to create the J. I. Case Company: Massena Erskine, Robert Baker and Stephen Bull. These men soon became known as the Big Four. Two years later, the eagle trademark was adopted. This was based on 'Old Abe,' the emblem used by Company C of the 8th Wisconsin Regiment during the Civil War. In 1894 the eagle was depicted on top of a globe, and was to remain the company logo for the next 75 years.

In 1869 Old No.1, the first Case steam engine, appeared. Although the engine was initially mounted on wheels, it still had to be pulled by a team of horses and was only used for belt power to other attachments. It was another 15 years before the steam boom would truly take off.

The first Case traction engine came in 1876. Throughout 1878, Case doubled its steam engine turnover to 220 units. The company shipped its first thresher overseas during this year, and before being put to work on a farm, the Case thresher won First Prize at the Paris Exhibition that year. Two years later the J. I. Case and Company partnership was dissolved, and the J. I. Case Threshing Machine Company was born. By 1886 Case was the world's largest manufacturer of steam engines, and in 1890 the company opened its first branch office in Buenos Aires.

Jerome Increase Case died on December 22, 1891, and the town of Racine mourned one of the USA's industrial pioneers. One of Case's partners, Stephen Bull, took over as President of the company. That year the company employed William Paterson to produce a new internal combustion engine to power a tractor. What Paterson designed had an unusual layout: the engine had two opposing pistons in one cylinder, with a complex linkage between them and the crank. But the unreliability of the engine was not something the company wanted to entertain: it was abandoned and Case returned to steam power. It wasn't for some time that Case would venture into making a gas-powered tractor. Indeed, several other companies had already produced their own models. Case introduced its first all-steel thresher in 1904 and though heavily criticized, other companies followed this trend. Nevertheless, that year Case produced more farm steam engines and threshing machines than its rivals.

In 1910 the Gasoline Traction Department demonstrated a prototype to the Case board, who decided they liked it and gave the go-ahead to build. Late the following year, the Case 30-60 tractor was launched. The design was reminiscent of that of the steam tractors and it was heavy and large. The engine was an unconventional horizontal twin-cylinder unit, but it could manage the huge frame admirably. It wasn't long before a smaller 20-40 model was brought out. This used a flat-twin engine and was in production for eight years. Small was the theme by now, and Case produced the 12-25 for 1913. It was still heavy, however, and only stayed on the books for five years. That year the Case Tractor Works (known for a time as the Clausen Plant) was built near Racine to manufacture several sizes of four-cylinder, gasoline engine tractors including cross-mounted units.

These cross-mounted engines were a development that stemmed from the purchase of the Pierce Motor Company (not to be confused with Pierce Arrow). Case studied Pierce's four-cylinder engines and re-designed them so that they would sit crossways in the 10-20 model tractor of 1916. The units were water-cooled and were initially made as three-wheelers. However, the 9-18 that followed had four

The Case 12-25 model was the company's first move towards small tractor production.

wheels and a steel-fabricated chassis. The cross-motor, as it became known, went through many stages of improvement and enlargement over the years. For example, the 22-40 unveiled in 1919 was the most powerful tractor the company had yet produced, having a huge engine capacity. Although expensive, with this power these machines could also pull Case threshers and–such was the workload they could carry out–they paid for themselves handsomely. The biggest of the cross-motors was the 40-72 produced in 1920.

This is an excellent example of a four-cylinder, crossmotor model, produced by Case.

During World War I there was an increase in demand for labor-saving tractor designs, which in turn boosted sales for many tractor companies. By the mid-1920s, however, Case was struggling and new products were needed to keep up with the opposition. The man who saw this through had come from John Deere, and was installed as President of Case in 1924. Leon R. Calusen started by closing down the automobile section and discontinued steam engines, which were outdated. He then asked D. P. Davies to design a new engine to take the place of the cross-motors.

A new line of tractors was introduced in 1929, the first of which was the Model L. This example is an 8.2 litre model.

This is a 1936 Case model CC and was originally introduced in 1929. The model C and CC were made up to 1939.

This is the rowcrop version of the model R and designated RC. This model appeared in 1935.

As part of their new tractor line in 1939, Case introduced their four-cylinder, model D, in new Flambeau red.

Production of the model S started in 1940. It looked like the model D but was smaller.

Case introduced their first diesel-powered tractor in 1953. The 500 was a six-cylinder model.

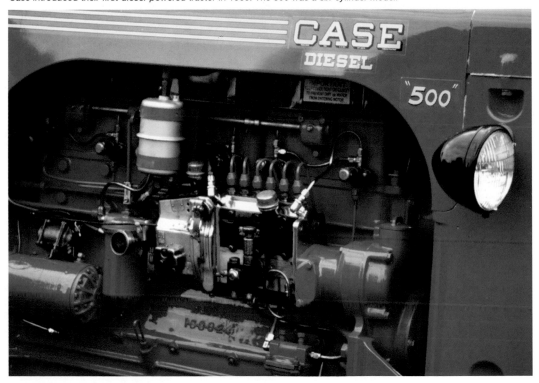

Case

This is a Case 400, which replaced the D series. The model was announced in 1955 with gasoline or diesel engine.

The new 300 series was introduced in 1955 and were available with Case or Continental four-cylinder unit.

Top of the range for 1957 was this eight-speed 600 series. Note the eagle and globe emblem, on the rear mudguards.

Two new machines arrived in 1929, the Model L and Model C. They both used four-cylinder engines, this time fitted longitudinally rather than across. All in all they were conventional tractors, exactly what Case needed to keep pace with its rivals. Both the Model L and the smaller C used a three-speed gearbox and chain final drive. The Model L was so popular in its various guises that it continued to be made through to the early 1960s.

In 1932 Case produced the little RC model, after much internal discussion. Clausen was not keen to produce this machine for fear of taking sales away from the Model L and C. The RC used a bought-in Waukesha engine (Case didn't make a unit small enough to suit) which ran on gas only.

In 1937 The Rock Island (Illinois) Plow Company factory was purchased and in 1939 'flambeau red' became the identifying colour for Case equipment. With this came the introduction of a new fleet of tractors, including the Model D. This was basically a restyled C but with additions such as mechanical motor lift to aid attachment of implements, disc brakes, and live PTO. It ceased production in 1953. There was also the model S, a two-plow general-purpose machine that replaced the RC. Unlike the D, the S had four-speed transmission. It was available in several different versions: S, SC, SO and SI,

depending on what type of work it was required to carry out. Another new model was the Model V, supposedly a lightweight but in fact was heavier–and more powerful–than its competitors.

World War II saw Case supply all kinds of material for the war effort. It produced hundreds of thousands of 155mm shells and 40mm anti-aircraft gun carriages, as well as B-26 bomber wings and after-coolers for Rolls Royce aircraft engines.

After the war production continued with pre-war models, though by now the model V had been replaced by the VA fitted with the new snap-on Eagle Hitch. Many other tractor companies were already fitting diesel engines when Case decided to introduce the 500 model. This wasn't a completely new machine–much of it harked back to the model L–but it did have the new six-cylinder engine. This was a strong and durable unit and one of the most powerful available to the farmer in the 1950s.

A new President, Mark Rojtman, joined Case in 1956 when Case absorbed the American Tractor Company. Current models were already going through an updating stage, and in 1955 the 400 model was introduced with the new colour scheme of 'desert sunset' orange sheet metal and 'flambeau red' chassis. This used a four-cylinder version of the six-cylinder unit from the 500 and could be run on

The Case 930 of 1960 used a water-cooled, six-cylinder engine. It came with the Comfort King driver's platform.

The 1980s advertising of the 56 series clearly shows the new logo that the company adopted.

For large farms the Case 4894, with its 300 hp engine, was a powerful and ideal machine.

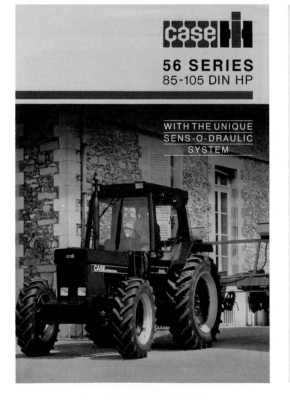

case

56 SERIES
85-105 DIN HP

WITH THE UNIQUE
SENS-O-DRAULIC
SYSTEM

case

MODEL 4894
Tractor

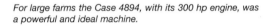

300 (223 kW) gross engine horsepower*
253 (188 kW) PTO horsepower*
225 (168 kW) d/b horsepower*

*Mfr's rating

gas, diesel or LPG. There was also a new eight-speed transmission. A new 300 model was introduced in 1956, which catered to the smaller farmer. In the meantime the 500 became the 600 with a new six-speed transmission.

This updating was already taking place when Rojtman arrived, but in 1958 he invited every Case dealer to Phoenix to view and test the latest products, something the company had never done before. The initial expense was covered several times over following the orders placed after the event. The most significant introduction to the models was the Case-o-Matic drive system. In 1964 the turbo-charged diesel, four-wheel drive 1200 Traction King tractor was introduced. This was aimed at high-production agricultural operations.

Things changed in the early 1960s. Mark Rojtman left the company after a boardroom bust-up, and in 1967 the company was taken over by Tenneco Inc. of Houston, Texas. This gave the company financial security and allowed it to continue producing in its many different sectors. With the change of ownership came other organisational changes. Old Abe was one casualty, being replaced by a bold 'CASE' logo.

The 1960s also saw Case change its designations. All models had the number 30 added, the model 900 becoming the 930 and so on. The six-cylinder diesel was now out of date and lacked power compared to other machines on the market. As with many of the other tractor companies, it was power that counted now. In response Case introduced the 1030 Comfort King model, which produced 102hp from its water-cooled six-cylinder engine. Turbo-charging was added at a later date.

As the 1960s moved to a close, new models came in the form of the 70 series, as in the 470 and 570 for 1969. That year also saw the introduction of the Agri-King line. These had fully enclosed cabs and included the four-wheel drive Model 1470, the largest tractor ever made by Case. In 1970 a family of four- and six-cylinder in-line/open-chamber diesel engines were developed, producing between 67 and 180 PTO horsepower. Case also started selling engines and hydraulic components to other manufacturers, and in 1972 the company experienced one of the most successful years in its history. In 1974, total Case sales surpassed the billion-dollar mark.

In 1982 there was excitement in the tractor world as the Panther 2000 tractor was introduced. This was the first model to have a twelve-speed, full powershift transmission, electronic controls, and PFC hydraulics. The following year a new line of 94 series, general-purpose tractors were announced, along with high-horsepower, two-wheel drive tractors, all in the 'power' red, black and white livery. That year the Super E was fitted with the newly designed Case four-cylinder diesel engine produced at its facility in Rocky Mount, North Carolina.

Also in 1983 David Brown Tractors was renamed Case Tractors and integrated in the Agricultural Equipment Group. A year later, Case introduced a

Another Super-tractor was this four-wheel drive, four-wheel steer, 2670 model. It used a 221 hp, engine.

Featured here is a Case International 5140, a mid-range model, produced in the 1990s.

new line of 94 series, four-wheel drive tractors. These included the most powerful Case tractor to date, the Model 4994, which boasted a turbo-charged V8 engine.

In a move to increase its market position, Tenneco Inc. acquired selected assets from the International Harvester agricultural equipment operation in 1985. Case now became the second largest farm equipment manufacturer in the industry. The letters 'IH' were added to the corporate 'CASE' logo.

A year later, Steiger Tractor Incorporated filed for bankruptcy protection and Tenneco Inc. snapped it up. The 94 series tractors were now being sold off at knock-down prices to make way for the new Magnum tractors, which were launched in 1987. A second series–the 7200s–followed in 1988. That year the new 9100 series Case IH Steiger tractors were presented in red livery.

On 24 June 1994 Case, trading under the symbol of CSE, were listed on the New York Stock Exchange for the first time.

In 1997 Case introduced its new range of MX tractors and moved its production plant in Neuss, Germany, to plants in Racine, Wisconsin and Doncaster in England. That year the company acquired Agri-Logic, a leading developer of software for agricultural applications. This helped to keep Case at the forefront of agricultural technology. Two years later, the Case Corporation merged with New Holland NV to create CNH. The year 2000 saw the introduction of the new STX series from Steiger, and Case covered the high-power market with its DX and CX range of machines.

With facilities all over the world, Case is now a world leader in the agricultural and construction equipment industries.

The spacious cab is clearly visible on this model 9280 Case. It has three front wheels, either side.

This model 5150 has both front and rear attachments ready for operation.

The 1170, part of the latest generation Case IH CVX range. Models range between 137 to 192 hp.

Seen here is the JX1070C tractor, which uses a three-cylinder Case IH engine.

The Case 4230 model is a 1990s mid-range machine, having four-wheel-drive.

Available in several widths, the JXN and JXV series tractors are ideal for vineyard work.

Caterpillar

1890-present

Three men were instrumental in forming one of today's best-known tractor companies. They each had thriving companies before their merger, and they both had interests in the farming community. They were Benjamin Holt, Daniel Best, and C. L. Best.
Born in New Hampshire, USA in 1849, Benjamin Holt was the youngest of eight brothers and sisters. The family owned a sawmill that processed hardwoods for the construction of wagons. These wagons and coaches transported people and goods all over New England.

Benjamin Holt developed the world's first practical track-laying tractor in 1904.

Daniel Best, on the left, was a great inventor of farm implements. His son Leo, right, also designed a crawler.

Benjamin and Charles moved out to San Francisco where they started a new company in Stockton doing business in hardwood, timber and wagon-making materials. Charles ran the day-to-day business side whilst Benjamin ran the production side.

One of Holt's original track-laying tractors, working the field somewhere in northern California

During the Gold Rush of 1848, thousands of people moved out to California in the hope of finding their fortune. When many failed to find gold, they started working the land, which was plentiful at that time. California covered a vast area and huge farms sprawled over thousands of hectares. These farms needed labour to manage their horses and to harvest their crops.
Benjamin Holt bought up patents for farm equipment, worked on his own ideas and designs, and increased the output of the Stockton Wheel Company. The first combination harvester and thresher, which was hauled by eighteen horses, was sold in 1886. The large number of horses needed to pull these machines was a problem in itself and so Benjamin set about finding a solution.
The first Holt steam-powered tractor made an appearance in 1890. Although large and heavy, it could be powered by burning wood, coal or oil. It ran on wooden wheels and became very popular for those harvesting large fields, the cost of running it being one-sixth of the horse-drawn method. All the same, there were difficulties with maneuvrability, and the wheels would on occasion get bogged down in mud. So Holt started experimenting, at first with larger and wider wheels, which only added to the weight and maneuvrability problem. Benjamin and Pliny took a trip through the US and Europe in 1903-1904 to study various ideas, including track systems, by a variety of people and manufacturers. His first actual attempt at a track system came in November

of 1904 when he instructed his engineers to remove the rear wheels from a steam traction engine and replace them with a set of tracks he had just designed. The company photographer at the time commented that it crawled like a caterpillar. In this way, the Caterpillar name and trademark was born. Gasoline-powered tractors were developed during 1906 and the first gas-powered models went into production in 1908, known as the Holt Caterpillar 40. By 1905 Benjamin's brothers had either moved on or died, and so he was left to run the company, by this time known as The Holt Manufacturing Company, which went from strength to strength. He was now making tracked vehicles for farming, road construction and the military. In 1915 his machines even saw action on the Western Front. Of all the tractor models his company produced, the Caterpillar 75 was the most popular.

But the other root of the future Caterpillar corporation, which would be formed by Daniel Best and his son Leo Best, has to be considered at this stage. Daniel Best was born in Ohio, USA, on March 28, 1838, the ninth child of 16 from his father's two marriages. As a youngster he lived for a time in Missouri, where his father also ran a sawmill. The family then moved to Vincennes, Iowa, to farm. One of his older brothers had already moved out west and

Daniel followed him in 1859. For the next 10 years he earned a living in a variety of ways, mostly connected with the mining and timber industries.

Whilst working with his brother, he designed and built a transportable machine for cleaning grain, which was able to clean up to 60 tons of grain a day. He patented it in 1871 and struck up a partnership with L. D. Brown. The 'Brown and Best's unrivalled seed separator' won First Prize at the California State Fair. Best went on to patent a seed-coating machine and continued to work in the corn separator market. He next went into partnership with Sam Althouse of Albany, Oregon, and in 1879 opened a branch of their business in Oakland, California. This place was chosen because it was not only a shipping port for grain and wheat, but also a broker's market. Best then moved with his family to Washington to pursue more mining and timber interests in 1879, while still a partner in the Oakland business. The demand for his inventions grew and he started manufacturing a variety of machines aimed at increasing productivity and mechanising farm work. In 1882 he worked for Nathaniel Slate for a few months; this is when he was exposed to a combined harvester and began his thought processes for his own designs of this machine. Growth of the business made him decide to sell some of his other

The name stuck when a photographer remarked that the machine moved like a caterpillar.

interests in Washington and Oregon, and he went on to buy the San Leandro Plow Company in 1886, renaming it the Daniel Best Agricultural Works.

During this period Best patented a combined header and thresher and a fan blast governor that allowed the machine to work at a constant speed, regardless of what speed it moved across a field. This was seen as a major step towards quality control in grain harvesting and cleaning, as well as combining two functions in a single machine. Best also noted that Californian wheat farms were much bigger than others, and that harvesting was a labor-intensive task. He was also aware of the possibility of mechanizing the harvesting process to save both manpower and horsepower. Steam power was already being used in two forms for agricultural purposes: the horse-drawn steam engine as a source of power, and the self-propelled steam traction engine. So Best bought the rights to manufacture the Remington 'Rough and Ready' steam traction engine, and re-designed it to tow his combine harvester and power its auxiliary engine. The successful machine was patented in 1889.

In 1908, and to the dismay of his son Leo Best, Daniel Best sold his tractor company to The Holt Manufacturing Company. Leo decided to start his own company, C. L. Best Gas Traction Company, and within a few years he was building his own crawler, similar to the Holt machine but which featured improvements.

During World War I, the Holt company supplied the military with vehicles, while the Best company supplied the farm community: each had its area of operations. After World War I and throughout the early 1920s there was a tractor slump, and although the Holt business went through difficult times, Best saw his sales increased by seventy percent. It was at this time that the two companies made a decision to merge and although there were many factors that brought about the merger, it was not the idea of either the Holts or the Bests. Benjamin Holt died in 1920 and never saw the merger, but in 1925 the Holt Manufacturing Company joined with the C. L. Best Tractor Co. and took the name Caterpillar Tractor Co.

The merger worked well, the products of the two companies complementing each other. With a little reduction in pricing, the company saw sales soar.

In 1927 a mid-size crawler, the Model Twenty, was introduced. This used an inline, four-cylinder engine and stayed in production until 1933. One year later the Caterpillar Fifteen was introduced.

The first Caterpillar diesel engine tractor, the Diesel Sixty, was delivered to its new owner in 1931. The Diesel Sixty was also the first tractor to be painted in the now familiar Highway yellow livery. This was for visibility when the machines were being used for road construction, but it wasn't long before every model was painted this color.

During 1935 there were new crawlers with diesel engines, designated with the letters RD and ending

Although Holt was seen to be the first to make crawlers, the Best company also produced this model 60.

Built between 1925 and 1931, the Sixty used a four-cylinder, gasoline engine of 1128.2 cubic inches.

with numbers that related to the power of the engine each carried: there was an RD8, an RD7, and an RD6 and the RD4 was introduced in 1936.

There were crawlers already around at this time that used angled blades. Caterpillar, looking to fit blades to their own machines, had struck up relationships with at least six blade manufacturers including LaPlant-Choate. Caterpillar did not fit these blades at the factory; the blade manufacturers made their products to fit onto the Caterpillar machines and Caterpillar encouraged their dealers to sell these products.

In 1938 the company introduced its smallest crawler, the D2, which was designed for agricultural work. A variation followed which could use paraffin or gas power, and this was designated the R2. In 1940 Caterpillar was producing motor graders, blade graders, elevating graders, terracers and electrical generating sets. By 1942, when America came into World War II, track-type tractors, motor graders, generator sets and a special engine for the M4 tank were being supplied by Caterpillar to the US military.

The war over, production got back to normal and the old pre-war models reappeared. On the financial side, a significant event had occurred in 1950, when Caterpillar Tractor Co. Ltd. set up office in the UK.

This was to be the first of many overseas operations, and was created to help manage foreign exchange shortages, tariffs, and import controls, and to allow the company to better serve its customers around the world. Nineteen years before that in 1931, the company had created a separate engine sales group to market diesel engines to other equipment manufacturers. This group was replaced in 1953 with a separate sales and marketing division to better serve the needs of a broad range of engine customers. At this time engine sales accounted for about one third of the company's total sales and revenue.

In 1963 Mitsubishi Heavy Industries Ltd. and Caterpillar formed one of the first joint ventures in Japan which was also to include partial US ownership. Caterpillar Mitsubishi Ltd., as it was named, started production just two years later in 1965. The company was renamed Shin Caterpillar Mitsubishi in 1987 and became the second largest maker of construction and mining equipment in Japan.

By 1966 construction machinery was the company's biggest market. However, it hadn't forgotten the farming community, and introduced the D4, D5 and D6 in SA (Special Application) form. The engines for these machines were positioned further forward

This is the Thirty, of the late 1920s. The marking on the radiator gives it away.

The Sixty had three forward and one reverse gear. The high operator's seat gave better visibility.

Probably the ideal machine in the circumstances and showing how capable the Sixty could be.

to counterbalance the drawbar work. The D3B SA began production in 1985, the D4D SA in 1966, the D5 SA in 1966, the D6C SA in 1970, the D7G SA in 1977, and the D8L SA in 1984.

In 1976 the company introduced sealed and lubricated tracks to its vehicles. This had the effect of reducing track wear, though this didn't really help

Both ends of the market were catered for, even when it came to crawlers. This Ten was aimed at the small farmer.

Manufactured between 1934 and 1942, the Caterpillar R2 used a four-cylinder, 251 cubic inch, gasoline engine.

the farmers, who were looking for greater road-hauling speeds and greater comfort. This was remedied in 1987, when, after much development, Caterpillar produced its Mobil-trac system. This was made of tough rubber and was close to the comfort

and speed attained by rubber tires. These tracks were initially fitted to the Challenger 65 tractor. They were so successful they were soon fitted to the other Challenger models too. This success also led to other manufacturers developing similar systems.

The RD 6, later to become the D6, was manufactured from 1935, initially using a three-cylinder engine.

Weighing some 4,700 pounds, this is the 2 Ton model, which used the company's four-cylinder engine.

The D4 originated as the RD4, and was modified on various occasions during its lifespan.

The recession that hit many industries in the early 1980s also had a huge effect on Caterpillar. At one point the company was losing the equivalent of one million dollars a day, and it had no option but to make dramatic reductions in the workforce. The Caterpillar Leasing Company expanded and changed its name to Caterpillar Financial Services Corporation in 1983, offering equipment-financing options to its customers world-wide.

This is the D4 engine, a four-cylinder unit with a 4.50 x 5.50 inch, bore and stroke measurement.

A Caterpillar with semi-enclosed engine and high-flotation, low-pressure tires.

The D8H model was more suited to earth moving duties and not specifically for farm use.

Described in the brochure as a total field machine, this is the Challenger 65B tractor.

The Challenger of 2001. This machine is very versatile and can be used all round the farm.

The bigger Challenger machines were followed by smaller Challenger machines – 35, 45 and 55.

In 1986, the Caterpillar Tractor Co. changed its name to Caterpillar Inc., and the following year a 1.8 billion dollar plant modernisation programme was launched to streamline the manufacturing process. The company began to expand once again. It acquired Germany's MaK Motoren in 1996 and the UK-based Perkins Engines in 1998. The company was now one of the world leaders in diesel engine manufacturing and in the same year introduced the world's largest off-highway truck, the 797, at the company's proving ground in Arizona.

As the new millennium approached, Caterpillar exhibited new lines of compact, more versatile construction equipment at the 1999 CONEXPO show. The year 2000 saw the company celebrate its 75th anniversary. Currently the company is the first engine manufacturer to offer a full line of clean diesel engines, fully certified by the US Environmental Protection Agency. The machines sacrifice none of their performance, reliability or long life thanks to the Caterpillar emission control technology, known as ACERT. With the world becoming more and more aware of the need to keep pollution under control, these machines represent a significant advance.

For 2005 Caterpillar announced their new T-Series, Track-Type tractors. This D9T is powered by a Cat engine.

Claas

1913-present

 The Claas story began in 1913 in Westphalia, Germany. August Claas, in association with his brothers Franz and Theo, saw the need for a mechanical straw-binder. Their improved knotter turned the poor quality twine available at the time into a binding firm enough to secure the sheaves. In 1934, Claas produced the first pick-up baler. However, the company fortunes did not really take off until 1936, when the first combine harvester suitable to European conditions went into production.

The Claas Ares 862 RZ uses a 6.8 litre, six-cylinder turbo-charged engine with fuel injection.

It was this machine that enabled Claas to reach a wide market, and the company has since become synonymous with harvesters of all kinds. Following its incorporation into Renault Agriculture in 2003, the Claas Group has expanded substantially and now employs some 6000 staff world-wide.

Clayton

1911-1928

This English firm, which was based in Lincoln, unveiled its first internal combustion tractor in 1911. Intended for ploughing, this machine had a big four-cylinder engine producing 80hp on paraffin and 90hp on gas. It could achieve speeds of up to 4 mph (6 kph) on the road and 2.5 mph (4 kph) in the field. Five years later, a crawler was launched: the Clayton Chain Rail Tractor, powered by a 6.3 litre Dorman engine. A bigger crawler, the Multipede, had a 100hp National motor with three-speed transmission. It was capable of speeds up to 7 mph (11 kph). Steering was by a single front wheel,

Made in England, the Clayton company made caterpillar type machines for many years.

and there were individual brakes on each track differential. In 1926 Clayton was taken over by Marshall. Tractor production ceased two years later.

Cletrac

1916-1965

Cletrac, or Cleveland Tractor, started life as the Cleveland Motor Plow Company in 1916, and was founded by Rollin H. and Clarence G. White. The Cleveland 20, known also as the Model R, was one of the company's first tractors. In 1918 the Whites renamed the company the Cleveland Tractor Company, and Cletrac–as it came to be known–was born.

The first Cletracs were advertised as 'geared to the ground' to stress their superior traction over conventional wheeled machines. In the 1920s, crawlers were gaining in popularity, and Cletrac was soon at the forefront of crawler makers. From 1920-1922, four versions of its Model F were introduced. This was designed especially for use with cultivators and other front-mounted units, and was driven by a

Better known for its crawlers, Cletrac also made the odd tractor like this GG General tractor.

The first Cletrac was the R, followed in 1917 by the H. Early machines had front mounted pulleys.

The Cletrac/Oliver BD model used a Hercules diesel powered engine rated at 27/37hp.

floating roller chain travelling between the drive gears and tracks. The F range also included the small Hi-Drive Model F 9-16, which was suitable for use on small farms.

Between 1926 and 1930, the company offered the Model 30A (30-45) and the Model 30B. However, production of both was limited. The Model K-20, by contrast, had a fairly long production life. Manufactured between 1928 and 1932, engineering refinements on this tractor included a simplified track layout and an instantaneous oiling system where the entire track could be oiled using a plunger. The K-20, like the Models W and F, used Cletrac's

The Cletrac HG: the basis for the Oliver OC3. Cletrac was purchased by Oliver in 1951.

own engine. However, most Cletrac models used engines made by Buda, Weidley, Wisconsin, Hercules, Continental, or Cummins.

Cletrac introduced its first diesel-powered crawler, the Diesel 80, in 1933. This had an electric start, and used a six-cylinder Hercules engine with about 90hp. Combined with differential steering, which allowed full power turns, these features made the model highly popular with farmers and industrial users alike.

In 1944 the Oliver company purchased Cletrac, though the tractors continued to be made in White's old Cletrac factory. (Oliver's HG crawler was effectively a continuation of the Cletrac track-layer line.) Then in 1960, the White Motors Corporation (the same White family who founded Cletrac) re-purchased Oliver, and moved operations to the former Hart-Parr works in Charles City, Iowa. But changes in the tractor market, and stiff competition, saw the end of all Cletrac-style crawlers in 1965.

Cockshutt

1882-1962

In 1882 the Canadian James G. Cockshutt founded the Cockshutt Plow Company in Brantford, Ontario. By the 1920s the company had become one of the leading tillage tools manufacturers. Initially, Cockshutt sold Oliver-built tractors with great success, but in 1946 the company unveiled its own Model 30. The Models 40, 20 and 50 followed this, and then the 35 Deluxe, a model falling between the 30 and 40 power sizes. In 1958 the '500' series was introduced. Departing from the streamlined styling of the Model 30, these had a bold, squared-off look. The last true Cockshutt was the powerful 570 Super. But the company had fallen victim to corporate raiders, and in 1962 it was purchased by the White Motor Company.

This is the Cockshutt 40 deluxe model, lovingly restored. It uses a six-cylinder Buda engine.

Co-op

In the USA and Canada, farmers' co-operatives have sought to maintain a supply of good tractors, and keep down prices, by contracting out to established manufacturers. For example, the original Allis-Chalmers Model U was created for a farmers' union based in Chicago. In Canada, farm co-operatives had a particularly fruitful relationship with Cockshutt, the Canadian Cockshutt 30 being sold as the CCIL. The little Cockshutt 30 was taken up by the American Farmers' Union and sold as the E3. The E3 was identical to other Cockshutts, though it came in Pumpkin orange. The Pumpkin deal worked well, and other Cockshutt models were sold by the AFU.

The Co-Op E4 was its version of the six-cylinder Cockshutt 40, while the little Cockshutt 20 was sold as the E2.

Looking a little like a machine built from Meccano, this later Co-op tractor is standard tread.

A typical rowcrop layout of one front and two rear wheels, this Co-op uses a four-cylinder engine.

D

David Brown

1939-1983

The original David Brown Company, which made wooden gears used in the textile mills of Huddersfield, England, was founded in 1860. As technology progressed, Brown began producing steel gears, and by the 1930s the company had become the biggest manufacturer of gears in the UK.

The David Brown company first became involved with tractors in 1936. It was then that, as a subsidiary of the local family firm David Brown and Sons, it collaborated with Harry Ferguson to manufacture the now legendary Ferguson-Brown Tractor. Ferguson needed someone to build the tractor he had designed to go with his new three-point-hitch system, and approached David Brown. The David Brown company agreed. In addition, it was understood that Ferguson would sell the machine that David Brown produced.

This model was built at Park Gear Works, Huddersfield, and later at the nearby Meltham Mills tractor factory. It had a four-cylinder water-cooled gasoline or gas/TVO engine. The first 500 tractors built had a Coventry Climax-type E engine, while the remaining 1350 machines had a David Brown engine of 2010cc capacity. The transmission was equipped with three forward and one reverse gear, and the tractor had independent wheel brakes.

Sales were good for a time, but tension set in following a downturn. Harry Ferguson was against changes, while the David Brown company felt the tractors could be improved with small alterations. David Brown won out for a time, and the Ferguson-Brown model was the world's first production tractor to be equipped with hydraulic lift and converging three-point linkage. Approximately 1,350 of these improved models were built before Ferguson and Brown parted. Ferguson himself had travelled over to America to see Henry Ford, and they were on the point of striking up their famous deal sealed with a handshake. This in turn left David Brown free to get on with developing its own tractor.

In September 1939 the new model came on to the

A fine example of a David Brown VAK 1 tractor. David Brown built it after Ferguson had left.

market. The David Brown VAK 1 had elegant styling, sleek lines and proved an immediate success. It used a four-cylinder, water-cooled, gasoline or gas/TVO engine and had four forward and one reverse gear. The track was adjustable by dished wheel centers–a David Brown patent–and implement depth was controlled by a patented depth (gauge) wheel system. In World War II, many of these machines played their part as aircraft tugs and crawlers, while also being used in their more familiar role on farms. Just before the war, David Brown had purchased a redundant textile factory outside Huddersfield at Meltham Mills. The intention was to build the tractors there, which indeed the company did for a while, but the war put a stop to that and instead it produced munitions and aircraft parts.

When peace finally came, production of the VAC 1 was once again taken up. In 1945, however, an uprated version, the VAC 1A, was introduced. This featured an improved engine lubrication system and a more precise governor. A patented automatic load-controlled hot spot, for rapid TVO engine warm-up, was introduced, and the now universally used turnbuckle top link–another David Brown feature–was also fitted.

In 1947 the company introduced the Cropmaster. With it came the popular policy of including in the standard specification many items normally regarded as extras: hydraulic lift, swinging draw-bar and electric lighting. The two-speed PTO, six-speed gear-box, and coil ignition were all introduced by David Brown in this period. The Cropmaster Diesel

This is the David Brown Tug, used by the RAF to pull aircraft during and after the war.

The VAK 1C, outwardly still looking the same as the original VAK 1 machine.

The VAK models used a four-cylinder, water-cooled, gas or gas/TVO engine.

tractor was powered by the four-cylinder, water-cooled, direct ignition, cold-starting OHV engine. The cylinder block was a single piece casting fitted with four detachable wet sleeve liners of close-grained iron, and the camshaft bearings and main oil galleries were integral to the cylinder block. The long production run of Cropmaster tractors (1947 to 1953) saw many new features pioneered added, and the machines themselves did much to enhance the reputation for reliability and quality enjoyed by David Brown.

From 1953 to 1958, the 50D model was produced. This was the first David Brown model to be available only with a diesel engine. It was based on a six-cylinder, 50hp power unit developed for a track-laying machine. A rugged, heavy tractor, it was ideally suited for towing operations and featured a four-speed PTO unit. It was unique amongst David Brown tractors in having a side-mounted belt pulley instead of the more familiar rear-mounted unit.

The 30C and 30D were introduced in the same year as the 50D. The 30C, a gas/TVO model, and the 30D with its diesel engine, had overhead valves and coil ignition or direct injection. By 1954 these models were equipped with TCU–Traction Control Unit–and the first controlled weight transfer system for tractors. In 1955 a special hitch to give the advantage of TCU in hauling heavy trailers was introduced. The 25C and 25D models, also

operated by compressed air, while the two front lift cylinders could be operated independently.

The next model, the 900, also came on the market in 1956. This was available with four alternative engines: diesel 40hp; TVO 37hp; gas 40hp; and high-compression gas 45hp. The diesel model pioneered the use of the distributor-type fuel-injection pump, and also featured dual category linkage with the David Brown-patented ball-type top link and the detachable bonnet. In 1957 the 900 Livedrive was introduced. This was the first David Brown model with a dual clutch, which could give live hydraulics and live PTO. The 950 'T' and 'U' series were similar in design to the 900 but had increased power.

A farmer studies his plow set, attached to his Cropmaster model David Brown tractor.

introduced in 1953, were the first small tractors to have the advantage of TCU. They too featured a two-speed PTO and belt pulley unit and had a six-speed gear-box.

In 1956 a completely different machine, the 2D, was introduced. This was made until 1961, and was ideally suited to precision market garden work and as a specialist row-crop machine on larger farms. The 2D used a lightweight, rear-mounted, air-cooled two-cylinder diesel engine, while rear lift and PTO were available as options. Both lifts were

The introduction of the 950 Implematic in 1959 offered farmers the opportunity to use the depth (gauge) wheel system or draught control with equal facility. Automatic weight transfer was available through the Implematic draught control or controlled weight transfer through the TCU engine. In 1961 the 'V' and 'W' series were superseded by the 950 Implematic 'A' and 'B' series, which had improved front axle clearance and multi-speed PTO to provide both 540 and 1000rpm standard speeds. The 'A' and 'B' series 850 Implematic tractors had a four-

The 25D, shown here was introduced in 1953 and benefitted from TCU and a PTO.

cylinder diesel engine but gasoline versions were also offered. The later 'C' and 'D' series had diesel engines only and featured multi-speed PTO and improved front axle clearance. From April 1963 height control was included in the hydraulic system. In September 1964, both the 950 and the 880 Implematic models were superseded by the 'E' and 'F' series 880 Implematic with a new three-cylinder engine. A choice of 11/49 (high-speed) or 9/50 (low-speed) final drives gave speed ranges similar to those of the old 950 and 880 Implematics, but the high torque of the new engine gave a much-improved lugging power.

With the introduction of the 990 Implematic in 1961, the company first used the principle of a cross-flow cylinder head in conjunction with a two-stage front mounted air-cleaner. The 990 was powered by a 52hp, direct-injection diesel engine. In 1963 height

This is the David Brown 2D rowcrop tractor, in production from 1956 to 1961.

The D2 used a 14 hp, four-stroke, air-cooled, two-cylinder, diesel engine and four-speed gearbox.

David Brown also made crawlers, this is the TD50, made between 1953 and 1956.

David Brown also made crawlers, this is the TD50, made between 1953 and 1956.

The David Brown 900 was launched in 1956. An improved version was introduced in 1957.

control was introduced in the 990's Implematic hydraulic system, the wheel-base was increased, a front-mounted battery fitted, and a twelve-speed alternative transmission brought in. This tractor was also equipped with a roll-over cage.

The next model, the 770, was a machine powered by a three-cylinder 35hp diesel engine. It had a patented two-lever twelve-speed gear-box as standard equipment, and was the first tractor to feature the outstandingly simple Selectamatic hydraulic system. This proved so successful that it was introduced on all tractors in the David Brown range in October 1965. At the same time the 770 was up-graded to 36hp and re-styled in a new orchid-white and chocolate livery. It remained on sale until 1970.

Also in 1965, the 880 was re-rated at 46hp and the 990 at 55hp. Both were equipped with multi-speed PTO and differential lock, and both were fitted with the Selectamatic hydraulic system and re-styled in the white-and-chocolate livery. (The twelve forward,

four reverse speed gear-box was also an option.) A four-wheel drive version of the 990 was introduced in 1970, while full-flow filtration of hydraulic oil was incorporated on all models in 1970.

The 67hp, 1200 Selectamatic tractor of 1967–uprated to 72hp in 1968 – was the first David Brown model to have a separate hand clutch controlling the drive to the PTO. In addition, the hydraulic pump was mounted at the front of the engine and it had three-point linkage. A luxury suspension seat was fitted as standard. Then in 1970 the four-wheel drive 1200 was announced. The 72hp 1212, which followed, was the first tractor to be equipped with Hydra-Shift semi-automatic transmission.

In 1971 the Synchromesh twelve forward and four reverse gear-box became standard equipment on all David Brown tractors except the 1212. The 885 superseded both the 780 and 880, taking the best features from each, including its availability in 'narrow' form. The 990, now equipped with the

The David Brown TVO(Tractor Vaporising Oil) model, which used a cheaper form of tractor fuel.

The 850 Implematic was available up to 1965. This is the four-cylinder engine.

The three-cylinder David Brown 780, fitted with the simple-to-use Selectamatic hydraulic system.

Taking over from the 880 was the 885, which used a three-cylinder, 164 cubic inch engine.

With David Brown now part of the Case IH corporation, many models were re-branded as Case.

Synchromesh gearbox, continued to be produced, while the 995 and the 996 filled the gap between the 990 and the former 1200 class. The 996 featured a hand-operated PTO clutch although, unlike the 1200 class, its hydraulic pump was retained behind the gear-box. The 1210 Synchromesh took over from the 1200. The David Brown-designed safety feature, Weatherframe, was also introduced in 1971, while the alternator became a standard fitting in 1973.

This is the popular David Brown 990 Selectamatic. It replaced the 950 model in 1961.

In 1972 the David Brown Tractor Company was sold to Tenneco Inc. of Houston, Texas, and became affiliated to another world-famous Tenneco subsidiary, the J. I. Case Company of Racine, Wisconsin, USA. The year 1988 was a sad one for all David Brown enthusiasts: the Meltham factory was to close, bringing to an end another significant piece of tractor history. Even so, under the Tenneco banner David Brown Tractors and Case were now successfully expanding their combined production, marketing and distribution facilities.

The 500,000th tractor made, the 1974, 91hp, model 1412, their first turbocharged tractor.

Deutz (Allis/Fahr)

1907-present

The Deutz company was formed by two of the pioneers of the internal combustion engine, Nikolaus August Otto and Eugene Langen. In the early to mid-1860s they developed a four-stroke engine which was finally exhibited at the Paris World Exhibition of 1867. The pair then formed a company, Gasmotoren Fabrik Deutz AG. They went out of their way to employ the best German engineers of the time, men such as Gottlieb Daimler and Wilhelm Maybach.

In 1907 the Deutz company produced its first tractors, as well as a motor plow which was then considered to be of advanced design. In 1926 the MTZ 222 diesel tractor was unveiled. The diesel's single-cylinder produced 14hp and was water-cooled, using a simple hopper system rather than a radiator.

The diesel engine had effectively changed the face of tractor manufacture in Germany, and Deutz was at the forefront of diesel engines for agricultural use. At the beginning of the 1930s the company produced the Stahlschlepper ('Iron Tractor') models. This range included the F1M 414, the F2M 312 and the F3M 315, which had single-, twin- and three-cylinder diesel engines respectively. The smaller engines were started by an electric mechanism, while the larger ones started with compressed air. When running, the largest displacement model produced 50hp. By this time Deutz was selling its engines to other tractor makers. One of these was Ritscher, which used Deutz diesels in the construction of what was then the only tricycle-type tractor built in Germany.

The Deutz tractor evolved throughout the early 1930s, and by 1937 the company was making one of the first mass-produced mini-tractors.

This too was powered by a single-cylinder diesel engine, which now produced 11hp, and had a 540rpm PTO. Now merged with the engineering firm Humboldt and engine-maker Oberursel, and operating under the name Klockner-Humboldt-Deutz, the company made a variety of vehicles during World War II, most of which used air-cooled engines.

Deutz used diesel engines early-on, in single, twin and three-cylinder engines.

The 1950 F1L 514 and F2L 514, were both equipped with air-cooled diesel engines.

A beautifully restored, single cylinder, diesel engined, Deutz D15, seen in Holland.

By the early 1970s the D80 06 was being manufactured with a 73hp, six-cylinder, diesel engine.

After the war, mass production was resumed, and Deutz soon made its 50,000th tractor. The company's machines were the best-selling tractors in France, which emphasised the popularity of single-cylinder diesel machines in Europe. Encouraged by this success in Europe at least, Deutz looked to expand its production base. In the mid-1960s, the company linked up with the implement-maker Fahr. The two merged in 1969.

In 1967 Deutz had begun to export tractors to USA, which would include the D5506 and D8006, even though air-cooled machines were not common in the States. By the mid-1980s Deutz had acquired the ailing Allis-Chalmers company. It was thought that

Seen here is a Deutz D80 06 at work in a field in Holland. The engine was reputed to be very noisy.

By the mid 1980s, Deutz had acquired Allis Chalmers. This is the Deutz-Allis 6265.

this famous brand name would improve company fortunes in the USA–giving Deutz access to Allis-Chalmers's big dealer network. The first Deutz-Allis machines were a combination of German imports and the surplus inventory of the Allis range. In 1986 the Deutz-Fahr DX range became the Deutz-Allis 6200 series, which ranged from the 43-PTO-hp 6240 to the 71-PTO-hp 6275. All these models were powered by Deutz air-cooled diesels. Then, adapting and re-badging models from the old Allis-Chalmers line, the company produced the Deutz 5015, 8010, 8030, 8050, 8070 and 4W-305.

Over the next few years, the Deutz content was increased as old Allis stocks ran low. In 1987, the 7000 series was brought directly from Germany, the air-cooled diesels offering up to 144hp. In 1988 it was announced that the White-New Idea company would build a range of 150hp-plus tractors for Deutz-Allis. These appeared the following year as the 9130, 9150, 9170 and 9190. However, all were powered by Deutz engines ranging from 150 to 193hp, and all had 18-speed transmission with three-speed powershift.

The following year, Deutz-Allis was bought by the new AGCO corporation, and in 1992 it was decided to brand the Deutz-Allis tractors AGCO-Allis. However, it would be another four years before AGCO-Allis ceased to use Deutz engines.

Imports from Germany came, like this Deutz-Allis 7145, after Allis parts ran dry in the US.

The 9100 series was top of the range for 1988. Seen here is the 9130 hard at work.

Also a part of the Deutz-Allis 9100 range, the big 9150 model used a Deutz, six-cylinder engine.

In Europe, meanwhile, the other arm of the old Deutz concern, Deutz-Fahr, was attracting the attention of a number of large corporations. It was finally bought up by the Italian group SAME in 1995. Given this financial backing, the company went on to develop and manufacture a number of high-tech machines. The outstanding model was the Agrotron. Launched in 1995, this looked positively space age when compared to other tractors of the

time. The long sloping nose would prove an extremely influential styling, while a water-cooled diesel engine, designed by Deutz itself, powered the big frame. The cab had a huge expanse of glass, giving the driver a high degree of visibility, and one of the machine's prime features was electronically controlled hydraulic lift. The Agrotron did experience a number of early performance glitches, but its eventual success ensured the survival of

Bottom of the range, the 9130 still used the Deutz, six-cylinder engine of 374 cubic inches.

The Agrotron models of the mid 1990s had a huge influence on future tractor design.

69

Deutz within the SAME fold. However, it was no great surprise to see that the next tractor, the Agroplus, was much simpler in concept. The Agroplus was modelled on the SAME Dorado tractor, but would be supplied with a Deutz range of engines between 60 and 95hp.

Deutz continue to operate under the SAME banner. Since its earliest origins in the early twentieth century, it has proved itself to be one of Europe's most durable tractor brands.

The Deutz 2012 engine, which has a power range of 75-147kW, and a choice of four or six-cylinders.

With a power range of 90-186 kw, the Deutz 1013 has water-cooled, four or six-cylinder versions.

The Agrotron series comprises fifteen models with countless features and equipment options.

The Agrotron 108-165 models use a powerful, high performance Deutz engine.

Sloping cowling and a panoramic cab allow excellent views of the front-mounted implements area.

Modern machines have air-conditioning and sealed cabs to counteract dust and heat.

E

Eagle

1906-1940s

The American Eagle Manufacturing Company built its first tractor in 1906. This was a heavyweight twin-cylinder machine rated at 32hp. It had a special cooling system in which water, flowing out of a tank and over a metal screen, cooled the engine as it evaporated. The next Eagle, of 1911, was not a great success, and it was 1916 before the company produced another machine–a big four-cylinder machine that could run at a speed of 2.5 mph (4 kph). After this, Eagle then set about making a series of smaller models. There was the 8/16 (also of 1916), the engine of which was governed to 400 rpm–unusually low for a machine of this kind. There was the twin-cylinder 16/30 made between 1916 and 1932. And there was the 12/20 twin–later uprated to 12/22, then to 13/25–which was produced from 1917. But it was the 20/35 tractor the company was really proud of, claiming in publicity that 'any man can run it and keep it in repair.'

In the 1920s Eagle's heavyweight twin-cylinder construction began to look outmoded (though the company continued with the 20/35 until 1934 and the even bigger 20/40 until 1938). In 1930, partly as a response to this criticism, Eagle built the very modern-looking 6A. At first this had a six-cylinder Hercules engine, but this was to be replaced by a six-cylinder Waukesha. Developments of the 6A included the 6B, meant for row-crop work, and the general purpose 6C.

Eagle continued to build tractors into the early 1940s. However, production was suspended during the war and was never resumed.

The Eagle model 6 took the place of the big 20-35 due to size and maneuverability.

The Eagle 20-35 model. A twin-cylinder machine that became unpopular due to its size.

Eicher

1936-2005

The German Eicher brothers, who were engineers, started small. Between 1936 and 1941 their company only built about 1,000 machines. All these were small and relatively simple in concept. Powered by Deutz engines, they were similar in frame to the machines produced by Fendt and indeed by Deutz itself. After World War II, however, Eicher developed its own range of air-cooled diesels. From 1948 onwards, these machines were offered in two-, three- and four-cylinder versions. Typical Eichers of the period were the EKL11, powered by a 1.5 litre engine, and the

The Eicher tractor company started off small by making machines similar to Deutz.

26hp twin-cylinder tractor, which used Eicher's own 2.6 litre diesel. By 1968, the company was making a six-cylinder diesel for use on the big Wotan tractor. In the 1970s, Eicher were doing well enough to attract the attention of Massey-Ferguson, who proceeded to acquire a stake in the company. Massey-Ferguson also owned Perkins, and so Eicher began to use water-cooled Perkins engines for its tractors. Soon after this, the company began to specialise in four-wheel drive machines. By the mid-1980s it had built its 120,000th tractor, and was producing some 2,000 tractors a year. But Eicher, like many firms in the West, was finding the economic climate increasingly frosty. The Far East was seen as a fertile new market, and so the company moved a large part of its operations to India. In May 2005, Eicher was taken over by the Indian firm TAFE. This acquisition strengthened TAFE's position as the second largest tractor producer on the subcontinent.

The Eicher catered for smaller farmers: Note the grass cutting attachment on this machine.

During the 1970s the Eicher tractor became a little squarer in shape and had a cab.

Emerson-Brantingham

1909-1928

In the mid-nineteenth century, one John H. Manny of Rockford, Illinois, USA, invented a horse-drawn reaper. With the help of investors Waite Talcott and Ralph Emerson, he formed a company to produce it. Though Manny died shortly afterwards, his partners carried on as Talcott-Emerson. In 1895 this company expanded, introducing new lines for farm implements. In the meantime, Emerson had hired a young grocery clerk called Charles Brantingham. Such was his impact on the company that by 1909 Talcott-Emerson had become Emerson-Brantingham, and Charles Brantingham was the company president.

Emerson-Brantingham soon began to absorb other firms, and this was the beginning of its interest in tractors. From the Gas Traction Company it inherited the Big Four 30. This was a four-cylinder, 21,000 pound monster that produced 60hp. Similarly, from Reeves & Co the company took on a 40/65 machine which it produced until 1920. Emerson-Brantingham also began to design its own tractors. In 1916 it introduced the Model L, a three-wheeler which produced 12/20hp and had a three-plough pulling power. This was superseded by the four-wheel Model Q 12/20, which remained in production until 1928. In 1917 the company built the little 9/16, aimed at a market now dominated by the Fordson. However, it failed to compete and was discontinued. There were other EBs, such as the 1918 Model AA and the 20/36 of 1919–a big machine powered by an L-head four-cylinder engine. However, the 1920s were to prove difficult for the company. In 1928 it was taken over by J.I.Case, and all EB tractor production ceased.

The model L was the first of a series of small machines introduced by Emmerson-Brantingham.

F

Fate-Root-Heath

1919-1954

In the late 1800s, Pennsylvania brickyard worker J. D. Fate and his business partner were attracted to Plymouth, Ohio, USA, by the community's promise to help them found an industry that would bring jobs to the area. In 1882 the Fate and Gunsaullus Company started building clay-extruding machinery for making bricks. Ten years later, Fate bought out his partner and formed the J. D. Fate Company. In 1909, Fate started the Plymouth Truck Company, but this wasn't a great success and went out of business in 1915.

At about the same time that trucks were being built, a customer asked Fate if he could build a machine that would replace the mules he was using to move rail cars around his railroad yard. Fate's yard locomotive proved very successful, and laid the foundation for what would become the company's primary product, Plymouth Locomotives.

In 1919 Fate joined Root-Heath Manufacturing Company and formed Fate-Root-Heath. The new organization continued to build clay machinery, yard locomotives and added a line of sharpening equipment for reel-type grass mowers. Business was good, and the company prospered until the economic crash of 1929.

By the early 1930s, orders for expensive locomotives had slowed substantially. In order to keep the factory doors open, Fate-Root-Heath needed a product that people could afford to buy in quantity. The town of Plymouth was located in the middle of prime Ohio farmland and a tractor seemed the natural addition. Charles Heath, general manager of the company at that time, presented the idea of building a farm tractor to get the company through the Depression. Accordingly, Floyd Carter, chief engineer of the locomotive department, designed a huge, heavy machine powered by a big, slow-speed Climax engine. Unfortunately, this was just the kind of tractor farmers were turning away from in favour of lighter, more maneuvrable machines. Several new engineers were hired, and once again design work began on a new tractor.

The result was an innovative new tractor, the Plymouth. The new machine was light and used a small, high-speed motor with four-speed

This model 42 of the mid 1940s has rubber tires, available prior to World War II.

Remove the mud from the wheels and you can see what a neat machine the Silver King is.

The company initially made tractors under the Plymouth name but changed to Silver King.

transmission. It was powered by a Hercules IXA engine and was a one-plow standard tread machine. Fate-Root-Heath engineers had found a silver paint that adhered well and gave protection against rust. This was used on the company's other products, so it seemed natural therefore to use it for the Plymouth tractors. The wheels were painted blue for contrast.

Luke Biggs, a farmer who had built his own tractor, then joined Fate-Root-Heath. One of the more original features of his machine was its single front wheel, and once he had shown Charlie Heath a

The name on the tank is Silver King but the mudguards are branded Faith-Root-Heath.

Sitting in the evening sun, a model R44 of 1937. The R signified the tractor had rubber tires.

picture of it, he was offered a job on the spot. Biggs brought his farming and tractor building experience with him to the tractor department and within weeks, he was made superintendent of the tractor division.

The most revolutionary thing about the new Plymouth tractor was that it was the first tractor that could be used with rubber tires. Even so, though the company sales literature promoted the use of rubber tires, steel wheels were the standard equipment and tires were purchased at extra cost. The first Plymouths were given one of four model numbers (R-38, R-44, S-38, S-44) determined solely by the tread width and type of wheels used. A model R-38, for example, was a tractor on rubber tires with a 38 in (95cm) tread, while an S-44 came with steel wheels with a 44 in (110cm) tread. As the model line expanded, so did the quantity of model numbers until, at one time, there were no less than 10 model numbers to describe two basic tractors.

The Chrysler corporation had been using the Plymouth name for their automobile since 1928, and had not complained about the Plymouth name on locomotives. But seeing little tractors with the Plymouth name buzzing down the road at 25 mph (40 kph) did cause a stir. In 1934 Fate-Root-Heath and Chrysler tangled over the use of the name but the single Plymouth car built by Fate-Root-Heath back in 1910, way before the Chrysler Corporation

even existed, saved the day for the tractor company. Chrysler indeed was forced to buy the right to use the Plymouth name from Fate-Root-Heath, and reportedly paid one dollar for it!

The company now had to come up with a new name. The tractors had always been silver, and the men at Fate-Root-Heath thought their tractor was king, so Charles Heath suggested the name 'Silver King'. The name stuck. It was proposed that all tractors after serial number 314 would carry that name.

By 1936 the tractor business was booming: the machines were going out the door at the rate of four or five a day. Biggs and his crew had developed a three-wheeled tractor, which borrowed heavily from his homemade design, designated model R-66. Designed as a row-crop cultivator tractor, the three-wheeled model featured a unique steering arrangement of levers and chains that formed a bulky appendage located in front of the radiator.

The low, stable design of the four-wheeled Silver King, along with the lights and horn available, made it popular for a wide variety of uses including towing movie sets around movie lots.

Throughout the late 1930s, tractors rolled off the assembly line at a pace that did more than just keep Fate-Root-Heath out of bankruptcy. The assembly line had been fine-tuned, and when all the necessary parts were available, a tractor could be turned out every 30 minutes. The year 1937 was the best ever for Silver King production, with over 1000 tractors being built. The year 1938 saw the three-wheeled tractor fitted with a new rounded radiator grille, and in 1939 the four-wheeled tractor also received the new grille.

The first major mechanical change in the production of Silver Kings came in 1940. The Continental-built engine was given to the three-wheeled tractor, while a Hercules IXB-3 engine was fitted to the four-wheeled tractor for a time before it too received the Continental engine.

The canister looking part is an excuse for a silencer on this four-cylinder Hercules engine.

Very few tractors were built during World War II, as the materials for farm tractors were in short supply. Besides, the US War Department had other plans for Fate-Root-Heath. There was huge demand for Plymouth yard locomotives, and so the company worked at nearly full capacity building locomotives and other equipment for the war effort.

Despite this concentration on war work, the first big changes in the Silver King line were introduced in 1942, an improved Continental F-162 engine being installed in all models. Newly designed sheet metal was added to the tractor, and now it really did look streamlined. The steering on the three-wheeled version was changed, a simple idler arm replacing the chain and sprocket.

After the war, demand for yard locomotives remained strong, and competition was much less fierce than in the tractor sector. Building locomotives now became the company's principal business. Nevertheless, that didn't stop other companies from approaching Fate-Root-Heath for help in meeting demand for tractors. Cockshutt bought several tractors to evaluate and was

favorably impressed, resulting in a request for Fate-Root-Heath to produce chassis and final drives for a tractor to be built by Cockshutt. However, lack of interest scuppered further arrangements.

Even as support from management was eroding, engineers in the tractor division were constantly at work improving the Silver King. Biggs and the other engineers had moved on, but most of the men working on the line were farmers and there was no shortage of ideas for improvements. New hydraulics and other improvements were added in the post-war period.

In 1954 Fate-Root-Heath management ran out of tolerance for the tractor division and parts and tooling were sent to the Mountain State Fabricating Company in Clarksburg, West Virginia. Unfortunately, even though Mountain State restarted the serial number series at 50000 and built approximately 75 tractors, Silver King couldn't keep it in business. The company ceased production and sent all remaining parts back to Plymouth, Ohio. There, the parts were sent to a local junkyard. Fate-Root-Heath had finally washed its hands of the tractor business.

The Silver King name appeared in the middle of the front of the radiator also.

Fendt

1928-present

When the Fendt brothers, Hermann, Xaver and Paul, of Weimar, Germany, started to build tractors in a blacksmith's shop in the 1920s, they could hardly have foreseen the huge changes that would transform the industry in the twentieth century. In 1928, Hermann Fendt built a mower that was little more than a stationary engine with transmission mounted on wheels. In 1930, he and his brothers introduced a small tractor with a 6hp engine, mounted plow and independently driven mower. For the first time, small and middle-sized farming operations could afford to replace their horses. The name of the tractor program, appropriately enough, was Dieselross ('diesel horse').

On December 31, 1937, Xaver Fendt & Co was established, and the following year the 1000th Dieselross tractor, a 16hp F18, left the production line. The following year, the Model F22 was introduced. This had a two-cylinder engine, a conventional upright radiator and a four-speed gearbox, and foreshadowed future developments in tractor production. In 1942, shortage of diesel oil and the prohibition of diesel tractor operation led to the development of the methane generator tractor with 25hp. In fact, shortages encouraged Fendt to produce tractors that could run on almost any kind of combustible fuel.

Following World War II, the company enjoyed rapid expansion. (Over 1000 Dieselross machines were turned out in 1946.) At the same time, the company changed its engine supplier, using MWM engines rather than Deutz ones. One of the last Deutz-powered Fendts was the 18hp F18H of 1949, which used a single-cylinder engine. A contrast was provided by the more powerful Dieselross F28, which was powered by a twin-cylinder MWM diesel. Both tractors, however, remained faithful to the original Dieselross concept.

The name Dieselross was used for a whole series of tractors. This is the model F15 of 1950.

1950

Dieselross F15

This is the little 6hp machine, with plow, that Hermann Fendt and his brother built.

The 12hp Dieselross F12L was first introduced in 1952 and went into series production in 1953. The 12hp Fendt tool-carrier also came on to the market in 1953. The Favorit 1, trend-setting in form and boasting technical features such as the 40hp engine and the multi-gear close-ratio gear-box, was produced in 1958.

In 1961 the 100,000th Fendt tractor, a 30hp Farmer 2, rolled off the production line. With about 60,000 models sold to date, the Tool Carrier, a mechanised system for tasks such as seeding and harvesting, reflected a particularly successful development. A technical breakthrough came in 1968 with the Turbomatik, which was provided with a stepless automatic transmission.

With the introduction of the Favorit range with up to 150hp in 1976, Fendt addressed a new market sector. In 1979 it could offer one of the most powerful machines available, the MAN-engined 262hp Favorit 626. This was followed in 1980 by the Farmer 300 range, which could be purchased with Turbomatik and featured innovations such as a speed of 25 mph (40 kph) and a rubber-supported cab. In 1984, the 380 GTA System Tractor, an all-round vision vehicle whose secret was an under-floor engine, came on the market. The following year, Fendt took the market lead in Germany for the first time. High-tech, and in compact dimensions, were the distinguishing features of the 200 range available from 40 to 75hp, which was produced as a standard tractor or as a special tractor for wine and fruit

growers. The 800 range was the first heavy-duty tractor with turbo-shift, hydro-pneumatic cab and front-axle suspension, and a speed of 50 kph. The top-performing machine was the Favorit 824 with 230hp. The Favorit 500 C-series (90-140hp), also introduced in 1984, incorporated successful features such as a speed of 30 mph (50 kph), springy suspension and turbo-shift.

In 1995, the groundbreaking system vehicle Xylon (110-140hp) made its appearance. This vehicle could be used for agricultural, landscape and municipal applications, and carried on where the famous MB-trac had left off. It was essentially a systems tractor with a mid-mounted cab, and could carry front and rear implements simultaneously. In fact it had four mounting positions, giving it the potential to perform several operations in a single pass. With four-wheel drive and almost equal-sized wheels, the Xylon was powered by a turbo-intercooled MAN four-cylinder diesel engine offering up to 140hp. It had a Variofill turbo-clutch that brought the turbo in and out of engagement as required. The complex transmission gave 44 speeds (20 crawler speeds and 24 for other work), allowing up to 50 kph on the road. With four-wheel braking, front-axle suspension, and a fully insulated cab, the Xylon was a thoroughly modern tractor that took many of its components from Fendt's conventional Favorit range. In 1996 it was followed by the Vario 926, the first heavy-duty tractor to have stepless Fendt Vario transmission.

By the mid-1990s, Fendt had become the best-selling make in Germany, claiming 17 percent of the market. But a total output of 10,000 machines a year still made the company small in world terms, and vulnerable to takeover. This happened in January 1997, when Fendt came under the wing of the

The Dieselross F 12 L was first introduced in 1952 and went into series production in 1953.

This is the Fendt 309 LSA, which used Turbomatik stepless transmission, a Fendt development.

A truly multifunctional machine, the Fendt Xylon is happy carrying out many chores on the farm.

The new 300 Ci has a brand new engine. A four-litre, four-cylinder turbocharged unit.

The first Vario 700 was introduced in 1998. The 700 Vario became the bestselling tractor range.

corporate giant AGCO. That year the company also introduced the Favorit range with Vario from 170 to 260hp and stepless drive technology. More importantly, it brought in the new Farmer 300C (75-95hp) tractor generation. The following year, with the introduction of the new Favorit 700 Vario range with 140-160hp, Fendt set new standards in tractor technology, the innovative control system receiving international awards. Also in 1998, the 380 GTA-Turbo and the 370 GTA with 75hp came on the market. In 2002 the Favorit Vario was offered in two

Built between 1995 and 2004, the Xylon is seen here happily cutting the long grass.

The 930 Vario is designed for the toughest operating conditions, with its 310 HP engine.

The 206V. Fendt have specialty, standard and Vario tractors, ranging from 65 to 310 hp.

ranges with variable speeds – 1-20 mph (2-32 kph) and 1-31mph (2-50 kph). In theory the Vario system allowed road speeds of 27 mph (44 kph), but in practice the purpose was to allow relaxed cruising of 1,680 rpm at 31 mph (50 kph). In fact the 2002 version was much easier to use than the original Vario, and was more efficient. It remained the only stepless automatic system available on tractors of this power. (The 926's six-cylinder, turbo-intercooled MAN engine produced a massive 271hp.) Fendt had come a long way indeed from Dieselross, and it continues to be one of the solid European performers.

The 200 V, F and P series – 14 models starting with the narrow vineyard tractor.

Extra-short crop cut, high compression capacity, with well-formed, dense round bales.

The mid-range Vario tractors in the high output range, like this 400 model, have stamped their mark.

Ferguson

1884-1960

Henry George Ferguson was born on 4 November 1884 in the small Irish town of Growell, County Down, near Belfast. He showed an aptitude for all things mechanical at a very early age but, much to his father's dismay, had no desire to get involved with farming. The exploits of the Wright Brothers fascinated the young Ferguson and he visited many air shows and exhibitions around Europe. Returning to Belfast, he persuaded his brother Joe that it would be good for their garage business to build a plane! Throughout 1909 construction took place, with various changes and improvements being made as work progressed. When the day of the first test flight arrived, the aircraft was towed through the Belfast streets up to Hillsborough Park. Initial efforts to get off the ground failed due to propeller trouble and bad weather. Finally, on December 31, 1909, the plane was ready. A reporter from the Belfast Telegraph described the scene: 'The roar of the eight cylinders was like the sound of a Gatling gun in action. The machine was set against the wind and all force being developed the splendid pull of the new propeller swept the big aeroplane along as Mr Ferguson advanced the lever. Presently, at the movement of the pedal, the aeroplane rose into the air at a height from nine to twelve feet, amidst the cheers of the onlookers.'

Henry Ferguson had made the first flight in Ireland, and was the first Briton to build and fly his own plane.

Henry Ferguson, who was known as Harry, married his wife Maureen in 1913. Assisted by the engineer Willie Sands, he went on to design the Belfast plow. It was designed for use with the Eros, a tractor conversion of the Ford Model T car. By 1917, it was ready for use as the first wheel-less plow: the first demonstration took place in Coleraine in front of the farming public.

Ford had announced its intention to build a tractor plant in Cork, but unfortunately it decided to import 6000 of its latest Fordson F tractors from America before the factory was ready. The Model F was the most widely used tractor after the Eros, and was lighter than most other tractors of the day. It under-priced the Eros and sold in vast numbers. Fordson F's came flooding on to the market: the Ferguson plow was effectively redundant.

However, Ferguson didn't dwell on his misfortune, but set about selling his remaining stocks of Eros plow. He then devoted his energy to designing a plow that could be attached specifically to the Fordson F tractor. The result of this work was the famous Ferguson 2-point hitch, later referred to as the duplex hitch. One of the main advantages, besides being comparatively light, was that if the plow struck obstructions and halted the tractor, it was prevented from toppling on to the driver. This design established the basic principle of all subsequent Ferguson linkages, namely the concept of a 'virtual hitch-point'. The 1919 Ferguson Hitch, with its simple top and bottom links, enabled Ferguson's own plough design to become a unit pulled as if its point of hitch was close to ground level and near the center of the tractor. It could also be raised and lowered from the seat with a spring-

A demonstration of the Ferguson three-point-hitch, a design that was often copied.

A close-up view of the famous Ferguson three-point-hitch mechanism.

Harry Ferguson was looking for someone to sell his design and the Brown-Ferguson was the result.

assisted lift. The ingenious geometry of the Ferguson System allowed a lightweight implement to gain penetration without built-in weight.

In 1925, Ferguson came up with a second crucially important invention–draught control. This enabled the depth of an implement to be automatically adjusted by reference to the effort needed to pull it through the soil. It complemented the 'virtual hitch-point' invention perfectly. Further development changes, including the addition of a third arm, finally culminated in the Ferguson three-point linkage.

The quest to find a company that would adopt this new system was not easy–the Depression was hitting hard and money was short. The Morris Motor Company was interested, but pulled out at the last moment. Ferguson decided to design his own tractor to fit his own attachments. The machine was assembled at his Belfast workshops during 1933, many of the components, such as the Hercules engine and David Brown gear-box, being bought in. The tractor was completed with Ferguson three-point linkage and draught control systems. A three-speed constant-mesh gear-box took the drive to a spiral bevel rear axle, and independent brakes were fitted to assist turning. It had spoke-type wheels, similar to those on the early Fordsons, and it could be operated on gasoline or paraffin. The tractor was

Basically the same as the original 'black' tractor, except the Brown-Ferguson used a Coventry Climax engine.

called the Ferguson 'black'. Having now made the tractor, Ferguson needed someone to build it in quantity. This task was taken on by David Brown, who had already supplied parts for the machine. David Brown formed David Brown Tractors Ltd., and the colour of the tractor was changed from black to battleship grey.

In October 1938 Harry Ferguson took tractor number 722, with implements, to the USA. An American, Eber Sherman, who had manufactured the Ferguson plough with the duplex hitch in the 1920s, arranged for Harry Ferguson to demonstrate his tractor to Henry Ford Senior. Ford was impressed, and the two concluded a deal with a handshake. The agreement was that Ford would manufacture a tractor for Harry Ferguson incorporating all the latest Ferguson inventions and designs. After Ferguson returned to England, Ford built two prototypes, but they proved entirely unsatisfactory and were discarded. In February 1939 Harry Ferguson returned to Dearborn with a small team of engineers and under their supervision, work resumed on another new prototype designated the 9N. Ford production engineers got the new tractor on line in record time, applying the very latest production line techniques. Ferguson had to accept a Ford side-valve engine, although he would have preferred an overhead valve unit. Every effort was made to use stock items where possible and the gearbox was similar to the old 'A'.

The 9N did finally reach the UK, fitted with a modified Holley 295 Vaporiser to run on TVO (Tractor Vaporising Oil): it was designated the 9NAN. Wartime shortages caused a utility model to be produced, the 2NAN.

When Henry Ford II took over the Ford Empire in 1945, his first task was to put the Ford operation back into the black: his attitude to the production of a tractor sold by another organization was hostile. The sales agreement between Ford and Ferguson was terminated in 1947 and by 1948 Ford was building its own tractor, the 8N, which was simply an improved 9N with a new color scheme.

This whole affair ended up in court, the trial starting on March 29, 1951.

After long and costly proceedings, Ferguson accepted a settlement of $9,250,000, which was only to cover the unauthorized use of the Ferguson hydraulic system. The claim against loss of business was dismissed.

During World War II, the Standard Motor Company operated, on behalf of the government, a new 'shadow' factory making aero engines. This plant was in Banner Lane, Coventry, and stood idle when the war ended. Standard's MD, Sir John Black, and Harry Ferguson struck a deal in which Ferguson would be in charge of design, development, sales and service while Standard Motor Company would make the tractors. The TE20 (TE standing for Tractor England) was soon created, the first unit coming off the Banner Lane production line on 6 July 1946.

The little grey Fergie carries out its work, using grass type tires. Note the roll-bar.

This beautifully restored tractor is a TE 20 model, still in Surrey County Council colours.

It used an American engine, the Continental Z-120, until the 2088cc unit of the Standard Vanguard car was fitted from July 1948. A diesel version followed in 1951, the TEF20.

Ferguson also built a factory in Detroit, producing the TO20–an Americanized version TE. This was later uprated to the TO35, which had more power and six-speed transmission.

Massey Harris merged with Ferguson in 1953, and soon took over. A prototype Ferguson 60 was developed but never went into production. Once Harry Ferguson realized he was no longer in control, he bought himself out of the company. He died on 25 October 1960.

Depicted is a T20. The contraption over the wheels is a section boosting wheel cage.

This TE 20 model was produced by Ferguson after he had fallen out with Brown and Ford.

Featured here is a restored Ferguson TEA model, which generally featured a car engine.

This Fergie is a model TO, standing for 'Tractor Overseas'. They were built in Detroit, USA.

A rare tractor. An American-made Ferguson 35 with 135 cubic inch, Continental engine.

A foreign advertising poster for the diesel FE model, an upgraded version of the original T20.

The Ferguson 35 with a gold engine was only made for about one year.

The TE 20 hard at work. This model Ferguson was made by the Standard Motor company in England.

Not often seen, not even at tractor meetings, is this Ferguson Road Roller machine.

Fiat

1919-present

The First World War was still raging when, in a field outside Turin, a group of Italian industrialists and government members met the businessman Giovanni Agnelli to view Italy's- –and arguably Europe's–first agricultural tractor. The Fiat Model 702 went on sale in 1919 and was manufactured alongside cars and trucks in Fiat's Turin factory. Built for plowing and for powering stationary threshing machines, the Model 702 was soon rated one of the most efficient tractors in the world, and enjoyed very strong export sales. It played a major role in the mechanization of farm work that took place in the early twentieth century. The engine chosen for the 702 came from one of Fiat's 3.5 ton trucks. It was a four-cylinder unit that produced 30hp in the gasoline version and 25hp in the paraffin one. Over the next few years, different versions of this tractor were produced along with an up-rated 703 industrial model.

By the end of the 1920s, the smaller 700 series had made its debut in both wheeled and tracked versions that could be run on either diesel or petrol engines. The 700C crawler version of 1932 was probably the biggest selling Italian machine of the period and its success – along with the purchase of the Ansaldo, Ceriano, SPA and OM companies – helped to strengthen the tractor arm of Fiat. The crawler used a four-cylinder 30hp engine, and was equipped with a scraper blade on the front. In the 1930s the company also produced the 708C and the Model 40. The Model 40 had a Boghetto engine that could be started on gasoline and then switched to diesel once it had reached its working temperature. During World War II, these crawlers and tractors formed the basis of many machines used by the Italian military. The L6/40 tanks, for example, used SPA engines.

Italy was devastated by the conflict of 1939-45. Following the war, Fiat was able to sell many small cars, but selling tractors was another matter. There weren't too many large farms to serve, and Fiat tractors were too big and expensive for the average farmer. The solution came in the form of a tractor that could serve every kind of landowner. The Model 18 or 'la piccola' (the 'small one') as it was named, could deal with big jobs on little farms and little jobs on big farms. It was extremely popular: 2,500 were registered in the first year, and some 30

A beautiful example of a Fiat model 702 used mainly for plowing and working threshing machines.

Fiat were heavily into making crawlers too, for the construction industry and agriculture.

Making an appearance at a tractor pulling competition, this Fiat 1100 has slightly bulkier tires.

versions of it were eventually made. The little machine had a six forward and two reverse gear transmission, which was coupled to an air-cooled 18hp engine. Overseas sales also took off in Romania, Yugoslavia, Turkey and Argentina.

In 1962 Fiat created a joint venture with the Turkish company Koa Holding. By this time it was offering a huge range of vehicles of all sizes and types. Four years later, the Italian company established a Tractor and Earthmoving Machinery Division, and in 1970 Fiat Macchine e Movimento Terra S.p.A. was founded to pursue the company's activities in the earthmoving sector at Lecce, Italy. After this the new

Seen at a tractor meeting on the Continent was this rare model 18 'la piccola' Fiat.

Not as popular as the Fiat 500 car, this model 500 special tractor was popular with farmers

Made between 1965 and 1968, the Fiat 315 used a four-cylinder, 33hp, diesel engine.

The Fiat 505 crawler, a heavy-duty, rugged machine, capable of tackling difficult work.

The Fiat 780 model had a 224 cubic inch, four-cylinder engine and was made in 1975.

This is the Fiat 100-90 model. It had a six-cylinder engine and twenty forward gears.

company took over Simit, the leading Italian manufacturer of hydraulic excavators, and in 1974 Fiat Macchine e Movimento Terra created a joint venture with the American manufacturer Allis-Chalmers, creating the new corporation Fiat-Allis. That year Fiat Trattori S.P.A. was founded, and in

Made between 1984 and 1991 was this model 90-90, which used a five-cylinder, diesel engine.

1975 it became a shareholder of the Laverda concern.

It was in 1977 that Fiat took over Hesston, a move that gave the company entry into the huge American market. At the same time it acquired Agrifull, which specialized in small- to medium-sized tractors. A joint venture was set up with the Pakistani Tractor Corporation in 1983, and the following year Fiat Trattori became FiatAgri, the group's holding company for its agricultural machinery sector.

In between more mergers and acquisitions, all FiatAgri and Fiat-Allis activities were combined to create the new company FiatGeotech. Fiat then went on to acquire Ford New Holland, the name of the conglomerate becoming N. H. Geotech. Thus, through a complex process of integration, all the companies came together under a common flag.

The end of the 1980s saw the launch of the 90 series tractors that ranged from 55 to 180hp. The merger with New Holland had strengthened Fiat's grip on the larger modern tractor sector, and the New Holland 70 series machines were now being sold in some markets as the Fiat G series (in Fiat red rather than New Holland blue). But whatever its color, the tractor was the same, and its name was merely part of a re-branding exercise that could work both ways. For example, in some countries the Fiat 'L' series was being sold as the New Holland 5635.

The mid-1990s saw the introduction of the 66S series, which ranged from 35 to 60hp. All used three-cylinder diesel engines coupled to transmissions that ranged from 16 to 22 gears. Larger Model 66s ranged from 65 to 80hp, and the even bigger 93 series was able to offer up to 85hp plus turbo-charging.

With its articulating cab, this is the six-cylinder, turbo-diesel, Fiat 44-28 tractor.

But the complex process of corporate acquisition, which had transformed Fiat as a company, was far from over. When the Versatile Farm Equipment Company became part of Ford New Holland, N.H. Geotech's US division was further expanded. In 1993 N.H. Geotech changed its name to New Holland, a move which marked the beginning of the GNH, a global group which just seems to grow and grow.

Ford

1928-1994

Henry Ford, renowned for his major contribution to the automobile industry, was himself the son of a Michigan farmer and understood the need to apply the latest technology to farming. However, his success with the Model T car did not convince the Ford board of directors that tractors were worthy of investment. So in 1917, when his own workshop experiments began to bear fruit in the shape of the Model F, Ford was compelled to form a new company to market the machine (see FORDSON). In 1928, having achieved massive success with the Model F, Ford closed down American production of Fordson, transferring operations to Ireland and the UK.

But Ford had not abandoned the idea of tractor production in the USA. On the contrary, his engineers built and tested a number of prototypes throughout the 1930s. The eventual result was the Ford 9N, which used the Ferguson-Brown tractor as its template following a personal agreement between Ford himself and Harry Ferguson.

The Ford 9N was revolutionary in design. Low-slung, relatively lightweight at 2,340 pounds, it was a new kind of utility tractor that could be applied to all kinds of farm work. It had a smooth-running four-cylinder engine, its cab was quiet, and it came with

Henry Ford also made a significant impression in agriculture and tractor production.

From a farming family, Ford understood the needs of the farmer, but didn't get it right the first time.

The badge shows clearly the connection between Harry Ferguson and Ford.

an electric starter and pneumatic rubber tires. But the real improvement was the Ferguson System for implement attachment and control, which allowed the farmer increased speed and efficiency in the field.

The 9N, the result of collaboration between two major figures in tractor design, was an enormous success. Some 10,000 9N's were sold in the first six months following presentation in 1939, and this enabled the Ford company, which had lost out to rivals in this sector, to substantially recover its US market share.

The Ford 2N was introduced in 1942 and initially lacked electrics and rubber tires due to war shortages.

In 1942, however, Ford was forced to cease production of the 9N because materials bound for tractor production were diverted to the war effort. In its place for a short period came the 2N, a tractor designed to use materials that were not as scarce.

In April 1947 Henry Ford, the man who brought the motor car to the ordinary American, died at the age

Dearborn, USA, was Ford country and that was where his farms were too.

of 83. With his death, the agreement between Ford and Ferguson collapsed. Ford's grandson, Henry Ford II, announced that the company would be distributing an improved version of the 9N, cutting out Ferguson entirely. This decision was to be a costly one, since Ferguson was now in a position to compete directly with Ford. But that would be a few years away. In the meantime Ford increased its market share with the 8N. Indeed, this tractor would shortly become the company's best-selling model.

One of the most important developments of the 8N was the four-speed transmission. But the 8N still used the basic Ferguson System incorporated in the 9N line, and it was this unauthorized use that was the bone of contention in the lawsuit Ferguson filed against Ford. Despite high sales of the 8N, the lawsuit forced Ford to use a new hydraulic control system. This change was incorporated in the new Ford NAA, launched in 1953 and often called the Jubilee because its presentation marked the 50th anniversary of the Ford company.

The practice of a simplified assembly line, which Henry Ford had first introduced for production of the Model T car and which had also turned out Ford tractors, came to an end with the NAA in 1954. That year the 600 and 800 series were presented. The 600 series tractors were based on the NAA design and were aimed at the small farm equipment market, whereas the 800s were more powerful and aimed at larger farming applications.

Ford was now interested in pursuing every sector of the tractor market. Accordingly, the 700 and the 900 were introduced. These were three-wheeled models, and could be used for a wide variety of applications, including row-crop work. Otherwise, though, they were similar in design to the 600 and 800 series.

In 1957 Ford decided to spruce up the appearance of its product line. The biggest change was the addition of a section of bars across the front grille. All the existing models remained the same in terms of specifications, though the '1' suffix was added in place of the '0' at the end of each model number. Thus the 600 became the 601, and so on. In addition the engine size on the 601 and 801 series was augmented by the addition of the Workmaster and Powermaster engines respectively. Liquid petroleum gas was now also an option on all Ford tractors.

In the UK the Fordson New Major had been very successful, but the tractor was now considered rather large for some purposes. In 1957, Ford began to feel

The Ford NAN ran on gas and TVO and was manufactured in the USA in 1950.

Ford were determined to keep ahead. This advertisement shows clearly the push for extra power.

that the lack of an efficient small tractor was hurting its own position in Europe. To address this problem, Ford developed the Dexta, which was powered by a Perkins three-cylinder diesel engine.

As the Dexta story suggests, during this period Ford took its cue from the performance of Fordson in Europe. In 1958 the Fordson New Major was replaced by the Power Major. The Power Major, as the name suggests, had a more powerful version of the New Major engine that revolutionised the tractor industry in Europe, and introduced diesel at a competitive price. So Ford began to roll out upgraded versions of each of these models.

In 1959 Ford introduced the 501, single-row offset series, with 'red belly' paint scheme.

Replacing the 8N, the NAA was also named 'Golden Jubilee' to celebrate 50 years in the business.

Accordingly, when the Super Major replaced the Power Major in 1961, the Super Dexta was produced to replace the Dexta.

In 1959, Ford had introduced the Select-O-Speed transmission system. This was meant to provide a system with ten forward and two reverse speeds, and was designed to give farmers greater control over rough terrain. At first the project was something of a disaster, and the earliest models needed repair and redesign. However, after a long period of development, later versions of Select-O-Speed proved successful.

would the Ford Tractor Division be separated into Ford and Fordson.

In 1965 the range from the 2000 to the 4000 was revamped with a new three-cylinder diesel engine. The 5000 was equipped with a four-cylinder diesel, while the 6000 was renamed the Commander 6000 and redesigned to address the model's earlier technical problems. Over the next 10 years, the entire Ford line, now numbered solely in 'thousands,' was expanded. Nevertheless, many of these retained the original low 'utility' position, in which the driver sat astride the transmission.

In late 1961, Ford introduced the 6000 as the top of the line. It had a powerful six-cylinder engine.

In late 1961 Ford introduced the 2000 series to replace the 601 line, the 4000 to replace the 801 series, and the 6000, with a powerful six-cylinder engine, as the top of the line. (The Ford 6000 was a failure, however, and Ford was forced to replace every unit due to technical problems.) Meanwhile, in a move towards unification of the US and European tractor arms of Ford, the Fordson Super Dexta was imported from European plants and sold in the USA as the Ford 2000 Diesel, while the Fordson Super Major was brought in as the Ford 5000. The Fordson brand was dropped and all Ford tractors now bore the same brand and came in the same blue-and-gray color scheme. The world tractor line that Henry Ford had always favored was now a reality: no longer

As the advertisement clearly states, the 6000 certainly was big, powerful and comfortable.

The Ford 4000 had come out as the replacement of the 800/900 models in the early 1960s.

In the 1970s Ford also turned its attention to mini-tractors. In fact, so successful was its involvement in this sector that the company was offering an entire range by the end of the decade, from the 11hp 1100 to the 27hp 1900. All of Ford's smaller tractors now bore the '10' brand, which denoted three-cylinder diesels for most of the mini-tractors and a 16-speed option for the mid-range machines. Cabs, four-wheel drive, and front-wheel assist were other options.

In 1985 Ford bought out the implements manufacturer, New Holland. The company now had a full line-up of farm tools to go with its tractors. This was somewhat perplexing, since not long afterwards–no doubt for pressing financial reasons– Ford announced its intention to pull out of tractor construction in the USA altogether. Production of smaller machines would be transferred to Basildon in the UK, while that of larger ones would be based in Antwerp, Belgium.

The direction of the company, so far as tractors were concerned, remained somewhat confused. In 1987 Ford bought out the Versatile Farm Equipment Company and a range of super-tractors was introduced by what was now known as Ford-New Holland Inc. Versatile's existing machines became Ford Versatiles in the Ford blue-grey color scheme. They were powered by Cummins V8 engines and ranged from 193hp to 360hp.

In the late 1980s, highly sophisticated small tractors

The 5000 model tractor was a direct descendant of the Fordson Super Major.

The Ford FW 30 used a powerful 903 cubic inch, eight-cylinder, diesel engine from Cummins.

The 4610, made between 1975 and 1981, used the three-cylinder, 201 cubic inch Ford engine.

You could be excused for not thinking this was a Ford - in fact it's a 1982 model 334.

were being produced in increasing numbers. Ford's answer was the 20 series. Nine-speed transmission was included on models from the 1120 to the 1520, while front-wheel assist and hydrostatic transmission were options. In 1990 the mid-range 30

Not all tractors have to be big. This is the Ford 4110 mini tractor, ideal for lighter work.

After taking over New Holland, Ford also bought Versatile in 1985. This is the 276 from 1987.

A Ford TW-15 waiting while the combine fills its trailer. The TW range came in during 1983.

series was introduced. The four smaller models all had three-cylinder diesels and eight-speed transmission. By contrast, the 8530, 8630, 8730 and 8830 all had 16-speed transmission and replaced the big two-wheel-driven TW series.

In the early 1990s, the end of Ford tractor production, which had been looming for years, finally became a reality. In 1991 Ford sold 80 per-cent of Ford-New Holland-Versatile to FIAT. Three years later, the remaining share of 20 percent was also bought by FIAT, or FIAT-Geotech as it was now known.

This is the mid-1980s Ford model 8210, a four-wheel drive tractor, with a 110hp engine.

This Ford 946 has been painted in the Ford colors, but that would change again.

The 6610 industrial tractor produced by Ford. Pulling this beast had to take some effort.

The top-of-the-range Ford New Holland model 8340, now owned by Fiat.

Fordson

1917-1961

Henry Ford, the son of a farmer himself, began experimenting with tractor designs as early as 1907. However, he found it impossible to interest the directors of the Ford automobile company in the agricultural sector. In 1917 Ford was forced to set up another company–Ford & Son Inc, later simply Fordson–to market the tractor he finally developed. The Model F Fordson (the product, it is said, of up to 50 different prototypes) represented a great leap forward in tractor design. The engine and gear-box were taken from a Ford Model B car, and the steering adapted from a Model K. But unlike most tractors of the time, the engine, transmission, and axle housings were all bolted together to form the basic structure of the machine. What was more, the tractor was comparatively light at 2,710 pounds, and a small 4.1 litre engine was sufficient to power it.

At first the Fordson Model F was produced on a limited scale. In 1918, however, production was massively increased. The impetus came from the British government. The ravages of World War I meant that Britain was suffering from a shortage of men, horses and grain. Tractors and mechanized farming methods seemed to be the solution. Accordingly, following highly successful trials of the prototypes in the UK, the British government put in an order for 6,000 Model Fs.

In order to make machines on such a scale, Ford had to resort to the assembly–line methods he had developed for the Model T car. In the event, the Model F's compact frame made it perfect for this

The Fordson model F. Reputed to be the result of some fifty prototypes. It came right in the end.

kind of quick, cheap manufacture. Again, as with the Model T, cheap production meant the machine could be sold at a low price, one the average farmer could afford. When it first came on the market, a Model F cost around $750, but this was later slashed to $385–about a third of the price of comparable machines–and the price soon went down further to $285. Mechanized farming for the masses had truly arrived.

But the USA and Britain were not the only nations to benefit from the widespread use of the Model F. Post-revolutionary Russia was suffering from famine, and Ford steadfastly believed that a productive USSR would be a peaceful USSR. He therefore organised the export of 26,000 Model F's to Russia, while many thousands more were made there under licence. By 1927, it was estimated that over 70 percent of all tractors in the country were Fordsons.

In the USA, the Model F was selling in huge numbers. Rival tractor manufacturers were finding it increasingly difficult to compete with the low price of the Model F tractor, and indeed many companies went out of business as a consequence. This did not mean, despite its sturdiness and maneuvrability, that the Model F was the perfect tractor. In fact, perhaps because of the lack of weight on the rear wheels, it suffered from wheel-slip, and its draw-bar performance was no more than adequate. Another

problem caused by its light weight was its tendency to turn over on rough terrain, making it highly dangerous to the exposed driver. Finally, during performance tests in 1920 it recorded a bad fuel-efficiency rating in comparison with its rivals.

But these disadvantages scarcely seemed to register with customers. The Model F was reliable, cheap to buy and cheap to run, and by 1928 some 750,000 of them had been produced.

That year, however, Ford decided to stop making Fordson in the USA. His Model A car was almost ready, and he wanted to devote all available factory space to its manufacture. Production of the Model F was transferred to a new factory in Cork in Ireland. (Ford's grandfather was an Irish emigrant, and Ford was very proud of his Irish roots.)

In Cork the Model F was transformed into the Model N. The Model N was essentially an updated Model F, though it was more powerful, had stronger front wheels and better wheel-grip in general. It also had a governor, a water pump, and a high-tension magneto that replaced the Model F's rudimentary ignition. But the Irish relocation was not a great success. Ireland at that time was still a relatively isolated place, cut off from Fordson's two main markets, the USA itself and the UK. Furthermore, all raw materials had to be imported, which pushed up production costs.

In 1933 the Fordson plant was moved again, this

This 1929 model F has 'orchard mudguards'. These helped to prevent it from tipping backwards.

time to be incorporated in the new Ford complex at Dagenham in England. (Fordson, however, remained a separate arm of the Ford business.) The Model N did not undergo many changes, though the color was changed from gray to blue. The tractor sold well in the UK, but Fordson's sales in the USA now took a downturn. It seemed that Ford's competitors, such as John Deere, Farmall and Allis-Chalmers, had managed to develop machines that could equal and outdo the old Model F and the new Model N. Fordson's response was the All-Around, a general-purpose row-crop tractor. But though this was more powerful than the Model N, this too failed to impress the American market.

In 1939 the story of Ford tractors–which comprised both Fordson in England and the Ford tractor arm in the USA–effectively divided. The Dagenham arm did not choose to build the new 9N developed in the USA, preferring to continue with the old model which had acquired a loyal following in the UK.

In 1945, when the US factory was mass-producing the successful 9N, Dagenham chose simply to produce an update on the Model N theme–the E27N. The basis of the machine was an updated Fordson N engine with a three forward, one reverse gear-box, a conventional clutch and rear axle drive. The new tractor featured a spiral bevel and conventional

A good example of a Fordson N, the Perkins badge on the radiator signifies it uses a diesel engine.

Seen here is a beautifully restored Fordson N from 1939. This tractor was made in Ireland.

This Fordson was made at Dagenham, England, nearer to its main sales market.

One of the main advantages of the Model N over the Model F was a more powerful engine of 27hp.

Manufacturer's markings on the rear of the fuel tank of the Fordson N.

The Fordson Allround, produced in 1936. Ford's first tricycle type rowcrop tractor.

differential instead of a worm drive, while a single-plate wet clutch was also incorporated. The tractor was powered by an in-line, four-cylinder side-valve engine that produced 30hp at 1450rpm. It came in four versions, each with different specifications for brakes, tires and gear ratios. A variant using a Perkins engine was offered in 1948, and in that year over 50,000 E27Ns were made. Production

The Fordson E27N. E stood for England, 27 for the horsepower and N the model line.

The front end of the All-round. This could be used with a single or double wheel.

continued until 1951, with various upgrades and options–including electrics, hydraulics and diesel engine–being made available. A number of E27Ns were also imported by Ford in the USA and sold there as the Major. The Major was a bit of a novelty on the US market, having both the diesel option and the high clearance that many US-built tractors lacked.

A Perkins diesel conversion was available in 1950, following problems with the kerosene engine.

It may look odd but no doubt the farmer appreciated this cab in the cold weather.

The Fordson Power Major was made at the Ford works in Dagenham, England from 1958.

In 1952, the Dagenham plant replaced the E27N with the New Major. The New Major was larger and heavier than its forerunner, and its diesel, gas or TVO versions all used the same cylinder block and crank. All three versions had six-speed transmission and hydraulic three-point-hitch, though draft control was absent. The 1958 Power Major rectified this lack, increasing power to 43hp, and making power steering an optional extra.

No mistaking the model. This is undoubtedly a very smart badge for a mere tractor.

The next tractors to come out of the Dagenham plant were the Super Major and the New Performance Super Major. Both these models had differential lock, disc brakes and–finally–draft control. Later on, the Super Major would be sold in the USA as the Ford 5000, while the smaller Fordson Dexta, which had 31hp in diesel form, also became available on the American market. The Dexta and Super Major were the last tractors to bear the Fordson name. In 1961 Ford combined its US and UK tractor operations, and the two ranges were also fully integrated.

The Fordson Dexta, launched in 1957, was a completely new design.

The Dexta was fitted with a 30.5 hp, three cylinder, direct injection diesel engine.

Friday Tractor Company

1947-1957

Initiated around 1947, Friday presented their O-48 Orchard tractor. This remained on the market until the 1950s and had a Chrysler Industrial IND-5, six-cylinder engine with a displacement of 217.7 cubic inches. The tractor had nine forward gears and was able to reach a top speed of 32.4 mph. A second model was listed as being on their catalogue as late as 1957, this was the O-48. Little information can be found regarding the model and company.

The rather odd-looking 0-48 Orchard tractor, produced by the Friday Tractor Company.

G

Gaar-Scott

1909-1911

The Gaar-Scott tractor concern lasted only a matter of months. Based in Richmond, Indiana, USA, the company was better known for its threshing machines, which it had been producing since 1849.

It was in 1909 that the company announced its intention to build its first tractor. This appeared two years later as the Gaar-Scott Model 40-70. The machine used a four-cylinder engine unit and was by no means a lightweight. In late 1911 the company was acquired by the M. Rumely Company of LaPorte, Indiana, which sold the remaining stock of machines under the Gaar-Scott Tiger Pull name. Once all the spare parts had been used up, production ceased.

Initially threshing machine manufacturers, Gaar-Scott only produced tractors in 1911.

Garner

1907-1955

Henry Garner set up a business in 1907 and in 1915 imported a tractor from William Galloway of Waterloo, Iowa, USA, selling it under his own name. It had a four-cylinder, 30hp, gasoline/paraffin engine, three-speeds and a 5 mph top speed. Sales were poor and Garner ceased marketing the tractor in 1924. Sentinel of Shrewsbury acquired a majority shareholding of Garner Motors and by 1935 all non-steam-powered lorries carried the Sentinel and Garner badges—the company was wound up in 1937. Prior to World War II, a group of businessmen bought the Garner name and moved it to North London.

This pre-war Garner was manufactured in the West Midlands, England.

After the war, Garner designed a light two-wheeled tractor with its own range of attachments. Garner Mobile Equipment Ltd., was set up and the tractor was made from 1948. A year later a four-wheel tractor arrived, and a year after that a slightly larger, more powerful tractor was presented.

Production of the light tractors ceased in 1955 but Garner continued manufacturing all-weather tractor cabs and car trailers until 1968.

General Motors Corporation

1918-1922

In 1882 the Janesville Machine Company was started in Janesville, USA, to produce farm machinery. The company manufactured items such as the Janesville plow, the Janesville tractor plow, the Janesville corn planter and many more items.

In an attempt to compete with the success of Henry Ford's Fordson tractor, William Durrant, chairman of General Motors Corporation, decided that he too wanted to enter the tractor market, so in 1919 General Motors purchased and consolidated the Janesville Machine Company and the Samson Tractor Company of Stockton, California, in Janesville. The new company was called the Samson

Tractor Division of General Motors Corporation and began operating on May 1 of that year.

Production of the Samson Sieve Grip model continued for a while until GMC announced the new Samson model M. This model was priced at $650 and was equipped with mudguards, governor, belt-pulley and other extras that were not a standard fit on the Fordson. The Model A was to follow for 1919, but in fact was never put into production.

It was also in January of that year that GMC bought the rights to the Jim Dandy motor cultivator, which it modified and transformed into the Model D Iron Horse. Although innovative, the design was not a success and the machine was considered limited by farmers: the Iron Horse was a failure for GMC, and large losses were incurred.

Faced with a very competitive tractor market, financial losses and a change of corporate direction, the company pulled out of tractor manufacture in 1922.

This is the Samson model M, produced by General Motors to compete with Henry Ford's Fordson.

Gibson Manufacturing Corporation

1948-1956

 Based in Longmont, Colorado, USA, Gibson began to produce its Model D in 1948, though it is understood that it may have appeared even earlier. The machine used a Wisconsin model AEH single-cylinder engine unit, and had three forward gears. The Model H, using a Hercules IXB-3, four-cylinder engine was tested at the Nebraska trials in 1949 and was in production until 1956. It was capable of about 23 belt horsepower. A Model I was produced between about 1948 to 1956. This used a Hercules six-cylinder engine. By 1957 the Gibson tractors were listed under the Western American Industries name, which was also based in Longmont, Colorado.

This is the Gibson model 1 rowcrop, which used a six-cylinder Hercules engine.

Graham-Bradley

1937-1947

 The Graham-Paige Motor Corporation of Detroit, Michigan, USA, produced its first agricultural tractor, the Model 503, under the name of Graham-Bradley. This three-wheeler, which was sold by the Sears, Roebuck Company, was introduced in 1938 as the 504.103 and used the company's own six-cylinder engine. The following year the company introduced the four-wheel 503.104 model, but with the onset of World War II in 1942, production of this tractor ceased in favour of military equipment and was not resumed after hostilities ended. In 1944 Joseph W. Frazer joined Graham-Paige Motors and became its President. That year Graham-Paige acquired the commercial line of Rototiller. In February 1947, Graham-Paige stockholders sold out to the Kaizer-Frazer Corporation, which had been incorporated in 1945.

Graham-Paige were better known for their cars, but entered the tractor market too.

Gray Dort

1930s

During the 1930s Great Depression, very few farmers were in a position to spend money on new tractors, and so all types of innovative ideas were produced, of which one was the Gray Dort tractor. The person who designed this was Gerald Miller, who lived in a town called Addison, just north of Rockville, Ontario, Canada. His tractor–built specifically to cut hay–was based on a Gray Dort car, from which he kept just the chassis, engine, transmission and radiator. To produce more power it was necessary to gear the whole machine down and so he fitted two hay-mower gears to the rear–a small gear in the axle and a larger gear in the wheel. The engine was a four-cylinder Lycoming unit with 3 inch bore and 5 inch stroke and had a maximum of

The Gray Dort tractor was a one-off machine that was put together from car parts.

2000rpm – a conveniently slow running engine. The featured machine is very small and has been shortened and made thinner. At the time you could buy kits to make up your own tractor from pretty well any car chassis.

Gray Tractor Company

1914-1933

The Gray tractor was an unconventional-looking machine, and it changed little from the moment the company was incorporated in Minneapolis, USA, in 1914. Its origins lay in a small two-cylinder machine with single rear-wheel drive made by W. Chandler Knapp in 1908. Knapp was the first to use twin rear-drive wheels, positioned close together in order to eliminate the need for a differential. This also became a feature of the Gray tractor. The company also produced several other models of various sizes, including the 22-40 Canadian Special and the popular 18-36 of 1920, which used a Waukesha four-cylinder engine. A feature of these tractors, unlike others of the period, was that all gears and drive chains were enclosed. The company was dissolved in 1933.

This is the rather strange but unique Gray tractor, which used a 54 inch roller as the rear wheel.

Guldner

1904-1969

Hugo Guldner was experimenting with two-stroke engines as far back as 1894. In 1904 he founded Guldner-Motoren Gmbh. Although it was shown in 1938, the first Guldner tractor–the A40–did not go on sale until 1940. This machine had a single-cylinder diesel unit and could produce 20hp. The factory was bombed during World War II, but by 1947 it was ready for production once more. Along with the A(F)15, which was produced in 1949 (the F standing for four-speed), several other 'A' series, two- and three-cylinder engine machines were made. The 'G' series featured a variety of two- to six-cylinder machines. In the late 1950s, an agreement was made with Fahr and Deutz-Fahr for their tractors to be built at the Guldner works, but in 1969 all production of Guldner tractors ceased.

The Guldner model G35. They specialised in smaller models, but larger ones were available.

This is a happy farmer on his Guldner 15hp model. These machines were ideal for small farms.

H

Hanomag

1835-1971

Hannoverische Maschinenbau AG, better known as Hanomag, were based in Hanover, Germany. The company started in the heavy engineering industry back in 1835, manufacturing steam locomotives and later ships and trucks.

After the turn of the century, agricultural mechanisation was moving forward at a rapid pace, with new self-propelled machinery being made available to pull the implements used on a farm. Under the brand name of WD–an abbreviation for Ernst Wendeler and Boguslaw Dohrn–the company produced an 80hp machine with four-cylinder engine, of which some 1,000 were sold through the 1920s.

In 1919 Wendeler and Dohrn brought out the first European caterpillar, which was equipped with a 20hp, four-cylinder engine. It could operate on a mixture of fuels, used Bosch magneto ignition and had, unusually for the time, an air cleaner.

Hanomag presented the world's first full diesel tractor in the 1930s. This is the model R25.

Demonstrations during 1921 led to the further development of these machines with a 20hp version. This was followed by a 25hp model, and in the same year the 50hp type Z 50.

During the mid to late 1920s, the company produced the R26 and R28 models, but Hanomag were aware that diesel engines were becoming very important and a first choice for farmers, for many reasons. Soon the majority of tractors were fitted with diesel engines, many of which were developed by Lazar Schargorodsky. One of the better known models was the R40, which used a 40hp, 5.2 litre, four-cylinder diesel D 52 engine. These tractors were extremely well-equipped and had items such as windscreens and toe-hooks, that the customer could choose from. Times were hard though and the company was struggling.

There was an economic upswing after 1933, and Hanomag produced improved model types and supplied equipment to go with them. Pneumatic tyres, a new development for the time, were also available and made a huge difference which Hanomag benefited from. The company found itself with all its factories destroyed by the Allied bombing at the end of World War II. But they were soon back in business and the trusty R40 and RL20 were back on stream. The late 1940s and early 1950s saw the introduction of the R16 and R45, along with the K55 crawler. In 1954 the 100,000th model rolled off the production line.

During 1961 the company became part of the Rheinstal Group and new four-stroke models followed for 1964, the 300, 400, 500 and 600 series, with the new 800 as the flagship machine. Business wasn't good though. The tractor factory in Argentina was sold to Massey-Ferguson, Hanomag Trucks was sold to Daimler-Benz and finally in 1971 tractor

The Hanomag R12 combitrac model was a new tractor that was able to carry out a multitude of tasks.

You could be excused in thinking this is not a tractor. Hanomag tractors often looked more like trucks.

production ceased altogether. In nearly seventy years more than 250,000 tractors were manufactured, the remaining part of the company being taken up by Kubota.

In the early 1960s Hanomag were taken over and new models appeared. This is the Granit model 500 E.

A big and powerful tractor, the Brilliant 600 model was able to cope with heavy tasks.

Although Hanomag stopped making farm tractors, the name lived on in the construction world.

Happy Farmer

1915-1916

The Happy Farmer Tractor Company lasted only a very short time before being amalgamated. It was started in 1915 in Minneapolis, USA, and commenced producing tractors the following year. The Happy Farmer machine had an opposed twin, cylinder engine.

In 1916 the LaCrosse Tractor Company at La Crosse, Wisconsin, was founded. This was an amalgamation of the Happy Farmer Tractor Company and the Sta-Rite Engine Company of LaCrosse. The company's first machines, based very much on the original Happy Farmer, were the 8-16 Model A and 12-24 Model B, both having a twin-cylinder engine. The machines were named LaCrosse-Happy Farmer.

Only lasting a short period, this is the Happy Farmer tractor, which used an opposed twin cylinder engine.

Hart-Parr

1901-1929

Generally understood to be the birthplace of the tractor industry, Charles City, Iowa, USA, has been synonymous with tractors since 1900. Two university friends, Charles W. Hart and Charles H. Parr, moved there from Madison, Wisconsin after accepting an invitation by investors to expand their company in Charles City. The word 'tractor' was in fact coined in 1907, to describe the Hart-Parr invention by their sales manager, W.H. Williams.

An early Hart-Parr, used mainly for working threshing machines of the period.

The two friends developed a successful gasoline engine on wheels and obtained sufficient financial backing to build a modest plant. The first tractor–generally known as No 1–was produced during 1901/1902 and used a two-cylinder, oil-cooled engine. This was soon followed by Hart Parr No 2–the 22-45 model–also produced in 1902 and which helped the company to continue with its tractor development. Naturally No 3 followed the following year and was designated the 17-30. It too used a two-cylinder engine and developed 17hp at the drawbar and 30hp on the pulley. In 1907 the engine bore and stroke were made larger and the addition of an overhead cam and valves in the head increased the horsepower to 30 and 60 respectively. Designated the 30-60, this very popular tractor became known as 'Old Reliable' and was produced up to 1918.

The 40-80 model was introduced between 1908 and 1914, which used a four-cylinder engine located under a very forward positioned drivers platform. The model 15-30 was to follow, initially with opposed cylinder engine, which was then changed back to the vertical twin unit for general release. For 1911 the 60-100 appeared, this was a monster of a machine, one of the largest wheel-type tractors ever built and weighed some twenty-five tons.

For 1914 Hart-Parr introduced a new, lightweight tractor, called the 'Little Devil.' This tractor was aimed at the small farmer who had no need for the huge machines around at that time. It was powered by a two-cylinder engine and had a single rear wheel. A total of 725 of these tractors were made between 1914-1916 but they were a disaster. In order to protect

By 1918 Hart-Parr models were taking a different shape and the big machines were phased out.

The 12-24 model was produced from 1924 and replaced the earlier 20 model.

A fine example of a Hart-Parr 12-24E model. This was a new style of tractor.

was a two-cylinder model rated at 12-25 horsepower, later upgraded to 15-30 horsepower. The New Hart-Parr as it was known, was conceived in 1917 and had the fuel tank mounted on top of the radiator, this basic design continued until 1930.

In 1927 the company introduced a 28-50 model, which used two 15-30 engines mounted side by side on a single crankcase. Both of these tractors proved to be excellent machines, and were in use into the 1950s.

On April 1st 1929 the company joined with three others to form the Oliver Farm Equipment Corporation, therefore putting an end to the old Hart-Parr name.

their good name, Hart-Parr recalled and destroyed every one of these tractors they could find, giving the farmers a used 30-60 'Old Reliable' in exchange.

In 1918 Hart-Parr introduced a new line of smaller tractors, which immediately became popular with farmers. This model had been designed by Charles Hart who had left the company in 1917, after a long period of conflict with the principal investors. This

This is the bigger 28-50 model, built during the late 1920s. It had a four-cylinder engine.

Hatz

1880-1963

Although the Hatz company has been around for many years, only a few years in the 1950s and 1960s were dedicated to tractor production.

Hatz today is a major diesel engine manufacturer and that is, and has been, their core product.

The company's first tractor was produced in the early 1950s and was a small utility machine, similar to those being produced by other German companies

Hatz were better known for the manufacture of their diesel engines.

of the time. These initial tractors had one- or two-cylinder, air-cooled, diesel engines although a three-cylinder unit was produced in the 1960s.

The competition at the time was considerable and Hatz decided to pull away from tractors, and continue to concentrate on their diesel engine production.

Heider Manufacturing Company

1911-1929

The Heider tractor was made and sold until 1929, although the company had already been taken over by the Rock Island Plow Company of Illinois. John Heider made his company's first tractor in 1910, and with it he introduced a friction drive in place of traditional transmission. A strange arrangement where the engine moved back

John Heider produced his first tractor in 1911 and with it also introduced his friction drive system.

and forth, via a lever, gave the same gearing both forwards and backwards. The Model A was succeeded by the Model B in 1911, and in 1914 the Model C 12-20 was introduced. By now Heider had arranged for the Rock Island Company to build and sell his machines, and in 1916 Rock Island bought his company out completely. Rock Island continued to make the tractor under the Heider name until 1929.

Hela

1914-1983

Another tractor that carried the Lanz name was the Hela. The name Hela was made up of the first two letters from the constructor's first name––Herman–and the last two letters from his family name–Lanz. The name was chosen so that the tractor would not be confused with the tractor being produced by Heinrich Lanz, which was called the Lanz. The Hela company was based in the upper Swabian area of southern Germany and they produced their first example in 1914.

Not wanting to cause confusion, Herman Lanz named his company Hela.

The company's model D38, which used a three-cylinder, water-cooled AD1 engine unit of 3200cc, producing 38hp at 1650 rpm. The transmission, also made by Hela, had six forward gears and two reverse. The tractor weighed almost 4000 pounds (1800kg). Most of the tractors were the same in design and in 1983 the company went into bankruptcy.

HSCS

1869-1973

Hofherr & Schrantz was founded in 1869, in Vienna, Austria. They produced agricultural machinery, such as mowing machines and by 1891 had become a large company manufacturing threshing machines, portable steam engines and the like.

La Robuste 40 model was certainly a robust machine. These tractors were strong and reliable.

In 1912 a partnership was established with Clayton & Shuttleworth Ltd., a British traction engine and threshing machines manufacturer. In 1923 the company built its first, single-cylinder tractor and in the 1930s the La Robuste tractor was presented. In 1938 Lanz bought HSCS after acquiring a majority shareholding, and the company concentrated on building the Lanz bulldog. Under communist rule in 1946, HSCS became state-owned and later started using the Dutra brand name. Under this brand it started building larger four-wheel-drive machines like the Dutra 2500, launched in the late 1960s. In 1969 it joined with the Trauzl-Werke AG and in 1970 became a part of the Böhlerwerke AG.

Huber

1865-1942

The Huber company was started in 1865, in a small factory in Marion, Ohio, USA and by 1880 Edward Huber had built the company up to be a major builder of steam traction engines and threshing machines. In 1898 they bought the Van Duzen Gasoline Engine Company of Cincinnati. Their first tractor used a Van Duzen gasoline engine, fitted to a Huber steam traction engine chassis and wheels. The project was not a success and soon abandoned.

In 1911 the company presented their first Farmer's Tractor, a gas-powered, twin-cylinder machine of

A beautiful advertising poster for early Huber products. It was known as the 'Patriotic Edition'.

Seen at a steam meeting in the United States is this New Huber, making plenty of noise and smoke.

You wouldn't want to get in the way of this Huber steamer when at full speed!

5.1 litres. The following year another tractor, the Farmer's Tractor 13-22, was presented. This also had a twin-cylinder engine, with a two-speed transmission. This same year the larger model 30-60 was produced, a four-cylinder monster machine with wheels that stood eight feet high. This was in production until 1916 when it was replaced by the 35-70 model. A smaller model, the 20-40, was introduced in 1914.

For 1916 came the Light Four model, which used a four-cylinder Waukesha engine and between 1921 and 1925 the Super Four 15-30 model was presented. This initially had a Midwest four-cylinder engine and was replaced later by a Waukesha unit.

This is the Huber 18/36. The engine, which is mounted transversely, is a four-cylinder unit.

The New Huber still had exposed steering gear and flywheels, as seen here.

1922 saw the Master Four tractor with a Hinkley four-cylinder unit. Using yet another make of engine, 1926 saw the introduction of the 18-36 Super Four tractor, which used a four-cylinder Stearns engine. This same year also saw the Super Four 20-40 model, again using a Stearns engine.

Two years later the Huber 20-36 was presented, using a Waukesha engine fitted with a Ricardo head. This special-design head helped with better emission and gave the machine more power.

1935 saw the introduction of the HK 32-45 tractor, which had rubber tires as an option and was produced until the war stopped all production. The Modern Farmer was presented in 1933, a model L and SC in 1935.

For 1936 there were Huber L and S standard tread models, along with SC and LC tricycle models. The model B was also available, which had a streamlined bonnet, rubber tyres and electric starter and lights. It used a Buda, four-cylinder engine. For 1937 the Huber OB, an orchard tractor with semi-enclosed rear wheels, was available. The company continued to make tractors up to World War II, when production ceased.

Hurlimann

1929-present

Hurlimann produced its first tractor, the 1K, in 1929 and was one of several Swiss tractor companies to start trading around that time. This was a single cylinder machine producing 10hp. It had three forward and one reverse gear and a top speed of 9 mph. For 1945 the company produced the D 100, the first diesel tractor to use direct fuel injection. Its Hurlimann water-cooled four-cylinder engine produced 45hp. Then in 1951 came the odd looking four-cylinder, H12. Following the late 1950s, early 1960s D 90, was the T 6200. This had new styling, a four-cylinder Hurlimann 62hp engine and partially synchronised gears. Between 1977 and 1985 came the two/four-wheel-drive H 480.

Seen in the SAME museum in Italy, this is the four-cylinder Hurlimann H 12 of 1951.

Since 1977 Hurlimann have been a part of the SAME group and have a good selection of models, which include the XT 115 and 130 tractors. These use the new EURO II, 1000 Series 6 cylinder, liquid-cooled, turbocharged engines. The XE F model is a compact, versatile, all-purpose tractor, ideal for use in orchards and vineyards. These use the new Series 1000, EURO II engines, either turbocharged or naturally aspirated. The XS machines specialize in narrow spaces. The compact dimensions allow easy access to narrow rows. The Euro II engines ensure plenty of power at the PTO and power is exploited to the full by the Overspeed gearbox with creeper and Fulldrive, giving a total of 45 forward and 45 reverse ratios. These are only three machines from their range.

This is the Hurlimann 1K 10 of 1930. It has a single cylinder engine producing 10hp.

There is a choice of two models in this range: XB-85 and XB-95, producing 81 and 91 hp respectively.

The XT 115 and 130 are driven by the new EURO II, 1000 Series, six-cylinder engines.

I

International Harvester

1903-present

The early history and background to the formation of the giant International Harvester concern is intriguing and certainly interesting. We could just start when the company first built tractors, but then we would be missing large chunks of its roots. So therefore there are one or two characters whose lives and work we need to follow, which will in their turn lead us gently into this maze of companies involved.

Cyrus Hall McCormick invented the reaper in 1831 and was instrumental in creating International Harvester.

Probably the most important factor was the birth of Cyrus Hall McCormick, the eldest of the eight McCormick children. He was born on February 15 1809 to Robert Hall McCormick and his wife Mary Anne, in Rockbridge County, Virginia. USA.

By 1831, and now at the tender age of twenty-two, Cyrus had taken over the design of his father's rather unsuccessful reaper. There was a will to succeed and within a six-week period he had modified, built, tested and remodeled the design down at the family smithy at Walnut Grove. The reaper was successfully demonstrated on a neighbour's farm at Steeles Tavern in late July of that year, and after carrying out various changes to the design, Cyrus patented the machine in 1834.

A view of the day the first McCormick reaping machine was tested near Steele's tavern, in 1831.

During June of this year Cyrus had also been granted a patent for yet another of his inventions, a cast and wrought iron plow–the Patent Hill Side Plow–a popular piece of equipment that was used extensively by the local farmers.

The demand for the McCormick reaper was so great that the Walnut Grove smithy was soon unable to cope and so Cyrus formed a partnership with C. M. Gray to purchase land on the north bank of the

An early advertising poster showing McCormick machinery in full operational mode.

Chicago River. It wasn't long before a factory complex was built and the production of 500 reapers was started for the 1848 harvest–this Michigan Avenue site was later to become the International Harvester corporate headquarters.

In 1851 the McCormick reaper won the Grand Council Medal at The Great Exhibition at Crystal Palace in London. During the next few years, more awards were collected at the Hamburg, Vienna and Paris Expositions and Cyrus Hall McCormick was elected an officer of the French Legion of Honor and made a member of the French academy of Science.

Disaster struck in 1871 with the Great Chicago Fire, which destroyed the McCormick reaper works but fortunately the company safe was retrieved with all records intact. An insurance settlement was made, but the fire cost Cyrus a personal loss of US$600,000. In August of the following year, work was started on a new factory, which was completed in February 1873.

More first prizes for McCormick came in 1881–this happened to coincide with the 50th anniversary year of his reaper–this time from the Royal Agricultural Society, following a four day trial of his first twine binder at Derby, England.

Just three years later, on May 13, 1884, Cyrus Hall McCormick died. He was survived by his wife Nettie Fowler McCormick and his brother Leander, who had joined him in partnership in 1856. In the year of his death his company, the McCormick Harvesting Machine Company, sold 54,841 machines and introduced the McCormick steel twine

An early advertisement for McCormick machinery, including grasscutting manufacture.

binder–previously these were mainly made from wood. He was a great inventor but was also widely regarded as being an innovator of good business practices.

In 1851 McCormick had engaged Burgess & Key to manufacture and sell his reaper in England from their Brentwood works; by 1859 they had made and sold about 2,000. The agreement was terminated in 1880 and McCormick appointed Lankester & Company of London as sales representatives for Great Britain. Then in 1900 the McCormick Harvesting Company set up a general agency office in London.

During the late 1800s McCormick found itself increasingly challenged by competitors in a somewhat depressed market, its chief rival being the Deering Harvester Company.

William Deering, a veteran dry-goods wholesaler, had been doing business in Maine and New York and had established a rival harvester factory at Plano, Illinois. Then in 1880, Deering decided to move his factory to Chicago. During the late 1890s, weary of competition, the Deering and McCormick families began to talk about a merger of their companies. By this time McCormick had a plant at Blue Island and Western Avenues that employed over 5,000 people. The Deering Harvester works, on the other hand, had a factory on Fullerton Avenue on the city's North Side and employed about 7,000 employees. So it was that in 1902, McCormick and Deering merged to form International Harvester.

In the winter of 1860–1861, at Plano, Illinois, W. W. Marsh and John Hollister built a harvester that, beginning with the harvest of 1861, cut more grain than any other machine of its class. Arrangements were made to manufacture the machine at Plano and so the necessary money was advanced and George Steward and C. W. Marsh were hired to run the shop.

So for many years Marsh Harvesters were manufactured and sold all over the world. When in the early 1870s the Harvester Company passed into the hands of E. H. Gammon and William Deering, it was the Marsh Harvester that was turned out by the thousands. In 1880 William Deering moved to North Chicago and many of the Plano mechanics moved with him to work in his factory. However this was not the end of the story, as the people of Plano revived the old plant and organized the Plano Steam Power Company. The company turned the old Marsh Harvester buildings over to the Plano Manufacturing Company, and for eleven years until 1902, the Plano Manufacturing Company supplied the world in harvesting machinery. Then in 1902, the Plano Manufacturing Company moved to West Pullman, and with that became the third part of the newly–formed International Harvester organisation.

Completing the amalgamation of companies were two other small companies, the Milwaukee Harvester Company and the Warder, Bushnell & Glessner Company. The newly organised company was capitalised at $120 million and soon became the forerunner in the agricultural industry.

Cyrus H. McCormick junior was named President and Charles Deering, Chairman of the board.

In 1903 International Harvester built a plant at Hamilton, Ontario, Canada and two years later it built its first plant in Europe, at Norrkoping in Sweden, to manufacture implements.

The company unveiled its first production tractor in 1906, which was based on S S Morton's friction

Initially a rival to the McCormick products was the Deering company.

drive truck chassis–these trucks were very popular and were ideal for any gasoline engine fitted–and powered by an International 'Famous' single-cylinder engine. It was available in 10, 12, 15 and 20hp capacity and nearly 800 units were sold up to 1908. By late 1907 a second model, the single-cylinder type A, was available in 12, 15 and 20 hp, of which 607 units were produced between 1907 and 1911.

It was December 31, 1906 when International Harvester of Great Britain (IHGB) was inaugurated, initially with offices in Southwark Street, London, but then moved two years later to Finsbury Pavement, where it remained until 1926.

The initial IHGB works at Old Ford on the river Lea were merely assembly shops that imported parts from the parent company in America and its affiliates in Canada and Europe. Full servicing and supply of International Harvester equipment was up and running within three years.

A new site was also purchased in Neuss on Rhine, Germany during 1908, which was located between harbors 1 and 2 on the river Rhine. By 1911 production of implements under the McCormick name started, typical products being mowers, tedders, rakes and fertilizer distributors, and by 1912 the plant also started to produce binder twine.

IHC expansion in Europe continued in 1909 with the

This is an advertising poster for the Plano Manufacturing company.

building of factories at Croix, northern France and Lubertzy, Russia.

After the merger of McCormick and Deering, the US dealerships were quite insistent that they wanted to continue selling separate products, and this caused some concern. The government dictated that even though these companies were now under the IHC umbrella, they should be able to sell separate tractors and equipment. The resulting outcome was that McCormick dealerships would sell the new Mogul tractors and the Deering dealerships would sell the new Titan tractors.

So the Type C Mogul appeared in 1909 and two years later a 25hp model was presented. This was quickly followed by the 45hp model, which when revised–it used a twin, opposed cylinder engine–took on the 30-60 designation and was built up to 1917. Several other models were produced during this time, a single cylinder Mogul junior for 1911 and a Mogul 12-25 for 1912, a relative lightweight compared to the others.

The Deering dealerships were preparing to sell the Titan tractors and so in 1910 the type D single cylinder was introduced, initially as a 20hp machine but later increased to 25hp. Again like the Moguls, other Titan tractors appeared in the following few

years; 1911 saw the Titan 45, later to be re-designated 30-60 after being upgraded. By 1915 it had been given an enclosed cabin and production was ceased in 1917. Most of these Titan machines were being built at the IHC Milwaukee factory, whereas the Mogul's were being made at the Chicago factory.

Starting life as the 12-25 Titan in 1915, this tractor was upgraded as the 15-30 for 1916. It then became known as the International Titan 15-30 and was produced between 1918 and 1921.

With some 14,000 units sold, the Mogul 8-16 was a big success for the company. The engine was a single-cylinder unit and the tractor was in production until 1917, when it was replaced by a similar model, the 10-20. This machine used a single-cylinder engine and also had two forward speeds and mudguards were added over the rear wheels.

There always seems to be a particular product that people remember as their first, and the IHC Titan 10-20 tractor of 1916 falls into that category. Many farmers consider this two-cylinder tractor to be their first, and it sold phenomenally well through to 1922. It was 1917 that things changed once more. The US Justice Department noted that IHC had too many Deering and McCormick dealerships, contravening competition laws, and so ordered they should be consolidated. From then onwards, each sales territory would have one dealership to sell one brand

The Milwaukee Harvester company also became part of the International Harvester group.

Completing the amalgamation of companies was the Warder Bushnell & Glessner company.

of tractor, and that would now be an International. In this way, the International 8-16 was born in the same year. This was a radically different machine to its predecessors, with the company's own four-cylinder engine enclosed within its own compartment. In fact it looked more like an early automobile than a tractor. It is interesting to note that this tractor could be adapted for industrial work, for which it also had hard rubber tires fitted. This 8-16 tractor was a significant step forward for IHC as far as the advance of tractor design was concerned, and it helped to set them on the path to lighter and more economical machines. In 1921, International introduced their 15-30, an attempt to counteract the onslaught that the inexpensive Ford model F was having across the

The Mogul 12-25, produced in 1912, became the first lightweight International Harvester.

The 12-25 was a pretty simple machine and was produced through to 1918.

The International Harvester Mogul 8-16, single-cylinder model, introduced in 1914.

world. This too was a lightweight machine, using the company's own four-cylinder engine, which was completely enclosed. This was also the first IHC tractor to use a unit frame design and there were mudguards over the rear wheels. It wasn't as cheap as the Ford, but still sold well with some 128,000 being delivered to customers over an eight-year period. This was followed in 1923 by the new 10-20 model, again with a four-cylinder engine; this tractor was produced up to 1939 with some 215,000 examples being made. Rubber tires became an option in the late 1930s and the tractor was available with a variety of other special pieces of equipment.

Between 1916 and 1922, International Harvester (IHC) built some 78,000 Titan 10-20 tractors.

The pulley of the 10-20 model. From here a leather belt went to a threshing machine.

IHC were making good progress with their tractors but it was their next design that would help them truly to become market leaders. Farmers were somewhat restricted in what they could achieve with their tractors–there were only two types and they were both designed to carry out particular functions. The heavyweight machines were used for belt work, whilst the smaller machines were used for cultivating row crops. It was time for a machine that could carry out both functions, and so it was that the Farmall–the name itself describes the machine's capabilities–of 1924 was produced to carry out both these duties. The Farmall had to be a great success but it was only initially put on sale in limited

numbers. IHC had fears that it would stifle sales of the 10-20, but in fact both sold like hotcakes. The Farmall used a four-cylinder engine and was equipped with a good array of attachments, helping it to be a truly multi-purpose tractor. Unlike its predecessors, it had two conventional large, well-spaced, rear wheels, but the two front wheels were small. These were positioned at the front of the vehicle, close together in the centre, which also helped to give the tractor a better turning circle.

With the end of the run of the Farmall in 1932, a new machine was presented in the shape of the Farmall F-20, which was built up to 1939 and sold 149,000 units during that period. This was similar in design

This is the Mogul 90, which was replaced in the 1920s by smaller, lighter machines.

to its predecessor and also came with many accessories and adjustable wheel tread, something that other tractor manufacturers scrambled to copy. The Farmall made a name for itself, and was seen as a durable and useful machine by farmers the world over.

A more powerful version of the Farmall was presented in 1931, still with a four-cylinder engine but increase in bore and stroke, and designated F-30. It still used steel wheels, but later in its life rubber tires became an optional extra. This wasn't exactly what the small land-owning farmers of the period wanted though. What they needed was a nimble, light and small tractor, and so it was that the F-12 was produced in the following year of 1932. Initially the tractor was fitted with a Waukesha engine–the company didn't have an engine small enough in capacity–but within months it was equipped with a four-cylinder, 113 cubic inch, IHC engine. A standard tread version–the W-12–was made in 1934 and other versions too were available such as the I-12 industrial model and the Fairway-12, for use specifically on golf courses and large estates.

The standard tread tractors were also being improved, but more power was needed and in 1932 the older 15/30 was upgraded and re-designated as the W-30. This was the start of a new series and in 1934 the International Harvester W-40 was put on sale. This was the company's first six-cylinder engine tractor and some 6,500 units were sold. Just

This is the Farmall, probably the most significant machine ever to be made by International Harvester.

The McCormick-Deering 10-20, two plow machine was available from 1923.

The F-30 tractor was introduced in late 1931. Initially it had steel wheels.

The W-12 McCormick-Deering was the standard-tread version of the F-12, produced in 1934.

two years later the McCormick-Deering WD-40 was introduced, the first tractor in America to run with a diesel engine. Although it ran on diesel, it was started with gasoline and then changed automatically to diesel once the engine had reached a certain speed.

During this same period the company was also experimenting with crawlers, to compete with the ever-increasing Caterpillar products on the market. Their first attempts were based around the 10-20 and 15-30 tractor models, but in 1931 they finally came up with the TracTracTor designated the T-20. Its power unit was the basic Farmall F-20 engine and it remained in production up to 1939. In the meantime the International Harvester T-35, six-cylinder, gasoline model and TD-35, four-cylinder, diesel versions were also launched. Further models were seen such as the T-40 and TD-40, the T-D18 for 1938 and the T-6 and TD 6, which were launched in 1939. In 1936 International Harvester in the USA made the decision to produce tractors in Germany, and so on March 15 1937 the first tractor, a type F-12 rated at 12-15 hp, rolled off the assembly line. Between 1937 and 1940, 3,973 units of the F-12 family were built.

The year 1939 saw the public introduction of the second generation Farmall, known as the signature letter series. Letters A and B meant Small Size, H was for Middle Size and M Large Size. The modern styling of these tractors reflected the efforts of the internationally known industrial designer Raymond Loewy, who was hired to give the new Farmall

This is the W-30 model. Standard-tread tractors were badged McCormick Deering, as this is.

The McCormick-Deering WD-40 was the first wheel-type tractor in America to use a diesel engine.

The T20 TracTracTor, was introduced in 1931 and basically used the Farmall F-20 engine.

tractors and crawlers a distinctive and, modern family appearance. Both these product lines now shared the same radiator grille design, including the three silver stripes and three-dimensional Farmall or International name plate–these were product brands, with the master brand McCormick-Deering and the company name International Harvester. Loewy went on to design the prototype dealer facility, with vertical pylon, that unified the look of all 800 US dealers and company stores. Variations of all the letter series tractors were made and the Farmall M became one of the most popular tractors in America from its introduction in 1939. This was a four-

This is one of the larger TracTracTor models, the T40. This machine used a six-cylinder engine.

For 1939 IHC presented a completely new series of tractors. This period poster shows the Farmall A.

THE PACE SETTER SETS A NEW PACE

FARMALL Ⓐ
THE NEW McCORMICK-DEERING FARMALL WITH
CULTI-VISION

UTILITY   ECONOMY   PERFORMANCE   COMFORT

SMOOTH
4-CYLINDER
POWER

ALL THE POWER FOR THE SMALL FARM
REPLACES THE LAST TEAM ON THE LARGE FARM

INTERNATIONAL HARVESTER COMPANY

...s every inch a FARMALL

The 1948 Farmall C had a relatively short life. It used a four-cylinder engine.

cylinder model and was made up to 1952, during which time 288,000 were produced.

Wheatley Hall in England was purchased from Doncaster Borough Council in 1938, and warehouse buildings were constructed on the site a year later. Then in 1940 with the outbreak of World War II, the factory was requisitioned by the ministry of supply to assist in the war effort.

Due to activities during the war, production at Neuss was affected on several occasions when the complete timber yard was burned out in 1940, and an Allied bomber crashed into the iron foundry and burned it out in 1942. Despite these setbacks, 1945

Shown clearly by this World War II poster, IHC produced tractors and tanks for the conflict.

Both are weapons

our farm and fighting forces depend on YOU

Internationally renowned industrial designer Raymond Loewy designed tractors and sales offices.

EXTERIOR AND INTERIOR VISUALIZATION

BASIC STANDARD NUMBER ONE

was the only year in its sixty-year history of tractor production that no tractors were produced.

After the war the letter series tractors were upgraded and an even tinier model was introduced. The Farmall Cub went on sale in 1947 and was aimed at the farmer who had small landholdings. It became extremely popular, matching and very soon overtaking sales of the Farmall A. It used a small capacity 60 cubic inch, four-cylinder engine, and not only remained in production for many years but can also still be seen in daily use on farms today.

With the end of the war, the Doncaster site in England was also returned to IHGB and with the completion of the works, implement and service

The International W6 tractor hit the market in 1940. It used a four-cylinder, 246 cubic inch, gasoline engine.

The advertisement states: A cub in size....but a bear for work. Although small, it was robust and powerful.

parts production were started. Products were marketed under the McCormick or McCormick International brands. Also during this time the factory at Neuss was rebuilt and a first batch of 50 tractors were produced.

Tractor production finally started at Doncaster in 1949, when a McCormick International Farmall M, serial no 1001, was driven off the line on Sept 13 by the Minister of Agriculture. These first tractors were assembled from components shipped from America. Then in January 1951 tractor production was started

The Farmall M was one of the most popular tractors in America. It was introduced in 1939.

The McCormick 523 was manufactured in Neuss, Germany between 1965 and 1972.

The B275 of 1963 used a four-cylinder, 144 cubic inch, diesel engine unit.

Featured here is a 1957, four-cylinder, Farmall 450, which was made between 1956 and 1958.

The 1968 IHGB McCormick B 634, the last tractor produced in Britain to use the McCormick brand name.

Four-cylinder diesel engine, 281 cubic inch displacement and 66hp, from the International 634.

The DGD 4 was a four-cylinder tractor and part of a new series produced in Neuss, Germany.

The DGD 4 used a DD 132 engine and was manufactured from 1953 to 1956.

The main feature of the 986 was the cab, which had tinted glass and a hi-tech ventilation system.

International have had a good selection of crawlers through their history; this is the BTD 8.

at the new French factory at St Dizier, with the assembly of the Farmall model FC.

As world agricultural mechanisation requirements increased after the war, it was obvious that a new small tractor was needed. It was during 1954 that IHGB acquired the old Jowett car works at Idle in Bradford and started production of the McCormick International B 250 tractor. This was rated at 30hp and was Britain's first tractor incorporating disk brakes and differential locking system. In early 1965, all farm tractor assembly was transferred to the Carr Hill factory but component parts for McCormick International B-450 and B-614 were still made at Wheatley Hall Road and transferred daily by road. The first tractor off the Carr Hill production line was a McCormick International B-450 in May of that year. In 1968 IHGB launched the McCormick International B-634 tractor, which was Britain's first model incorporating lower link torsion bar hydraulics, and was also the last tractor produced in Britain to use McCormick as part of its brand name. Production actually ceased in 1972. That year, a decision was made to close the Liverpool facility at Orrell Park, and transfer its work to the remaining British plants. The last tractor

off the Neuss factory line to carry the McCormick name was a 624 in 1972.

IHGB started building a new tractor series at their Carr Hill factory in 1970. During October of that year, the first of the 'World Wide' range rolled off the production line. The range initially comprised the 454 and the 574, but soon the 474, 475 and 674 agricultural tractors, and 2400 and 2500 industrial machines were also included. As well as having syncromesh transmissions, these tractors were Europe's first models offering the option of hydrostatic transmissions too.

The US side of things must not be forgotten, where they were working on bigger machinery. The early part of the 1970s saw the unveiling of the 66 series, which had new rubber-mounted cabs with radios and eight-track sound systems. By now the race for ever more power was on and International used one of their V-8 truck engines to power their 1468 model. Even bigger models such as the 4366 were based on the Steiger machines, which International had purchased 28 percent of in the early 1970s.

In 1976 the Pro-Ag 86 series of two-wheel-drive machines was introduced, with machines ranging from the 886 through to the 100hp Hydro.

In 1978 IHGB launched their 84 series tractor range, which featured flat deck cabs and four-wheel-drive models. These tractors used engines that were produced at the Neuss factory in Germany. The 85 series, available with the new XL cab or low-profile L cab, was launched in 1982 and continued in production until 1987.

Then in late 1984 Tenneco, owners of the Case and David Brown brands, declared its intention to purchase certain assets of International Harvester's Agricultural Division. The deal was concluded in 1985 and Harvester was placed under the control of the Tenneco Case division. Following this, all products from Case's agricultural division were re-branded Case International.

In 1999 Case became interested in merging with New Holland and once agreed by the shareholders, the new company became known as Case New Holland Global N.V. (CNH). European Union regulatory authorities rubber-stamped the merger, provided that CNH divested themselves of the Doncaster Wheatley Hall Road plant, and the 50 to 100hp C, CX and MXC tractors it produced, along with the MX MAXXUM production and engineering know-how. After negotiations with various interested parties, the Doncaster plant was purchased by ARGO S.p.A of Italy, who announced that the plant would become the global headquarters for McCormick Tractors International Ltd., and that products from there would be sold world-wide under the McCormick brand name.

Often referred to as the 'Super Snoopy' the 7488 was the last of the big four-wheel drive machines.

A new Doncaster-built tractor range was introduced in 1994. The 3200/4200 series models were equipped with low profile or deluxe cab versions, in two and four-wheel-drive. Then in 1997 the new CX tractor series were introduced and built at Doncaster, which were available with low profile or standard cabs as well as platform versions. The following year the Doncaster plant started building the MAXXUM MXC models, which used the MAXXUM transmission and hydraulics, powered by the same series of four-cylinder engine used in the CX tractors.

In April 2001 it was announced that CNH had sold their transmission plant at St Dizier to ARGO, and so this now became McCormick France, and the headquarters for operations in that country.

In 2005 McCormick distribution covers all Europe, Australia, New Zealand and South Africa. McCormick USA has recently been established to distribute their products into the United States.

And with this we complete the circle and return back to the name of the man who started it all off back in the 1800s.

Ivel

1902-1920

Dan Albone was born in Biggleswade in 1860. He became interested in cycling at an early age. It was in 1880 that he started his own cycle business–the Ivel Cycle Works. His bicycles were much favoured by many well known racing cyclists for their speed and light weight–Albone also became a racing champion in his own right.

Albone was also the man who first brought the internal combustion engine tractor to the ordinary farmer. His tractor–named after the nearby river, the Ivel–was introduced in 1903. It was a three-wheeler and had a twin-cylinder, horizontally opposed, petrol engine, which produced 20hp. Being a very versatile machine, it could be used for a multitude of chores on the farm. Reportedly, some were made in the USA. Unfortunately Albone died in 1906 and without its inventor and guiding hand, the company went into receivership in 1920.

Thought to be the world's first practical tractor, this is the Ivel. It was made in England by Dan Albone.

J

JCB

1945-present

The phenomenal global success story of JCB started in Staffordshire, England from humble beginnings. The business was founded on October 23 1945, when the late Joseph Cyril Bamford, CBE–known universally as Mr JCB–launched the construction and agricultural equipment manufacturing company that bears his initials. He made his first product in a rented lock-up garage, measuring 15 feet by 12 feet, in Uttoxeter, Staffordshire, England. With the help of a £1 welding set and some wartime scrap, he produced a screw-tipping trailer, which he sold at the town's market for £45.

By 1948, six people were being employed by Bamford, and it was then that he turned his attention to producing a hydraulic machine–Europe's first hydraulic tipping trailer. This was developed into a hydraulic arm for tractors, called a Si-draulic, which was to become a big hit for the company.

This is JCB 1, a diesel digger, manufactured in 1964. Restoration took 2 years.

The first product to carry the JCB initials, as we know them, was in 1953. It was a backhoe loader, the machine that most people today know as a JCB. The company went from strength to strength, with Mr JCB using his marketing skills to the full. The 1960s saw the 3C presented, which became a big seller for them. Publicity stunts were carried out to show how maneuverable and versatile the machines were. One maneuver was to run a car under a machine that had its feet fully extended.

The diesel engine of the JCB 1 – completely removed, restored and replaced after restoration.

Not exactly hi-tech, but for 1964 this was innovative. The JCB 1 had front and rear implements.

Today, they can not only extend their feet but can even roll on their sides, although that isn't recommended! The unmistakable JCB backhoe loader can often be seen on the side of motorways, on industrial sites, building sites and pretty well anywhere earth needs moving, digging or redistributing. Today the model range starts with JCB's smallest ever model, the Mini X, which can be easily transported on a trailer. This is a machine that can be operated with ease and by an operator of any experience level. It is powered by a 20hp diesel engine and has a hydrostatic drive on the rear axle.

The compact 1 and 2CX models are versatile and agile. The 3 and 4CX models are suited to larger tasks.

At the top of the range, (skipping the 1CX, 2CX and 3CX) is the 4CX, a machine for high productivity and complete with four wheel drive to the four same-size wheels. With four wheel steering, the machine also has great maneuverability and a large cab, giving a good working environment. The cab has over six square meters of glass for better visibility, and as you would imagine, it has a very high level of instrumentation.

The array of JCB wheeled loaders runs from the 407 ZX, a compact, uncomplicated, quiet and comfortable machine, through to the huge 456 TX. This machine is equipped with the latest Cummins 6CT8.3C engine, giving some 216hp, which is connected to a fully-automatic transmission. Again the cabin has a high level of visibility, fully adjustable seat and steering column and air conditioning comes as standard. There are 15 models to choose from.

The JCB Fastrac is probably the best known tractor that the company produces today. It has a unique suspension system, which gives an unrivalled level of comfort and control for extra speed and productivity. With higher in-field operating speeds the Fastrac tractor can cover up to thirty percent more ground than the conventional machine. There are three models–the 142hp 2140, 155hp 3170 and the top of the range 178hp 3190/3220, which is

The 456 XZ model, is top of the range and has a maximum engine power of 216hp.

equipped with all the latest technological refinements–all use a Cummins engine of differing capacity and power. These are just a few of the company's products.

JCB is privately owned by the Bamford family and the Chairman, Sir Anthony Bamford, is the elder son of the late Mr JCB. Sir Anthony took over the running of the Company in January 1976 at the age of 30. Mr JCB sadly died on March 1 2001, at the grand age of 84.

Today JCB is one of the world's top five construction equipment manufacturers and has 14 plants on four continents–ten in the UK, two in India and others in the USA and Brazil. JCB has also announced plans to build its first Chinese factory in Pudong, south of Shanghai. There are also subsidiary companies in France, Germany, Italy, The Netherlands, Belgium, Spain and Singapore. As Europe's premier manufacturer of construction equipment, JCB exports seventy-five percent of its UK-made products to 150 countries.

The company's worldwide Headquarters are in Rocester, Staffordshire, which are thoughtfully landscaped in 175 acres of countryside with three lakes, wildlife and sculptures.

The company employs more than 5,000 people and manufactures 186 different machines in 12 product ranges: backhoe loaders; telescopic handlers; tracked and wheeled excavators; wheeled loading shovels; articulated dump trucks; rough terrain fork lifts; mini–excavators and Robot skid steer loaders and Robot tracked skid steer loaders. In addition, the company produces a range of telescopic handlers and the unique Fastrac tractor for agricultural markets, JCB also manufactures the Teletruk forklift for the industrial sector.

The Fastrac was a great success and was at home in the field as well as on road haulage duties.

The company opened a $62,000,000 plant, on a 1,000 acre site, in Savannah, Georgia, USA, where backhoe loaders and skid steers are manufactured. In 2001 a Brazilian assembly plant was opened to produce backhoe loaders for South America.

In 2003, JCB announced an £80,000,000 investment

With higher in-field operating speeds, Fastrac can cover far more ground than a conventional tractor.

The unique suspension system allows superior comfort and control for extra speed and productivity.

to develop and manufacture its own diesel engines. A new company–JCB Power Systems Ltd–was formed to produce the engines and production has now begun at a new plant in Derbyshire, England. The company has won more than 50 major awards for engineering excellence, exports, design, marketing, management and for its care for the environment. Among them are 16 Queen's Awards for Technology and Export Achievement, the latest being a Queen's Award for Enterprise in the International Trade category in 2005 for JCB's Backhoe Loader Business Unit.

In 2004 the company celebrated an historic milestone–the production of the 500,000th JCB machine–and in 2005, JCB celebrates its 60th anniversary.

JCB's famous yellow backhoe loaders and excavators have become part of the global construction landscape and part of the English language. The name JCB is even listed in the Oxford and Collins Dictionaries as a type of construction machine, with a hydraulically operated shovel on the front and an excavator arm at the rear. From humble beginnings, this is now a truly international company.

JCB are better known for construction equipment but they introduced Fastrac in 1991.

Beat that! JCB have been making these machines for many years and they are proud to show them off.

John Deere

1825-present

The history of the John Deere tractor company starts way back, during a period when early settlers were moving to the Midwest of America. During the nineteenth century, this area of America was seen by the settlers as a land of opportunity that held great promise for them. There were vast open areas just waiting to be farmed and cultivated.

It was in the small town of Rutland, Vermont that John Deere was born on February 7 1804, to William R. and Sarah (Yates) Deere, the fifth of six children. He became an apprentice blacksmith at the age of seventeen and when he had finished his apprenticeship in 1825, he began his career as a journeyman blacksmith, soon gaining considerable fame for his careful workmanship and ingenuity.

Two years later he married Demarius Lamb, but times were hard during this period and by 1836, like many others, business was not going well for John Deere and his new family. Demarius already had four children and was pregnant with their fifth when John decided to move to Illinois. Many who had settled in Vermont had already moved there and when John got whispers of the opportunities in the West, he decided to move there too. He sold his shop

John Deere developed the world's first commercially successful, self-scouring, steel plough.

to his father-in-law and left the proceeds to his wife, who was due to join him later. He arrived in Chicago with a bag of tools and a small amount of money. He continued onto Grand Detour, a new village that had been settled by others from his native Vermont, where he found more than enough work to keep him busy. Here there were no blacksmiths and so he became very much in demand. The following year of 1837 saw John construct his new shop on a piece of land he had rented, where he would shoe horses and oxen, and repair the plows and other equipment that the pioneer farmers used.

Associating with the farmers also gave him access to their conversations and it was clear that the farmers found very fertile, stickier types of soils to cling to the bottom of their cast iron plows. This meant that they had to clean the soil from the plow before continuing, which made for an even slower process than plowing already was. In addition, this meant having to use more oxen and horsepower than normal. The plows that the farmers had brought with them were made for the softer, sandier soil of New England and couldn't cope with the heavier soil in the West. Discouraged and frustrated, many of the farmers gave up and returned to their homes back in the East.

John Deere spent time looking at the farmers' problem and became convinced that a plow with a properly shaped moldboard and share should be able to clean itself during the ploughing process. So it was that in 1837 he found an old broken steel saw, shaped and molded it and then went on to test it at the Lewis Crandall farm, not far from Grand Detour. Two further models followed the success of this initial plow and so the John Deere name, and his 'self-polishers', started to spread throughout the West and beyond.

In 1843, with demand increasing every year, John Deere had to find a way of obtaining large volumes of steel, and he started by importing it from the steel mills in Sheffield, England. This involved a hazardous and very long journey over the Atlantic Ocean, up the Mississippi and Illinois rivers and then overland for some forty miles to Grand Detour. By the following year he had found a company in St Louis that would supply steel for him and finally in 1846 the Jones and Quigg Steel Works of Pittsburgh produced the first slab of cast plow steel made in the United States. This was far superior to any other steel on the market at the time.

The railroad reached the area in 1843 but it by-passed Grand Detour, and John Deere decided that the town would not thrive without it. He struck up a partnership with John Gould and Robert Tate and moved to Moline, seventy-five miles southwest of

John Deere listened to the problems that the farmers had with the fertile soil they encountered.

Grand Detour. Here he was able to tap into the waterpower from the great Mississippi River and the transportation facilities. A new building was constructed in 1848, and in 1849 a workforce of sixteen built 2,136 plows.

In 1852 John Deere bought out his two partners and during the next sixteen years the company became known by the titles: John Deere, John Deere and Company, Deere & Company and the Moline Plow Manufactory.

In 1853, John Deere's son, Charles, joined the company as bookkeeper at the age of sixteen–he would become president of the company at a later date. Well-educated, he soon climbed the rungs of leadership, heading up the position of vice president and treasurer. He was seen as a great businessman and provided the company with the entrepreneurial spirit to propel it to the forefront of farm machinery manufacturers. Production grew each year and diversification into other products was also taken up. It was only the Panic of 1857 that slowed things down, and it was during the following year that John Deere handed over the reigns of leadership to his twenty-one-year-old son Charles.

In 1860 the company was trading under the Moline Plow Manufactory name and the following year the American Civil War started. With crop failures in Europe the farmers of the Midwest found themselves having to produce more than ever before and so both

The Sulky corn cultivator, produced during the mid 1880s. One advantage was the high operator's seat.

farmers and their suppliers prospered during this bloody period. With the large amount of farming needed to keep soldiers and animals fed, machinery was improved to cope and so even the smaller farmer was able to expand. In 1863 the company started producing their first implement adapted for riding–the Hawkeye riding cultivator–under license from the inventor Robert Furnas.

During this period a farmer using a walking plow

Gilpin Moore developed the Gilpin Sulky plow in 1875, finally allowing the farmer to sit.

The first logo to be produced for the John Deere company, with the classic leaping deer.

Charles Deere was an outstanding businessman who established marketing centers to serve retailers.

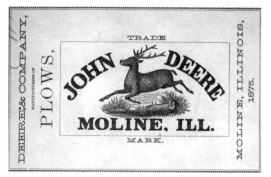

could expect to cover something in the region of one to one and a half acres per day. It was now, though, that the idea of fifting more than one mouldboard to a plow–the two bottom gang, as it was known– was taken up. With this the farmer was now able to farm nearer five to five and a half acres of land per day. In 1867 the Walking Cultivator was patented– the farmers liked to ride but the cost difference was too much for some. By 1870 the company had five basic lines that would see them through to the end of the nineteenth century: plows, cultivators, harrows, drills and planters and wagons and buggies.

Fighting through the Panic of 1873, triggered by the failure of a New York bank, and which led to the depression of the 1870s, Deere and Company, as they were now known, continued to thrive. In 1874 grasshopper attacks made the economic conditions for the Midwest farmer extremely difficult, but still the company continued to grow. The following year the Gilpin Sulky (riding) Plow was developed, probably the most significant piece of machinery to be presented by Deere in the post Civil War years. Because it was so practical and well made, it became a huge success and was one of the best-selling sulky plows of the period in the USA. But by 1876 it was clear that business was not doing well and debts were mounting, so a wage reduction was brought in. Also this year saw the introduction of the 'leaping deer' trademark. This first trademark depicts a deer bounding over a log with the words John Deere above it. The words 'Moline, Ill' are written below the figure, Moline, Illinois being the location of the company. It is interesting to note that this original trademark represented a type of deer not common to North America but from Africa, and it was only in the future trademarks that the native North America white-tailed deer was portrayed. A trademark was essential and stopped others from copying the John Deere products.

Sadly in 1886 John Deere died at the age of 82, and his son Charles took over the presidency, a position

John Froelich's machine, the world's first tractor with an internal combustion engine.

The emblem of the Waterloo Boy tractor made by the Gasoline Engine Company of Waterloo, USA.

Waterloo Boy was acquired when they bought the Waterloo Gas Engine Company in 1918.

The Waterloo Boy was imported to England and Ireland. One importer was Harry Ferguson.

he held until he died in 1907. His two daughters married in 1892–Katherine to William Butterworth and Anna to William Wiman. Butterworth would take the reins of the company when Charles died and Anna's son, Charles Deere Wiman, would take control after him.

During the fiscal year 1899–1900, aggregate business exceeded $2 million for the first time.

By 1915, equipment makers were looking at the new tractors using gasoline engines and wondering if this was the way forward. If they were, should they purchase them from the manufacturers or should they build their own? So it was that the following

year, Deere started building some experimental and prototype models, but these never went into production.

Back in 1893, John Froelich–credited with being the creator of the first gasoline tractor–and a group from Waterloo, Iowa, formed the Waterloo Gasoline Traction Company to market the Froelich machine. Four experimental tractors were built, of which two were sold and then returned. Then in 1895 the company re-organized itself as the Waterloo Gasoline Engine Company. In 1902, they and the Davis Engine Company formed the Waterloo Tractor Works; their aim was to manufacture gasoline

When imported to England and Ireland, the Waterloo Boy tractors were given the name Overtime.

The John Deere model C tractor, which was built in relatively small numbers from 1927.

When Model D production finished in 1953, it had the longest production run of any tractor in history.

engines and three-cylinder automobiles. Withdrawing from the company just two years later, the Waterloo Gasoline Engine Company offered a redesigned engine they called the Waterloo Boy. These farm tractors first came on the scene in 1913, with the model LA. Then came the model R, and in

1915 more than one hundred were sold. The model N was introduced in December 1916, which included enclosed transmission and two forward speeds. The company was building two Waterloo Boy tractors by now–its model R and the model N; both were kerosene burning, with two-cylinder engines. It wasn't long before the Waterloo Boy tractor was one of the most popular in the industry, which allowed the Waterloo Gasoline Engine Company to concentrate on farm tractors as their major product line. So by 1918 they had a tractor manufacturing facility, filled with machines, in Waterloo, Iowa.

The first model D was presented in 1923 and had a two-cylinder engine, this one is from 1938.

The Deere & Company board had shown their reluctance to make tractors; they had dabbled but nothing had come of it. Then after a while a compromise was agreed. On March 14, 1918, by a unanimous resolution, they agreed to purchase the Waterloo Gasoline Engine Company. So it was from these events that the Deere Company started selling its first commercial tractor. The following year there was much labour unrest, with workers wanting union recognition. A strike ensued but the company resisted the installation of a union. By 1920, the economy was starting to take a dramatic dive and there were many bankruptcies in the farming community. Even well–known companies like General Motors had decided to pull out of making tractors. There was worse to come the following year: the sales of Waterloo tractors plummeted from over 5,000 in the previous year, to a miserable 79. Lay-offs followed along with wage reductions in an attempt to keep people employed and the company trading. These were hard times not just for Deere but all the other tractor manufacturers too. Ford had once again reduced their prices and benefited from that action. Others companies followed suit and so the Waterloo Boy model N was reduced to a selling price of $850 for July of 1921.

This is a GP, standard-tread model. In rowcrop form, it became the first John Deere rowcrop machine.

The model N had not had much in the way of updates or changes during the period it had been around and the company decided the time had now come to make these changes. As Model N serial number 30400 rolled off the production line on June of 1923, it was followed not by another model N but by the new model D, with serial number 30401. This was also the first production tractor with the John Deere name on it. This first

The model C became the GP, seen here. It used a 311 cubic inch, twin-cylinder, side-valve engine.

model D used an improved version of the two-cylinder, horizontal, water-cooled, Waterloo Boy model N engine fitted to it. The early models had a welded front axle, a two-speed transmission and left side steering. The tractor was a great success for the company and remained in production until March 1954, during which time it went through much updating, including fitting rubber tires prior to the World War II. By the late 1940s, electric starting and lights became option too. Farmers loved the simplicity and low cost maintenance of the machine, and the fact that it would run on most

The engine of an AO machine, generally known as an Orchard model. It was streamlined in 1936.

kinds of cheap fuel, whilst still capable of pulling a three-bottom plow in most conditions. Some of the last examples of the model D were assembled on the roadside, next to the factory, and for this reason are known as 'streeters.'

This is a model AR, presented in the mid 1930s. The model was styled in 1941.

The design for the GP (General Purpose) model tractor was started in 1925 and in 1929 the GP Wide-Tread, row crop model was put on the market. This was not a replacement for the model D but an alternative that was more versatile. It was fitted with an exclusive feature, a mechanical lift that was foot operated, a John Deere first which would be copied by many of the other companies. Although the first GPs were rated at 10hp at the drawbar and close to 20hp at the belt when running at 9000rpm, these figures were increased during its lifetime. The tractor was started on gas and then would continue to run on paraffin. The first John Deere orchard

The biggest rowcrop machine so far appeared in 1937, the model G, with a two-cylinder engine.

tractors were based on this model and had all-encompassing rear wheel, belt pulley and flywheel covers, which helped to prevent any accidents with limbs and the like. There was also an XOGP model produced for 1930–the XO standing for a new crossover style manifold.

The economic downturn had by now worsened and the Great Depression started to hit hard. Once again wages were cut and now there were huge lay-offs, pensions were cut and there were shortened working hours. By 1933 business was poor and sales were plummetting but somehow the company struggled on. Despite all the doom and gloom, a new model tractor was produced for 1934–the model A–which was followed a year later by a smaller version, the model B. The model A was advertised as a brand new tractor with greater adaptability, new outstanding array of features and greater economy of operation. One of its new features was the adjustability of the rear wheel track. Generally up to this time the rear wheels of a tractor were 40 to 42 inches apart, now they could be adjusted by sliding them in and out on their splined axles, allowing spacing between 56 and 84 inches. The styling on the model A was changed for 1939 and electric starting was added as an option, only to be made a regular feature by 1947. Just one year after the model A was presented, the smaller version model B– advertised as a one bottom plow tractor giving the daily work output of six to eight horses–was also put on the market. This machine was aimed at the larger farmer who needed a tractor to carry out smaller tasks on the farm, whilst at the same time it also introduced the smaller horse-bound farmer to the idea of a small and inexpensive tractor. This model sold so well that it became the best selling two-cylinder John Deere Tractor ever produced, with well over 306,000 sold.

The model A was one of the first tractors to have adjustable wheel tracks. Note rear spindles.

A crawler conversion made by Lindemann Brothers, was mounted on the model BO tractor chassis.

An operator's view of the controls and instruments of the Lindemann BO crawler.

In 1935 John Deere, who now had a strong tractor division, paired up with the Caterpillar Company, who had a very strong crawler division. The two companies decided to sell each other's products, with particular emphasis in California. This agreement went well at first but over time it started to fade, finally breaking in the 1960s.

As the depression started to lift and the 1930s came to a close, industrial designer Henry Dreyfuss started work with the engineers at Deere to streamline the A series tractors. It was from this time onwards that more attention would be paid to the attractiveness of a John Deere design, as well as its utilitarian requirements.

The model L, introduced in 1937, used a two-cylinder engine designed by Deere but built by Hercules.

The model 60 was introduced in 1952. It used a two-cylinder 321 cubic inch engine.

military tractors, ammunition and aircraft parts, along with other items for the war effort. Some 4,500 employees went to war, many of whom served in the 'John Deere' battalion, a specialist ordinance group who also saw action in Europe.

In 1945, with the war now over, the board at John Deere approved the purchase of 730 acres of land near the town of Dubuque, Iowa and the building of a new factory was started. During 1942 and 1943 the company had been working on the Model 69, and after much testing and refining the 69 turned into the model M tractor, which was presented in 1947 and built at the new factory. The original Ms were rated at 14.39 hp at the drawbar and 18.21 hp at the belt. A new model–the MT, very similar to the model M –soon became available and had wide front, dual tricycle front or single front wheel. Touch O Matic

It wasn't until 1949 that John Deere introduced their first diesel model, the model R.

Late in 1937 John Deere introduced their model L, which directly replaced the older model 62. This still used the two-cylinder engine, although now it was a vertical unit rather than the usual horizontal one, it also featured a three-speed transmission. By 1941 a larger model L was introduced, the model LA, which had more engine power, weighed more and had higher crop clearance. Electric starting and lights were an option

When time came for men to enlist, Charles Deere Wiman, president of the company since 1928, answered the call to serve his country in the US Army during World War II. Whilst he was away, Burton Peek was made president until Wiman's return in 1944. During the war years Deere produced

As shown here the model 70 was able to burn LP gas, note the tank, and was presented in 1953.

Several versions of the 420 model were made, which was introduced in 1956.

A wonderful period advertising poster depicts the two-cylinder, 420 rowcrop tractor.

This is the 520 model, in LP gas configuration. It was produced between 1956 and 1958.

During the early 1940s, John Deere started developing a tractor that would replace the model D. The new model MX was developed over a period of several years and it was this that would eventually turn into the model R. The late 1930s had seen the start of the use of diesel engines in tractors, but it wasn't until January 1949 that Deere finally presented its own version. Not only was the model R the first John Deere diesel tractor, it was also the first to have live PTO and the first to be equipped with a cab. Some 17,000 units were made during its lifespan–1949 to 1954.

Designation letters were now replaced by numbers and new models were known as the numbered series: the Model 40 replaced the M, the Model 50

hydraulics were also available as an optional extra on the MT. Two years after its presentation the M was also available as the MC. This was a crawler version of the model M, which once a front blade was fitted, became a bulldozer.

Just under 10,000 model 530's were made. Presented in 1958 they used a 190 cubic inch engine.

replaced the B, the Model 60 replaced the A, the Model 70 replaced the G and the Model 80 replaced the R.

The models 50 and 60 were introduced in June 1952 and the 70 came out in April of 1953 using a gasoline or all-fuel engine. It was Deere's first row crop diesel tractor and was rated at 54.7hp at the drawbar and 51.5hp at the belt. To start the engine, a new four-cylinder pony motor design was used. The driver would have to pull a lever, which then made the pony motor engage the flywheel ring gear, which would then turn the diesel engine over. As soon as the diesel engine was turning, the lever could be

moved forward, which then put the diesel on full compression and it would start.

For 1955 the model 80 was introduced, catering to farmers' requirements for more horsepower. This was a stop-gap machine until a new, more powerful and larger tractor could make its debut in 1960. The era of the two-cylinder engine was coming to a close. More powerful than both the model R, which it replaced, and the 70 diesel, the 80 had a water-cooled, twin-cylinder 475 cubic inch engine, and six-speed transmission. During this time the model 20 was also being developed but more importantly so was the New Generation of Power tractors, which

The 830 was the last John Deere big twin model. Production ran from 1958 to 1960.

The model 4030 was available in either gasoline or diesel version, the diesel being the bigger.

The Generation II tractors arrived in 1972. The big feature was the Sound Guard cab.

would make their debut in a blaze of glory in 1960. In 1955 William A. Hewitt was elected president and later became CEO, after the death of his father-in-law, Charles Deere Wiman. He would be the last of the Deere family to head-up the company. The following year John Deere built a factory in Mexico, to produce a small tractor. A presence was also made

Using a six-cylinder diesel engine and introduced in 1963, the model 5010 had 8 forward gears.

in Spain, a harvesting company was bought in Germany–in 1956, John Deere and Lanz became international partners, with John Deere's acquisition of a majority shareholding–and in the next few years Deere also moved into France, Argentina and South Africa. They were now a truly international company. The early numbered series were replaced in 1957, these were now changed from the model 40 to the 420, the 50 became the 520 and so on. Although similar in looks to the machines they replaced, there was the addition of the now familiar yellow stripe along the bonnet and side of the radiator. Horsepower was also increased along with driver comfort and many other operating aspects. A completely new model 320 was introduced, based on the M and MI models and was built at the Dubuque factory. A third version known as the Southern Special, was merely a variation of the 320S. Then in 1958 the 20 series were replaced by what would be the final numbered series, the series 30, the 420 would now become the 430 and so on. These were equipped with further improvements and refinements for the driver. A new series was also released for 1959 in the form of the 435. This same year the company introduced the 8301 and 8401 models which were aimed exclusively at the industrial market and were fitted with a Hancock scraper system. At the end of the 1950s the company introduced a monster of a machine–the 8010–a diesel powered, 215hp, tractor, much ahead of its time. This was the first four-wheel-drive to be produced by the company but unfortunately only a few were sold. Of those that were sold, all had to be recalled, were updated and returned as 8020's.

As 1960 dawned, a new 10 series was created with designations starting with the 1010 and 2010 models, but these weren't new models, merely the two-cylinder tractors with new engines. The models 3010 and 4010 though, were entirely new machines and became known as the 'New Generation of Power' tractors. Introduced at a huge show with much razzmatazz–the Deere Day show in Dallas in 1960 – some 6,000 people attended. It was back in 1953 that these new machines had been thought about and so this was the culmination of many years of development and design. Many thought that these tractors would kill off the company–how wrong they were! These machines piloted John Deere into prime sales position, just a few years later overtaking their biggest rivals International, for the first time. The 3010 was fitted with a four-cylinder engine, whilst the 4010 had a six-cylinder unit. These were diesel engines although both gasoline and LPG engines were also available. With the addition of power steering, power brakes, power implement raising

The 7520 super tractor of 1970 was an update of the original 7020 and had four-wheel drive.

capabilities and an eight-speed transmission, these machines became extremely popular. The following year a 5010 model–the industry's first two-wheel-drive tractor rated over 100hp–was introduced with 151hp. Three years after their introduction, the 3010 and 4010 were replaced with an updated 3020 and 4020. The latter would eventually become the most popular tractor of its time. The 91hp 4020 diesel truly deserved its reign, lasting from 1964 to 1972, with its ideal blend of power and performance.

The 7520 model had a six-cylinder turbocharged engine of 415 cubic inches.

Construction started on a new engine factory in 1961, at Saran, near Orleans in France. At the same time the Deere & Company administration centre was also being built in Moline. The following year the company celebrated its 125th anniversary and bought a majority interest in South African Cultivators, a farm implement company near Johannesburg. The following year of 1963, John Deere ventured into the consumer market with a decision to produce and sell lawn and garden tractors, which would include some attachments such as mowers and snow blowers.

Total sales surpassed $1 billion for the first time in 1966. Sales of farm equipment set a record for the fourth straight year. Industrial equipment sales gained their largest ever year-to-year increase, whilst lawn and garden equipment sales rose by 76 percent and worldwide employment hit a record high–without doubt a bumper year for John Deere and all its subsidiaries around the world.

By the end of the 1960s, overall sales started to level out, mainly due to a downturn in farm equipment sales, and although overseas operations expanded, no real profit was seen. For 1972, the same year that the 'Green Girl' was born, the 'Generation II' tractor model line was launched. New styling, Perma-Clutch and a Sound-Gard cab all went to make these an instant success for the company. John Deere had always been at the forefront when it came to safety

The little model 2120 was manufactured at the John Deere factory in Mannheim, Germany.

and was now putting a lot of emphasis on cab comfort and safety. These cabs were comfortable, sealed from the dust and dirt, and air-conditioning or heater were optional extras. Tinted glass, to stop glare, along with seat belt and adjustable steering wheel went to make this cab extremely desirable.

The engine of the 2120 model was a three cylinder, diesel unit. Deere were now truly international.

The proof was in the pudding, as they say–the best selling model was the 4430 and three–quarters of those who bought it paid the extra money to have the Sound-Gard cab fitted. The new 30 series tractors consisted of the 80hp 4030, the 100hp 4230, the 125hp 4330 and the 150hp 4630. The last three of these used the same six-cylinder, 6.6 litre diesel engine. Naturally aspirated they could be fitted with either turbo or turbo-intercooler.

A French advertisement for the new 2000 series tractors with engine capacities of 89 to 106hp.

Huge crop failures outside the United States spurred massive foreign buying of American grain and with it farmers prospered greatly. The demand for equipment also exploded and John Deere total sales increased to a staggering $2 billion for the first time. This same year, 1973, the board at John Deere decided on a more independent board structure and the first outside director was appointed. The demand for John Deere equipment continued to increase but inflation also increased costs in 1974. All the same the company began an extensive expansion program, with more than one billion dollars forecast to be spent on new facilities by 1979. In 1977 an agreement with the Japanese manufacturer Yanmar, allowed the sale of small tractors under the John Deere name. Along with a new Canadian headquarters in Grimsby, Ontario, a new engine works in Waterloo and new sales branch offices in Atlanta, company employment reached an all-time record high. Sales topped the $5 billion mark with earnings hitting a record $310 million–what a way to end the 1970s.

The 1980s kicked off with the introduction of a four-row cotton-picker, a machine that would increase the operator's productivity level by some 85–95 percent. This machine was an industry first. The following year two new super-tractors were unveiled, the 40 series, four-wheel-drive machines now being replaced by the 50 series 185hp 8450 and the 235hp 8650 six-cylinder models. Farmers with large holdings were

The Model 920 was another small tractor being produced in Mannheim.

now looking for bigger and more powerful machines to do their work. In addition to these John Deere added the even bigger 8850, a new powerhouse model producing 370 hp. This tractor used a turbo-charged and inter-cooled V8 diesel engine, that was designed and built by John Deere themselves at their

The model 920, three-cylinder engine was produced in the John Deere factory in Mannheim, Germany.

Waterloo plant. The 8850 had a wider grille and six small headlamps, compared to the four used on the smaller six-cylinder models. All three six- and eight-cylinder models had their exhaust and air intake stacks moved to the right hand corner of the cab, which helped to improve field vision. Following the bumper 1970s, the 1980s saw a deepening recession, and the advertising for these machines reflected this when they were described as 'three new ways to

An advertisement for the new John Deere 3000 series, which consisted of four models.

tighten your belt.' You could be forgiven for thinking there was no recession going on though as this was the most expensive John Deere model and it was also the biggest to date.

Fortunately all the investment in new plant, facilities and machinery that the company had instigated in the 1970s paid off during these recession years, but not without casualties. Nearing the end of the 1980s the company was losing substantial amounts of money and the workforce was reduced dramatically. But due to good investment and forward planning the company came through the bad years in a strong position, now in control of over half the US tractor market.

During this period an updated series of the Mannheim-built tractors were also presented. These ranged from the three-cylinder 2150 model, through to the larger six-cylinder 2950 model. The Yanmar connection also came into play when Deere started importing one of these machines as the 1250 model, in corporate colours. Bigger models followed as in the 1450 and 1650 and some specialist models were also presented, for example the 2750 Mudder–a high clearance, four-wheel-drive machine–and a range of wide-tread machines used for such crops as tobacco. Other new machines followed and older models were updated, re-designated and improved as the 1980s and the recession moved to a close.

The 3400 telehandler, built by Matbro for John Deere. This type of machine was popular in the 1990s.

The 344H loader had a four-cylinder engine with a displacement of 276 cubic inches.

This is the nerve center of the tractor, with controls literally at your fingertips.

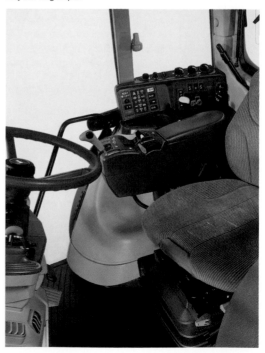

A bird's-eye view of the cab and all its features. The driver has complete control and great visibility.

In 1990 Robert Hanson retired as chairman and Hans W Becherer took over from him, having previously been both president and CEO. The following year SABO, a European maker of lawnmowers, was acquired. Then in 1993 the new 5000, 6000 and 7000 series tractors were presented, helping to put John Deere at the head of the table for tractor sales in the German market. The 5000 series used a three-cylinder engine, had hydrostatic power steering, nine-speed transmission and optional four-wheel drive. The four-cylinder 6000 series tractors (75hp 6100, 84hp 6200, 90hp 6300 and 100hp 6400) were being produced at the Mannheim factory in Germany, the six-cylinder 7000 series

were built in the USA at a new factory in Atlanta. Once again there was a state-of-the-art cab, which fitted all models and was claimed to be the quietest on the market with more space and more glass area. Three further models–6600, 6800 and 6900, with a choice of horsepower–were also produced, which took the best from both series and fitted the 6000 with the small six-cylinder, water-cooled, diesel engine from the 7000 range. There were three models initially of the 7000 series (7600, 7700 and 7800) of which the 7800 was top of the range. This used a water-cooled, six-cylinder, turbo-cooled diesel engine and had a nineteen-speed, power-shift transmission.

It would seem you might need a degree in tractor handling when you look at this lot!

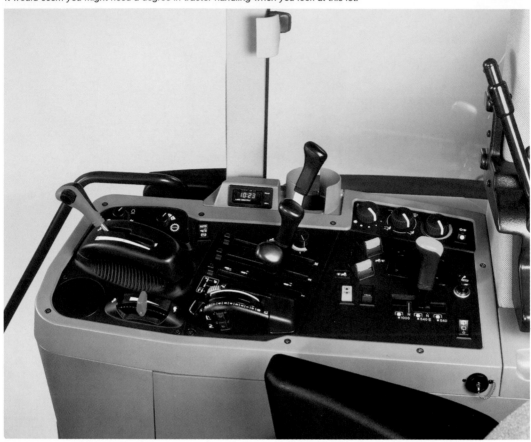

The model 5510 made between 1998 and 2000 came in several different specifications.

This model 5510 is shown in High-clearance form. All came with a three-cylinder diesel engine.

This is the 1993, 6420S version of the 6000 series built at Mannheim in Germany.

The 6620 model has an optional front loader capability, and can be adapted for various duties.

The 6920 tractor has a six-cylinder engine and was derived from the four-cylinder 6000 series.

One of the six-cylinder 7000 series machines being built at the Waterloo factory is the 7810.

The 8120, part of the huge rowcrop 8000 series. This machine could take on most tasks.

Clearly a monster in its class, this is the John Deere 8000T. It produces between 185-260hp.

It's not the similarities that upset our competitors . . .

NEW 136 to 191 kW (185 to 260 hp) John Deere 8000T Series Tractors

The mid-range John Deere 7000 series for 1993. They were row-crop tractors with attitude.

REDRAW THE BOUNDARIES OF POWER

NEW JOHN DEERE 7000 SERIES TRACTORS

7600
130 HP/
96 KW

7700
150 HP/
110 KW

7800
170 HP/
125 KW

For 2006 the lineup of tractors being produced by John Deere is sufficient to cater for pretty well any need. Their compact utility tractors range from the 23hp 2210 model, which John Deere class as their most compact tractor ever. It has a wide-open step-through platform, which gives plenty of room for the operator and a more comfortable ride. Comforts also include a multi-adjustable seat and thick rubber isolators, which help to tone down engine noise and vibration. Four-wheel drive, mid and rear PTOs, and a limited Category 1 three-point hitch are all standard. A variety of popular rear-hitch implement options like rotary cutters, tillers, blades, and rakes are available. Described as rugged and dependable, the 90 series tractors provide affordable power and productivity with durable, field-proven transmissions. The 27hp, three-cylinder diesel engine 790 and the high-torque, fuel-efficient

The huge 8500 model is making easy work of this. Rubber tracks were also available.

The John Deere 3210 model going about its daily business plowing a field.

Seen with a front loader, here is the John Deere 5400 model, a versatile, mid-range tractor.

A slightly bigger machine is the 6210 SE model, which is towing a modern, round bailer.

40.4hp, four-cylinder Yanmar diesel engine 990 models are available with four-wheel drive. The 4000 TEN series compact tractor received the prestigious Agricultural Engineering AE50 award, again a versatile little tractor that can cover a multitude of work. Last but not least is the 3000 and 4000 TWENTY series. There are four, three-cylinder, Yanmar diesel engine 3000 models and four, four-cylinder, John Deere, PowerTech, turbocharged, diesel engine 4000 series.

The 2005 Utility tractor consisted of the 5000 series machines with all three 03 model tractors using John Deere designed and manufactured diesel engines. The 5103 and 5203 tractors use naturally aspirated engines and the 5303 tractors use a turbocharged engine. Both the 05 model tractors use John Deere designed and manufactured, naturally aspirated, three-cylinder diesel engines. The 6000 series tractors consist of the 98-109hp 6003, 72-105hp 6015 and 65-90 6020 models.

Row-crop models are available in the 7000 and 8000 series. Smart controls include optional CommandARM and smooth performance comes from the shift-free IVT, available on all 7020 tractors. The John Deere 6.8 litre PowerTech engines deliver high-torque performance over a wide range of engine speeds.

The driver seems dwarfed in his spacious cab in this model 6810 from 1993.

This is the John Deere 7810, which is equipped with Infinitely Variable Transmission (IVT).

The more wheels you fit the less compaction you have. This 9000 series tractor has plenty!

The John Deere 8020 series tractor is the best-selling brand in its class. These tractors lead the way in power with up to 255-PTO horsepower. Exclusive ActiveSeat and front Independent Link Suspension provide outstanding operator comfort, which allows the operator to work at fast speeds with less fatigue. Five-wheeled and five-tracked models are included, the tracked models having a 'T' after their designation. All 8020/8020T series tractors feature reliable and proven 6081H engines. These air-to-air aspiration engines deliver constant power with a power bulge feature and excellent torque characteristics.

Taking tractor productivity and performance to the highest levels ever, John Deere have introduced the new 9620 and 9620T tractors rated at 500 engine horsepower. These new four-wheel drive and large-track tractors are the largest tractors ever built by John Deere and have all the industry-proven features of the smaller models. The new 9620/9620T tractors are powered by the 12.5 litre John Deere PowerTech engines, which meet Tier II EPA emission levels. These efficient engines feature a 7 percent power bulge at 1900-rpm and a 38 percent torque rise at 1600-rpm for a quick response in tough conditions. These machines also feature, as standard equipment, the 18-speed PowerShift transmission with Automatic PowerShift (APS). When APS is activated, the transmission automatically shifts up or down, based on tractor load, to maximize the tractor's pulling performance. Inboard planetary final drives with large diameter bar axles, 120-mm,

GS2 takes the operation and management of precision agriculture to a higher level.

The 8520, for the first time, offered ILS as an option, increasing comfort and traction.

Keck Gonnerman

1837-1946

Although the first Keck Gonnerman tractor was produced in 1917, John and Louis Keck and Louis Gonnerman had got together way before that, to produce steam engines, threshers and sawmills. This first machine was a twin-cylinder model and had the 12-24 designation; later it was upgraded to the 15-30. For 1928 the company produced the Kay-Gee 18-35 model, which used a Buda four-cylinder engine and was in production up to 1935. This model was revamped and fitted with a Waukesha engine and a four-speed transmission. Also for 1928 there was a 22-45 model, later uprated to 25-50, which used a LeRoi four-cylinder engine. The biggest tractor for 1928 was the 27-55, upgraded to 30-60, which also had a LeRoi four-cylinder power unit and was in production through to the late 1930s.

During World War II, tractor production ceased and never picked up again once the conflict was over.

are featured on the 9620 tractors. They provide a wide range of tread settings and assure dependable performance in tough conditions. The 9620T tracked tractors have a rear axle with inboard steering planetaries and five-pinion outboard final drive planetaries for superior strength and reliability. The rear axle is pressure-lubricated and cooled with the transmission hydraulic system.

There are also speciality tractors in the 91hp 5525 Hi-crop model and the 6020 Low Profile series with horsepower ranging from 65 to 95. The 6020 uses PowerTech engines, dual temperature cooling, and PowerCore air filters maximize economy and power. There is a choice of eight different transmissions, but only five for cab models. The 25 gpm pressure-and-flow-compensated hydraulics and modulated PTO, optimize implement performance. Cabs are available on 80 to 95 PTO-hp models.

There is no reason to question why John Deere is the biggest farm machinery company in the world. Their products and equipment are extensive, their tractors probably the best in the world and the company makes no bones about how much money they invest in research and development. They have outlets all over the world and whether you are looking for a mower to trim your lawn or a huge monster of a tractor to use on your acres of farmland, they can cater for these and pretty well anything in between. The company has come through recessions, farm worker unrest and stock market crashes. It is still with us today and will no doubt be with us for a long time in the future.

The Keck Gonnerman company started way back in 1837. This is a more recent four-cylinder model.

Kubota

1890-present

Kubota Corporation of Osaka, Japan, was established in 1890 and has become an international brand leader with a focus on contributing to society by offering environmentally compatible equipment, designed to improve quality of life. Kubota Corporation has subsidiaries and affiliates that manufacture, manufacture and market, or just market their products that are sold in more than 130 countries around the world.

The Kubota tractor has its roots on the Japanese farm and although Japanese farms are traditionally smaller than those in America, the need for high performance and powerful maneuverability is the same. Kubota Corporation introduced its first tractor to the United States in 1969. Filling a product void in the American marketplace, the Kubota 21hp L200 was an overnight success. As a result, Kubota Tractor Corporation (KTC) was formed in 1972, with headquarters in Torrance, California. The company introduced its first 12 hp, four-wheel drive tractor in 1974–although four-wheel drive was common among larger American tractors, it was unheard of in the compact sector and became a benchmark for the industry.

Over the past quarter century, KTC has continued to expand its product line, with four lines of tractors–the BX, B, L and M series. Kubota has successfully introduced compact construction equipment, turf equipment, lawn and garden equipment, pumps, generators and a variety of performance-matched implements and attachments. KTC is now the leading marketer and distributor of under 40hp tractors in the United States, offering more than 80 tractor models.

Like its bigger ME brothers, the ME5700 has virtually the same advanced technical features.

In its older blue livery, this is not a current machine. This is the B1200 model Kubota.

Kubota Manufacturing of America (KMA) was formed in 1988 in Gainesville, Georgia, as Kubota's North American manufacturing base. KMA manufactures and assembles Kubota lawn tractors, zero-turn mowers, sub-compact tractors, loaders, backhoes and other implements. The company employs 1,200 workers. Two master buildings offer 616,000 square feet of manufacturing space. Today, one-third of all Kubota branded equipment sold in the United States is manufactured or assembled at its 151 acre Gainesville, Georgia facility.

Kubota is a leading OEM (Original Equipment Manufacturer) of compact diesel and gasoline engines for industrial, agricultural, construction and generator applications. Established in 1999, KEA distributes and markets Kubota-Tough, 6 to 83hp, compact, lightweight, turbocharged options, liquid-cooled, low noise and low vibration engines, to other top-name manufacturers serving various industrial equipment sectors.

With turbocharged engine and advanced features, the M105S can tackle a range of farm tasks.

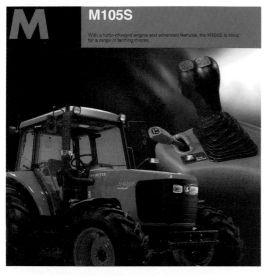

The Kubota Ultra Cab, fitted with all the latest technology, air conditioning and even a radio/CD player.

The Kubota flagship compact STV series tractor has been redesigned with a host of new features.

L

Lamborghini

1949-present

The Lamborghini company, named after its creator Ferruccio Lamborghini, didn't start by building high-performance cars. In fact he was building successful tractors long before he turned his hand to exotic sports cars. Lamborghini was born to a farming family and when he returned from World War Two, he started converting old Morris military engines and fitting them into tractors, which were much needed at that time. This work was initially carried out in an old barn but business was brisk and by 1949 he had moved into larger premises. He had a new factory built, which saw the birth of Lamborghini Trattori SpA in Cento, not far from Bologna, Italy. Now the re-used engines were being replaced by MWM, Perkins and even their own units and soon the L33 model was introduced.

An early, little Lamborghini tractor was an ideal machine for the Italian wine farmers.

Starting off building one tractor per day, the company grew over the next few years and by 1958 they were producing 1,500 tractors per year.
Eighty percent of the tractor parts were now produced at the factory; in this way Lamborghini was able to keep an eye on the quality of the materials. The tractors gained a good reputation as reliable and good quality and were very robust, which always showed up at the tractor pulling events that

Lamborghini organized with the local farmers. By 1969 the company was producing some 5,000 units per year and a further move was needed to cope with the increase in demand. This happened in 1971, by which time Lamborghini was the third best selling tractor in Italy.

Besides tractors, Lamborghini also made crawler, shown is the Cingolato DL30C, diesel model.

In 1968 high-powered models were added to the tractor range, like this Lamborghini R 480 DT.

A spacious but sparse cab on this Lamborghini R 235 DT, makes it look a little top-heavy.

This is the 2005, 141 hp, R6. It uses a Deutz 2012 engine and has 40 forward and reverse gears.

A crushing blow came in 1972 when a large order from a Bolivian company fell through, leaving Lamborghini dismayed with the tractor business; within a short time the SAME group of Trevigliano bought them out. The company continued to thrive under its new owners and by 1979 they were producing 10,000 tractors per year, worldwide. Today, the R1 range, the smallest machines, have excellent engine performance, outstanding maneuverability with a full complement of PTO speeds, giving a very versatile machine. At the other end of the scale, the R8.215 and R8.265 tractors use a Deutz 7146 cc, Euro II engine, with electronic adjustment, transmission with four-stage Powershift and hydraulic power shuttle, just two of the latest, comprehensive Lamborghini range.

Landini

1884-present

Landini is the oldest established tractor company in Italy and was founded by Giovanni Landini in 1884. As a blacksmith he set up his works in the small town of Fabbrico, near the Po river in the Reggio Emilia province of Italy. His skills as a blacksmith soon moved him onto manufacturing agricultural implements and wine-making equipment, shortly to be followed by steam engines and internal combustion engines.

In 1910 Landini had produced a 'testa calda' or hot bulb engine, often referred to as a semi-diesel engine due to the fact that it doesn't have an electric ignition system but instead a hot chamber in the head, which ignites the fuel.

Landini was never to see the fruits of his work though; he sadly passed away in 1924. However, all was not lost as his sons took over the business and from here the foundations that their father had laid would grow to be the successful Landini company of today.

It was only a year after their father's death that the first model 25/30 prototype was presented, which became the first authentic Italian tractor. The Landini 25/30 of 1925 was a well made machine and was not only easy to use but more importantly repairs were easily carried out by the farmers themselves. The engine was a single-cylinder, two-stroke, hot bulb model, which was water cooled. It was equipped with four forward and one reverse gear, which made it very versatile and able to cope with many different types of terrain and therefore a variety of workloads.

This tractor was upgraded to 40hp in 1928 and in 1934 the SL 50 SuperLandini model was announced, which produced 48hp and was the first to use a radiator. Again it had a single-cylinder, hot bulb engine with just three forward gears and one reverse. This was followed in 1935 by the VL 30 Velite models, which were produced through to World War II.

Post-war production was re-started and the L25, a 4300cc engine 25hp model, was announced. This machine was built at a new factory in Como. For 1955 Landini produced their most powerful hot bulb model tractor, the 55L, but the hot bulb engine was on borrowed time and two years later, after an agreement with Perkins engines, Landini gained a licence to produce and fit these engines in their tractors. This agreement has continued to the present day when Perkins engines are still fitted to the current range of machines.

In 1959 Landini moved into the crawler market with the introduction of their first, the C35 model. It was also this year that the company was taken over by Massey-Ferguson, who were keen to exploit the crawler division of Landini. The company did well under its new owners and a new plant was opened in 1968 at Aprilla, to manufacture heavy-duty industrial construction machinery.

The new 6500, 7500 and 8500 tractor models were introduced in 1973: these had redesigned transmissions which equipped the tractors with twelve forward and four reverse gears. This was followed in 1977 by the first 100hp Landini model, a four-wheel-drive machine that used a Perkins, straight six-cylinder engine. The range was increased to include outputs from 45hp through 145hp.

Giovanni Landini died in 1924, just one year prior to this tractor, the L25, being put on the market.

It was 1924 when Landini produced his 'Testa Calda' (hot bulb) engine. This is the model L25 engine.

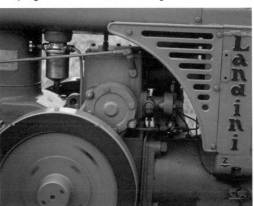

The Landini 9880, was launched in 1988 and uses the reliable 93hp, Perkins AT 4.236 engine.

Once the 1980s had arrived, Landini moved into yet another sector–it was in 1982 that they introduced their first Orchard model–and in 1986 a new Vineyard model was presented too. This was a whole new area for Landini but it wasn't long before they had a large share of that market, becoming sole suppliers of orchard and vineyard versions of both crawler and wheeled tractors, branded as Massey-Fergusons. With sales of over 13,000 tractors, not only was 1988 a bumper year for Landini but they also updated their mid-range models, now classified as the 60, 70 and 80 models.

Massey-Ferguson made the decision to sell off 66 percent of its Landini shares to the Eurobelge/Unione Manifatture holding company in 1989. They in turn later sold their controlling interest in its affairs to the Cameli Gerolimich Group, which finally took Landini SpA into the Unione Manifatture. Now at the forefront of the tractor industry, Landini began redesigning their tractors and produced a new series to be announced as the Trekker, Blizzard and Advantage series.

In February 1994 Valerio and Pierangelo Morra, representatives of the Argo SpA family holding company, became president and vice-president of Landini SpA respectively. They and Massey-Ferguson contributed to a substantial recapitalization of the Landini concern. March 1994 saw Iseki join

An English language version advertisement for the Landini Blizzard 95 of the late 1990s.

Built in 1985, this is the Landini 10000S, which had a 105hp engine and four-wheel drive.

The Vision series feature four-cylinder, Perkins engines that comply with EURO I standards.

Landini SpA, who announced an increase in tractor sales of more than 30 percent over the previous year. It was 1995 that Landini acquired Valpadana SpA, a prestigious trademark in the Italian agricultural machinery sector. Overseas markets were starting to open up too and distribution started through the AGCO network in North America. Landini Sud America was opened in Valencia, Venezuela, with the aim of promoting the brand in Latin America. During 1996, the Fabbricio factory was given an overhaul to cope with the extra production demand. A new assembly line was fitted which would allow double the previous production levels. This same year the new San Martino factory was also opened, concentrating purely on machining parts, such as gears and the assembly of prototype components. The following year the Legend II series was launched along with the Globus range. World distribution continued with importers being opened in Spain and Germany. The following year of 1998

The 2005 Ghibli 90, has a new cab with good all-round visibility and optional air conditioning.

The Landini Legend series have Perkins green engines that offer reliability and high performance.

saw the introduction of the Discovery and Minstral range, with a new transmission system, the Deltasix, being launched in 1999.

As the new millenium came in, new models appeared in the form of Rex Orchard and Vineyard, Mythos, Ghibli, Atlas and new Trekker. In 2005 the Landini range includes a variety of different models, with power outputs ranging from 43-123 PTO hp.

The Trekker series of crawlers use fluid-cooled, four-cylinder, Perkins engines.

Landini tractors are distributed in North America by AGCO and the current range includes the Trekker, Mistral, Atlantis, Ghibli, Mythos, Legend, Globus, Vision and Rex series.

The REX series has been designed for true professionals and uses three- and four-cylinder engines.

Lanz

1860-1960s

Heinrich Lanz was born in Friedrichshafen in 1838 and was the third child of Johann Peter Lanz. He was taken into the family business, based in Mannheim, Germany, in 1859 and was soon involved with importing mainly English agricultural machinery and implements. By 1860 he had started up a small workshop, repairing second-hand machinery, with the help of two assistants. The business went well and in 1867 J. P. Lanz was manufacturing agricultural machinery itself. Two years later the company was importing John Fowler steam plows and in 1879 the company saw their first 2.5hp steam machine leave the premises. It wasn't long before some 3,000 people were being employed by the company to produce steam threshing machines and other agricultural machinery for world-wide distribution. By the turn of the century Lanz farm machinery was well known throughout the world and at the 1900 World Exhibition in Paris, their largest steam machine, with an output of 460hp, astonished the public.

On February 1, 1905 Heinrich Lanz died but the company continued production as normal. During World War II the company supplied 120hp gas driven tractors to the war effort.

It was in 1921 that Lanz exhibited a new prototype to the public at the agricultural show in Leipzig. This machine was designed by engineer Dr Fritz Huber and used a hot bulb, two stroke engine with the designation HL12. This was the beginning of a

A sectional view of the low pressure tired 'All Purpose Tractor,' with six forward speeds.

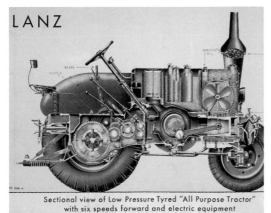

Sectional view of Low Pressure Tyred "All Purpose Tractor" with six speeds forward and electric equipment

long-lasting line of tractors known as the Lanz Bulldog–it was given this nickname because it looked like a bulldog. The 38 hp, two-cylinder, hot bulb model with four-wheel drive was produced for 1923 and a further Grossbulldog was presented as the HR2 in 1926. By the late 1930s the Bulldog model range consisted of six groups (15, 20, 25, 45 and 55hp) in various versions such as general-purpose, and some supplied with pneumatic tires. World War II approached and the tractor had to be designed to run on wood, by law, as there was an acute shortage of fuel. On April 14, 1942 Dr Fritz Huber died and in this same year the 100,000th Bulldog was delivered to its new owner. The war took its toll on the factory but manufacturing was soon taken up once again with what remained of the factory. During 1949 the hot bulb system was replaced by a semi-diesel system engine, allowing the engine to be started with gas via an electric starter.

A powerful advertisement for a powerful tractor, produced by Heinrich Lanz of Germany.

John Deere gained majority stock control in 1956 and basically took over Lanz, renaming it John Deere Lanz AG in 1960. By 1965 a whole new range of machines with new engines and new looks were

A Lanz Bulldog doing what it does best, whilst the farmer keeps an eye on the plough.

presented–the type 310, 510 and 710 models. 100 years of the company had been celebrated in 1959 but soon the name was to be dropped, except in the home market. The end of an era but not the end of the factory at Mannheim, which still thrives today.

A 1957 model 6006, with 7300cc, single-cylinder engine, producing some 60hp.

The Lanz Bulldog was built in several European countries. This one is a French version.

The single-cylinder engine also had a size limit; it was then that Lanz built conventional tractors.

Latil

1898-1955

Georges Latil was building vehicles as early as 1898, having pioneered front-wheel drive in the Blum-Latil truck, before establishing Cie des Automobiles Industriels Latil in 1914.

The French company specialized in all-wheel drive, all-wheel steer truck-like tractors, the first of which was produced in 1914. The French military showed a great interest in these during World War I. After the conflict further development led to these machines being used on the land by farmers and for forest clearing. The 1930s saw the JTL model, a petrol-driven machine with six speeds and in the 1950s this machine was presented as the H14 TL Navette, with bigger 5.6 litre engine and eight-speed transmission.

Mainly used for hauling, the Latil four-wheel drive could also be used for field work.

Latil tractors were licence-built in the UK by Shelvoke & Drewry as Trauliers. After the World War II Latils comprehensive range was mainly diesel-powered and until 1955 Latil remained independent, but it was then swallowed up by Saviem.

Leader

1946-1950s

There were several Leader tractor companies–Leader Engine Company from Detroit and Leader Tractor Manufacturing Company of Des Moines–but the Leader Tractor Manufacturing Company of Chagrin Falls, Ohio made tractors after the Second World War. A Hercules, four-cylinder, 2.2 litre engine was used and a belt pulley and take-off shaft was fitted as standard. It seems that the Leader tractor was built by the Brockway brothers of Auborn, Ohio and never built in Chagrin Falls. The nearest post office was in Chagrin Falls and as the postmaster knew everybody for miles around, they could get their mail there. The company was in business through to the 1950s. There are plenty of these being restored in the United States today.

This is the little Leader model D of 1950. It used a 133 cubic inch Hercules engine.

Le Percheron

1939-1956

Heinrich Lanz gave the French company Societe Construction National Aeronautique du Centre, located in Colombes, a licence to build a copy of his tractor because they lacked production capacity to satisfy the French demand for the Lanz 25hp model. Pre-war models varied from post-war models in a variety of details–for example the 'systeme Lanz' badge was absent, and often parts were not exactly the same on one tractor as they were on another, although still based on the 25hp Lanz.

The later logo, common to almost all Le Percherons, is a big rampant horse–Le Percheron is a famous breed of French draught horse, which can be found in the Perche region of northwest France. Some 3,700 examples were built during its lifespan.

Looking just like the Lanz Bulldog, this is a Le Percheron, sold under license.

Leyland

1968-1981

The Nuffield tractor business had been created by William Morris (later Lord Nuffield) of Morris cars fame. This had become a part of BMC, the British Motor Corporation, an amalgamation of well known car companies, which was then eaten up by British Leyland in 1968. There had been positive mention that the Nuffield tractor would continue but that the products would be consolidated, like so many other products under the Leyland banner, and that new models would probably be produced. By now the production line was based in Scotland at the new Bathgate factory.

Typical Leyland styling of the period, this is the grille and front lights on the 245 model.

In November 1969, three new machines were unveiled, but there had without doubt been some major changes. The Nuffield orange livery had gone, as had the Nuffield badge. In their place was a two-tone, blue paint scheme, and the name 'Nuffield' was replaced by 'Leyland.' There was a small sticker under the badge with the Nuffield name on, but this too would shortly disappear.

The first three new machines–154, 344 and 384–with their new blue paint scheme, were not completely new but carried over many features from the old Nuffield stable. The designation numbers these tractors were given had a significance of their own; for example the 384 denoted a 3.8 litre engine, and the 4 denoted that it had four cylinders. The 384 diesel was the biggest model, whereas the 154 only had a 1.5 litre diesel engine, but retained the four cylinders.

At the bottom of the range was the model 154. The one featured is a 1960 vintage model.

Front-end of the Leyland 245 tractor. It used a 2.4 litre, three-cylinder engine.

The engine size was distinguished easily by the 145 designation: 1.5 litre, four-cylinders.

configurations were made available, the venture didn't last long. Production ceased in 1979 when Leyland tractors finally sold out to Marshall and Sons in 1981.

A pretty impressive sight, this large-wheel Leyland tractor. Production ceased in 1979.

Several other models were produced; the model 2100 was a six-cylinder diesel that was fitted with a transmission that had ten forward and two reverse gears. This model was made from 1973 through to 1979, during which year the model 462 was introduced, with a four-cylinder diesel engine. In 1973 the 245 model was introduced with a three-cylinder diesel engine and that was preceded by the model 253, which had a three-cylinder Perkins engine and was put on the market in 1972. Although a good array of models with varied

M

MAN

1924-1962

The MAN–Maschinenfabrik Augsburg-Nurnberg company was a well established organization when it first decided to enter the tractor construction business. Their roots went back as far as 1758 when Franz Ferdinand Domherr von Wenge founded the first heavy industry enterprise in the Ruhr region of Germany– the St Antony Ironworks–near Osterfeld.

From humble beginnings a monster of a company emerged and tractors were just a tiny part of their history. MAN are best known for their trucks and the diesel engine that powered those trucks also served to power the tractors they built. The company had worked closely with Rudolph Diesel back in 1897, to help develop the diesel engine.

It was in 1924 that their first tractors were made, using four-cylinder diesel engines, but the time wasn't right and the company decided to suspend tractor production after only a few years. Their next attempt was in 1938 but by now Germany were gearing up for World War II and so they had to concentrate on making trucks and other military equipment for the war effort.

Being right in the heart of industrial Germany, the MAN factory was hit hard by the Allied bombing

MAN were better known for their trucks. This tractor has a grass-cutting attachment.

The pretty front end of a 1950s MAN. A passenger seat rails can be seen at the rear.

during the war and it took some time for tractor production to regain momentum. This time though they produced more advanced machines with the choice of two- or four-wheel-drive. These machines were available through the early 1950s, their engines ranging between 25 and 45hp; larger tractors followed in the following years.

In 1958, MAN tractors was linked up with the Porsche tractor concern. Four years later, and by now under the Mannesmann umbrella, the last MAN tractor was made.

This is the MAN Ackerdiesel of the 1950s. The company sold out to Porsche in 1958.

MAP

1945-1955

For a period of about ten years Manufacture d'Armes de Paris (MAP) were involved in the production of tractors and also produced a car for the Le Mans 24-hour race. Their first tractor was powered by a Latil engine and introduced in 1945. It was only a couple of years later that the company replaced the Latil engine with their own design, which was a twin, opposed-cylinder, two-stroke, diesel unit with supercharger attached. MAP entered their diesel car at Le Mans in 1950 but due to engine problems (a cooling system leak) the car did not complete the race. The MAP was the first mid-engined car to race at Le Mans–the engine was located immediately behind the driver–and was a two-cylinder, opposed-piston, two-stroke unit, with rocking levers connected to a single crank.

A fine example of a diesel powered MAP, who also made a race-car for the Le Mans 24 hour race.

In 1952 the company was acquired by the SIMCA group, who used the MAP tractor as the basis of the first SOMECA tractors of 1953. MAP tractors sold through to 1955, during which time some 15,000 were made.

Marshall

1908-1991

Marshall were well-known for their steam engines with their Britannia Iron Works situated at Gainsborough, England, and it was here that they constructed their famous boilers. The company was never afraid to pick up a product, look it over, improve it and then re-market, it and this was more or less what happened with their first tractor. They had taken a Lanz tractor, studied it and then produced their own version. One major change was that they made it all diesel, therefore running on engine compression rather than a hot spot, which the Lanz and other hot bulb engines of the period used. This machine took the 15/30 Model E designation and had a single-cylinder, two-stroke,

Marshall were already well-known for their steam engines when they entered the tractor market.

A line-up of the Field Marshall diesel models. Very British tractors-note the Union Jack on the front.

diesel engine, which was started by using ignition papers placed in a holder, which protruded from the combustion chamber. There were three forward and one reverse gear. This became a very popular tractor and its distinctive engine noise could be heard on many farms around England. A smaller, more economical and cheaper version was to follow in the mid-1930s, the 12/20, to compete with the Fordson, which was more than competitively priced and winning many orders. Just prior to World War II, the designation of the 15/30 was changed and with both internal and external modifications, it became the model M.

Once hostilities had ceased, Marshall had an organisational changearound and designated their products by name. In this way the Road Marshall would become the name for the road construction equipment and the Field Marshall would denote the tractor division machines.

The pre-war model M was once again upgraded and designated Marshall series 1 in 1945. Just two years later, and in an attempt to compete with the multi-cylinder opposition, the company produced the series II, a water-cooled, single-cylinder, diesel producing 40hp. An upgraded series III and even a Series IIIa with several detailed engine changes and

Marshall built its first gas tractor in 1908 but it was some years before it got seriously involved.

These single-cylinder machines were powerful and often seen working threshers of the time.

electric starter was produced, again in an attempt to keep up with the competition. There is only so much you can do to a single-cylinder engine to make it bigger and more powerful, and still be able to fit it to a smallish tractor. The company was encountering a specific problem: the transmission housing kept cracking. Unfortunately even though the new series IIIa did rectify this problem it was never a good enough tractor to compete with the multi-cylinder machines of the day. The writing was clearly on the wall: change or die! Although a series IV with supercharging was planned, it never made the production stage, and 1957 saw the single-cylinder models finally pushed to one side. Over their long period of production they had served the company well.

The Field Marshall Series III was launched in 1949. It had six forward and two reverse speeds.

The decision for Marshalls now was what should they do. It would be hugely expensive and time-consuming to develop a brand new tractor from scratch, and so the decision was made, like many others before them, to purchase an engine off the shelf and construct their own tractor around that. The engine they decided on was the Leyland UE350, a unit used by Leyland in their trucks. So in 1954 Marshall launched its all-new model MP6, using the six-cylinder, water-cooled, Leyland diesel engine. The tractor was not like anything they had produced before and might have sold well had it been aimed at the US market. In America they had vast tracts of farmland that needed big powerful tractors, but in

England the MP6 just seemed too big and too expensive for the average farmer. In total 197 left the Gainsborough works, ten being sold to the home market. The rest went around the world, in particular to the West Indies for sugar cultivation. After this Marshalls decided to concentrate on manufacturing crawlers. There was one last attempt at selling tractors, when the company bought the Leyland Tractor concern in the 1980s. They re-badged the machines and painted them a different colour. These were built up to 1991.

Leyland eventually were bought by Marshall, the influence can be seen here on the 904XL.

904XL MARSHALL TRACTORS

MARSHALL 904XL

The Marshall 904XL is the new 92HP four wheel drive tractor for those heavier farm jobs. It combines well proven Marshall engineering with a host of new features designed to suit every farmer's requirements.

Engine

Power is provided by a 4 cylinder turbocharged 92HP diesel engine offering an impressive torque ratio of 240 lbs/ft @ 1600 engine RPM. This long stroke high torque unit produces power with maximum economy.

Transmission

The synchro transmission offers 15 forward and 5 reverse gears. It includes 6 forward and 2 reverse creep speeds and allows a range of forward speeds from 0.3 to 20 m.p.h. This versatility in conjunction with a 2 speed PTO, offering 83HP @ 2200 RPM makes the tractor compatible with a wide range of equipment.

Stability and ease of handling are assured by a long wheelbase. Limited slip differential on the 4WD axle means less wheelslip, increased traction and greater fuel efficiency.

Hydraulics

Dual assistor rams give a maximum hydraulic lift of 6400 lbs. Heavy duty lift rods with quick coupling lower linkage are standard. One single and two double acting spool valves are fitted with quick release couplings and hydraulic trailer braking is also a standard feature.

Cab

The luxury Explorer cab is fitted with radio and clock and provides excellent all round visibility with the high level of comfort and convenience that you have come to expect on a Marshall tractor.

Contact your Marshall dealer now for further information on the superb new 904XL.

The later Marshall certainly looked more modern than their single-cylinder models.

MARSHALL TRACTORS

Massey-Ferguson

1847-present

Massey-Ferguson came about mainly through the merger of three different agricultural companies: Massey, Harris, and of course Ferguson.

This was the company that took on the mighty forces of Henry Ford, who was taking the tractor business by storm in the early years, just as he did with his motor cars. The Ford Motor Company finally moved away from tractor production in the 1960s and so allowed Massey-Ferguson tractors to become dominant in the market, but it had needed great strength and determination to succeed.

The Massey family immigrated to the United States from England in 1630 and by 1795 some of the family had moved to Watertown, New York, on the east side of Lake Ontario. A few years later, Daniel Massey, along with his wife Rebecca Kelley and their infant son Daniel, moved across the lake to Haldimand Township, near the village of Grafton. Here, he purchased 200 acres of land and started clearing the forest and constructing a family home.

At the age of six, young Daniel was sent back to Watertown to live with his grandparents, where he was given an education, after some years returning home to help his father on the family farm.

Alanson Harris, a farmer and mill owner, had a talent for designing and building.

By the age of twenty-one Daniel had purchased his own 200 acres of land, near his parents farm, and had also married his childhood sweetheart, Lucinda Bradley.

During the following years he continued to purchase and clear woodland, until in 1830 he returned to farming. Throughout this time he had also made several trips to the USA, to visit family and friends, and he had become fascinated by the agricultural tools and machinery available in the USA, that couldn't be found in Canada. Very soon Daniel had started a small workshop on his farm, repairing tools and machinery not only for himself but for the local farmers too. On his frequent visits to the USA he would always bring back more and more new implements and tools, and the time soon came that he was so busy in his workshop he no longer had time to tend the farm, which he finally turned over to his son Hart.

As Daniel's company grew, he had to move premises and struck up a partnership with a family associate, Robert Vaughan, but it wasn't long before Daniel bought out that half of the business too. By 1848, the company had grown even bigger and larger premises had to be found. He chose a spot north of the newly established village of Newcastle, along with extra land on which he would build houses. A year later the implement works were moved into Newcastle and renamed the Newcastle Foundry and Machine Manufactory, with the employment of more workers. By now ploughs, stump pullers, harrows and a mix of agricultural machinery was being produced by the company. Just two years later his son Hart joined

In 1847 Daniel Massey, a Canadian pioneer and farmer, opened a small machine shop near Newcastle, Ontario.

him, as once again Daniel found he could no longer cope on his own. Hart increased the production of the company further and after obtaining the rights to the Ketchum grass cutting mower, started producing them at the Newcastle factory, along with the Burrel reaper and Manney Combined Hand Rake reaper. Things really started to take off when the Grand Trunk Railroad passed through Newcastle, opening up all sorts of opportunities outside the local area. With the railroad, large new areas of America were now open for Hart to exhibit and export his products. These now not only included farm machinery but steam engines, boilers, castings, stoves and lathes, to name a few. In 1856, Daniel Massey died at the young age of 58.

In 1862 the company changed name once more to the Newcastle Agricultural Works and business was so good now that an extension had to be added to the original works, but disaster struck in early 1864 when the warehouse caught fire and burned down. Later that year a new building was erected and the following year business was as brisk as ever. With prizes now being won for their products, the company had spread its wings into Europe too, where many new orders were coming fast.

By 1867 there were over one hundred people working at the factory and in 1870 the company changed its name once more to the Massey Manufacturing Company. Hart Massey retired in 1871, his son Charles taking over the reins of the company. The Massey harvester was introduced in 1878 and it was this that took the company to Toronto a year later. Demand was so great that the factory in Newcastle was unable to provide the necessary amenities, such as gas lighting and public water supply, required by a large company.

Whilst all this activity was taking place, there was another man who was also making his mark, also in the Canadian agricultural business. Alanson Harris, a farmer and mill owner formed his own implement business back in 1857 in a town called Beamsville. In 1863 he was joined in partnership by his son John, and the acquisition of the Kirby mower and other well-known US agricultural machinery saw the A Harris and Son company become a big competitor for the Massey company. In 1872 Harris moved his company to Branford and during the 1880s the Branford binders became very popular, in fact one of the company's best selling products. Then in 1890 the company produced the open end binder, a product so popular that it prompted Hart Massey to propose a merger of the two companies. After a long period of competing against each other the two companies decided the time had come to bring it all to an end, Alanson Harris agreed to the merger. So it

was that on May 6 1891 the two companies became one, under the name of Massey-Harris Company Ltd. Smaller agricultural companies were also added to the duo over the next few years, increasing their versatility and product range. Even with all this might behind them, the company was slow to move into the tractor manufacturing business, which by now was starting to pick up pace around America.

Before they even thought of building their own engines, Massey-Harris were assembling Olds engines. It was in 1910 that the company bought out the Deyo-Macey engine plant of Binghampton, New York–producers of petrol engines-which set them on the road to building their own petrol engines. By 1914 Massey-Harris were making their own engines in the Binghampton premises and in 1916 they moved the Deyo-Macey plant and all its equipment to Toronto, where building started soon after.

Harris purchased a small foundry in Brantford, Ontario, in 1857 and began making and repairing machinery.

By now World War I was taking its full toll and food supplies to the troops, both friend and foe, was needed in abundance. Horses that pulled the guns and trailers full of ammunition and supplies also needed feeding. Without this supply, whole armies would grind to a halt and men would die of starvation, let alone from the deadly bullets and

This is the Massey-Harris No 2, a 12/22 tractor designed for M-H by Dent Parrett.

bombs that were being used. So it was a period when farm mechanisation suddenly had to step up a gear, and one way to increase productivity and supply was by using the tractor. This machine could cover more work in a day than a man and his horse did in a week. Massey-Harris weren't about to be left behind at this point–they were after all the biggest supplier of agricultural machinery in Canada–but unfortunately they didn't have a tractor in production. Canada also had large numbers of troops fighting in Europe, and so it was that in 1917 a search was started by Massey-Harris to find a tractor that could be imported into the Canadian market. The finance and set-up costs needed to design and build a new tractor during this period would have been enormous for any company, so the decision was made to import a current model. The tractor chosen turned out to be the Big Bull model of the Bull Tractor Company, also sold in England as the Whiting-Bull. The company was no stranger to the tractor market and its Big Bull tractor–based on their Little Bull model–had already established itself in America and England as a popular model. It used a 25hp, horizontally opposed, two-cylinder engine and was a three-wheel design–one at the front and two at the rear–delivering 10hp at the drawbar. The tractor was only sold for about a year by Massey-Harris, not because it wasn't a good tractor but because there were problems with the supply of parts. Without parts, there were no machines and without machines

there were no sales, so the import agreement between Massey-Harris and the Bull Tractor Company came to a premature end. Massey-Harris was now obliged to look elsewhere for a tractor or possibly even have to build their own. The decision was made to aproach another established company, and so an agreement was settled with the Parrett Tractor Company of Chicago. It was in 1918 that the two companies agreed that Massey-Harris would make the tractor themselves, and market them under their own name for the Canadian and some export markets. So Dent Parrett drew up designs for three models that would be made by Massey-Harris, these being the MH1, MH2 and MH3. The production of these was started in 1919 at the Massey-Harris engine factory in Weston, Toronto and the three models came in three different sizes–No1 was 12-25hp, No2 was 12-22 hp and No3 was 15-28hp. All three machines used a Buda, water-cooled, four-cylinder engine, with No1 and No2 having a 287 cubic inch rating and No3 having the larger rating of 397 cubic inches. These engines, capable of running on petrol or paraffin and fitted across a simple steel-frame chassis, used a two forward and one reverse-speed transmission system.

Despite being well-made machines, Parrett had designed these without thought for the future and as the pace of tractor development marched on, these machines were being left behind by the new lighter, more economical and better-looking models that

The Massey-Harris No 3 was a larger machine, rated at 15/28hp and also designed by Dent Parrett.

were being presented. Production finally finished in 1923, when sales took a sharp downward turn–just a year earlier the Parrett company had itself gone out of business.

Having burnt their fingers twice now, the company decided for caution and waited to see what would happen within the industry. World War I had seen great activity within the farming community, the need to supply not just soldiers but animals too, had created a boom in farming. But once the hostilities were over and people had returned from the war, they found there was less, or worse still, no work and a recession was creating problems around the world. This would not be a good time to re-enter the tractor market where losses were potentially disastrous, and could have put the whole company in jeopardy. Yet there was the dilemma that the tractor business was still moving forward at a fast pace and it was inevitable that they would at some stage have to rejoin the race to produce tractors–all the time they didn't have a tractor division they were potentially losing money.

As the world economy started to recover in the mid 1920s, the time seemed right to re-enter the tractor market, and so it was that Massey-Harris started looking for another partner to work with, to establish their position in the tractor production market.

The company opened negotiations with the J I Case Plow Works Company of Racine, Wisconsin in

1926, and this led to the acquisition of the company the following year. Although Massey-Harris had bought the Case company along with its name, it sold back the rights to the Case name, which eventually made the whole deal a very worthwhile one for Massey-Harris. What they had acquired through the Case deal was the Wallis family of tractors, which were well known both for their excellent fuel efficiency and their distinctive U-frame construction, a design that used a U-shaped steel frame to protect the underside of the tractor. It was also rather an opportune time to get into the tractor market, which had seen its major force, Fordson, decide to move away from tractor production, therefore giving more potential for a new company to establish itself. Massey-Harris continued the production of the Wallis tractors and established the old Case factory in Racine as their own, now in a position for the first time to infiltrate the American market too. The current Wallis tractor was the 20-30, which used a 346 cubic inch, water-cooled, four-cylinder engine and had a two-speed transmission. Other variations were produced, for example the Orchard model, which was distinguished by the semi-covered rear wheels, and the industrial model–equipped with solid rubber tyres and modified transmission. To satisfy the small tractor market, a smaller version of essentially the same machine was produced with the designation Massey-Harris 12-20. The model 25 followed in

This is a Wallis 20-30. M-H bought the J I Case Company in 1927, and with it acquired Wallis too.

1931, which replaced the 20-30 and was also known as the Massey-Harris 26-41, again using a four-cylinder engine.

During this period, Massey-Harris had also started working on their own tractor design. They had now been in the tractor business for some fifteen years but did not as yet have their own in-house designed machine.

The tractor that was produced as the first true Massey-Harris was the General Purpose machine, a name that was given to describe everything it should have been able to achieve. Unfortunately this wasn't quite the case. Besides the coming of the Great Depression, which would devastate the farming community like never before, the tractor failed in its attempts to be everything to everybody. There was no doubt it was a very advanced machine for the time, with its permanent four-wheel-drive and articulated chassis. The engine was a 226 cubic inch, four-cylinder, water-cooled Hercules unit with a three-speed transmission. But as good as four-wheel-drive was with its pulling power and traction, it restricted the turning circle of the tractor and caused frustration and extra work. Although the track could be adjusted it had to be pre-ordered and therefore eliminated that possibility for the farmer to adjust the track of the wheels, something that had been available for some time now and which was

essential to any farmer. Although not a complete failure, the General Purpose wasn't as popular as it should have been considering its advanced features. For 1936 the company launched two new machines, a row-crop tractor based on the earlier Wallis cub, and named the Challenger. This machine featured the single/two small front wheels and a Massey-Harris four-cylinder engine of 248 cubic inches with four-speed transmission. The other model was the Pacemaker; again this used the same engine and similar components as the Challenger but was a standard tread machine. In 1937 the Twin Power Pacemaker–the name was given due to its dual power rating, in this case 1200 and 1400 rpm–which was distinguished by its more streamlined and more enclosed engine cover. An Orchard version was available too.

Meanwhile the failed General Purpose machine was updated and renamed the Four-Wheel Drive. But even though it was now available with paraffin as an option, and an industrial model was also made available, disappointing sales once again saw it discontinued pretty soon after.

For 1938, Massey-Ferguson took time to update all its range and the model 101, a new tractor, was launched in that year too. This, and its derivatives, would see the company through the war years, when the series was replaced.

This is the GP model, the first tractor designed and made by Massey-Harris in Canada.

The GP had a very wide track, used four-wheel drive and had an articulated chassis.

The 101 was an all new machine and had a long sleek bonnet under which was incorporated a new Chrysler 201 cubic inch six-cylinder truck engine. A cast iron chassis now substituted the old familiar U-frame and it was produced in both row-crop and standard wheel format. The following years this model was joined by the 101 Junior, a smaller version with a four-cylinder, water-cooled, Continental engine of 124 cubic inches. Other derivatives were to follow during this period. The 201 was launched to replace the 25 model and also used a Chrysler 242 cubic inch engine, and then the 202 and 203 models were presented, all 101 derivatives. Two new models–the 81 and 82–were launched in early 1940, both smaller, lighter and less expensive machines than the 101 Junior, but which used the four-cylinder Continental engine. The tractors were available in row-crop or standard four-

Although the GP had a wide track, it could only be adjusted by the factory and pre-ordered.

Up to 1936 the GP was fitted with a Hercules engine, after which M-H fitted their own.

This is the 1936 Challenger, the first rowcrop machine released by Massey-Harris.

This is the Pacemaker machine, which was largely based on the earlier U-frame model.

The Pacemaker model was also released in 1936 and had a four-cylinder, 27 hp, engine.

This is the 101 model, which was produced in 1938 and had a powerful six-cylinder engine.

The model 101 came in Standard, Super, Senior and Junior versions, this one is a Junior.

Shown here is the Junior model, most had six-cylinder engines, including a choice from Chrysler.

wheel trim. Going smaller still, Massey-Harris struck up a deal with the Cleveland Tractor Company to sell their model, the General, in selective markets. The deal didn't work well and so lasted for only a short period, terminating soon after it was struck.

After World War II the 81 and 82 models were phased out and a model 20 was introduced, which was based on the model 81. This used a Continental F124 engine and was produced in row-crop and standard four-wheel format. A model 20K was produced during 1947 and 1948, which was specifically designed to use paraffin. New machines continued to come after the war and in 1946 a new 20/30 hp model 30 replaced the old 101 junior. This was a row-crop and standard tread machine of which several versions were made. It used a Continental four-cylinder engine and was made up to 1953, when it was replaced by the model 33. Next on the agenda in 1948 was the model 11 Pony, the only tractor that Massey-Harris built in any number in Canada. Even though they were a Canadian company most of their

The 102 Junior was derived from the 101 models and also used the six-cylinder engine.

After World War II, M-H introduced several new tractors, of which the model 30 was just one.

Massey-Harris launched the little Pony, 8/10 hp model, in 1947 but it was never a great success.

The Pony engine was a water-cooled, four-cylinder unit, of 62 cubic inches, producing 10.4hp.

tractors were being built either in the USA, France or England. At the time it was the smallest in the Massey-Harris line-up and used a Continental four-cylinder engine. Interesting to note that in France this was known as the model 811 and used a Simca engine. Later it was superseded by the 812 and 820 models, using Hanomag, Simca and even Peugeot engines.

By 1947 the 101 was replaced by the model 44, a future success story for the company. The 44 was a three/four plough machine and used the company's four-cylinder engine and came in row-crop–the better seller–and standard tread guise. For those who

A post-war poster showing a happy farmer with his new model 44 tractor.

preferred a smoother feel, the company also produced the 44-6, which used a Continental six-cylinder engine. The standard trim machine was phased out just a year later whilst the row-crop machine lasted until 1951. There were several other versions of the 44; an LP gas model was produced to keep up with the trend of the time. LP gas had

The Massey Harris model 44, released after the war, was the best selling tractor of a new line.

The 744 was one tractor that was built in Britain. It used a six-cylinder Perkins engine.

A smaller post-war tractor, an update of the model 20, was the model 22, produced from 1948.

The Mustang model was a successor to the 22 model and used the same four-cylinder engine.

With its long hood and clean looks, the Mustang looked good but wasn't a great seller.

Here is another tractor from Massey-Harris that was made in Britain, the model 745.

become popular with farmers as an alternative fuel and so many of the tractor producing companies had built tractors that would run on LP gas. Then there was the Orchard and Vineyard versions, both standard tread vehicles, with special bodywork that covered the rear wheels, and a screen-like shield to protect the driver. A Special Cane model was also built with high clearance, of which only a few were produced. In the European market the 44 was designated 744.

The year 1946 saw the introduction of the 55 model, which was the largest wheel-type farm tractor on the market during that period. The 55 used a four-cylinder petrol engine and was built up to 1955. A diesel version was presented in 1949, which used a 382 cubic inch, four-cylinder engine. It was built in standard four-wheel form only and there was a 55 Rice model and a 55 Wheatland model, again in standard four-wheel format. Two more models followed in 1952, the Colt and M23 Mustang. The Colt was only built for two years and used an F 124 Continental engine, the Mustang was a successor to the 22 model and used the same F 140 four-cylinder engine. Both tractors were available in row-crop standard tricycle, single wheel or adjustable-width, high arch front axle. They were also available in standard four-wheel format.

Massey-Harris were lagging behind in one area of the tractor market, and that wasn't an actual tractor but the equipment that they carried. Back in the late 1940s the company had turned down the offer made

to them by Harry Ferguson, to produce his TO-20, equipped with all his advanced attachments. Now they were having to look at ways of acquiring a similar but more modern tractor with those similar attachments. Ferguson had finally taken his tractor to America and approached Henry Ford with his novel ideas. They struck up a deal with a simple handshake. Now both Ford and Ferguson were reaping the rewards of that deal. Massey-Harris

Harry Ferguson sold out to Massey-Harris in 1953, and soon they were called Massey-Ferguson.

MASSEY-HARRIS

miracle-
powered 555

gives

big

jobs

the

full

$\rightarrow$ power

treatment

knew that if they couldn't buy in or build a similar tractor and system, they would lose no end of sales and they would lag dangerously behind the competition in the fast–moving tractor market.

In the meantime, things were starting to go badly wrong between Ferguson and the Ford Motor Company. Henry Ford, with whom he had struck up his deal, had died and the new Mr Ford was keen to build his own tractors. Finally, Ford and Ferguson split and Ford launched their model 8N. With this Ferguson filed a lawsuit–this pertained to the agreement he had made with Henry Ford, the simple handshake and man-to-man agreement they had struck up–that would take years to sort out and which Ferguson would win but not to his satisfaction. Ferguson had built up a large distribution network in America and he used this to sell his newly imported TE-20 tractor–the TE-20 had been launched in England back in 1946. Designated with the letters TO for America, he launched the tractor on the US market in 1948, where they sold extremely well. Obviously they were kitted out with the complete Ferguson system and along with the launch of his new 30hp, TO-30 in 1951, they grabbed much of the Ford market.

Ferguson had been a great inventor and involved himself in all sorts of daring feats as a young man

One of the first tractors produced under the Massey-Ferguson name, a high clearance 65.

but now he was of an age where all he wanted was a little peace and tranquillity. He enjoyed the marketing and engineering side of business, and so when he found himself having to handle the production side, he wasn't so keen. This resulted in him looking for someone to produce his tractors and put his name into the history books. How convenient that Massey-Harris should also be looking for exactly that kind of arrangement and in this way a second bite of the apple presented itself. The two got together and signed a deal in 1953, where Massey-Harris would buy out the Ferguson Tractor Company. They then changed their name to Massey-Harris-Ferguson, which was later shortened simply to Massey-Ferguson.

With the merger of two large companies, there are always problems. There are distribution networks to sort out, the production line of each company also had to be organised and sorted and so on. There were

This is a re-badged Minneapolis-Moline Gvi. This time disguised as the model 95.

Clearly seen is the axle of the four-wheel drive 97, which was an optional extra.

The model 97 was really a Minnepolis-Moline in disguise. M-F didn't have a 100hp tractor at the time.

problems to begin with but slowly they were sorted. In the meantime both brand names produced their tractors–the 44 became the 444 with extra power and dual-range transmission in 1955. The 33 also received a new transmission and became the 333, and the big 55 was re-numbered as the 555. The Ferguson TO-30 was upgraded to the TO-35 and also marketed as the Massey-Harris 50, whilst the Ferguson F40 was offered in tricycle format.

While all this was going on, restructuring was also happening and in 1957 Massey-Ferguson started its short and successful road to being the biggest tractor producer in the world. The new M-F tractors were now being painted in their new joint red and grey livery, with the Massey-Harris red and yellow livery relegated to the archives.

Some order soon became apparent; the M-F TO-30 brought up the bottom of the range, whilst the old Ferguson 35 was upgraded to the M-F 50 and a new M-F 65 was introduced with a Continental engine and six-speed transmission.

Some re-badging and buy-ins now happened to see the company through a period of new development. During this time the Minneapolis-Moline 75hp Gvi model was given new bodywork, painted in the new red and grey colours and sold as the M-F 95 Super. This was the ideal tractor for the farmers of the American wheatlands, and it sold very well. Another tractor that was brought in was the Oliver 990

This is a genuine 68hp, model Super 90, Massey-Ferguson from 1962.

The model 50 was a mid-range tractor. Note the mention to the Ferguson system on this poster.

model; again this was re-badged, re-painted and marketed as the M-F 98. Finally in 1959 M-F introduced their own large horsepower model, the 60hp M-F 88. This machine used a 276 cubic inch, Continental, four-cylinder engine, which could be run on either gas or diesel. The 88 was made through to 1962 and its stable-mate was the 85, a row-crop version for the US market. But with everybody screaming out for more power, these machines were still not hitting the mark and so until they were able to oblige, M-F resorted to bringing in yet another Minneapolis-Moline and disguised it as the MF97.

Up to 1959, M-F had been using engines that were supplied by several other companies, and had never built its own in great numbers. It seemed a good move that in 1959 they bought the Perkins Diesel Engine Company of Peterborough, England. Perkins had been making diesel engines for many years, had a very good reputation and had outlets all over the world–soon becoming the world's leading supplier

of diesel engines. This was a major step for M-F, not only giving them access to a variety of engines but also giving them the ability to supply. Hence they now became builders as well as suppliers to other companies.

Late in 1964, M-F introduced their next series of new small tractors, the Red Giants, as they were to be known. These would take the place of the now ageing 35, 40 and 50 models. The new machines would be recognized as the 100 series and consist of the 135, 150 and 165. These smaller tractors were being made in Britain and France whilst the larger M-F machines were assembled in the USA.

If this model 35 looks familiar, it's because it descended from the original all-grey Ferguson.

A farmer proudly displays his Massey-Ferguson model 130 at a local tractor rally.

Smallest of the new 100 series for 1964 was this Massey-Ferguson 135 model.

The Massey-Ferguson 35x, with the three-cylinder diesel, is a great piece of engineering.

The smallest of the series, the MF 135 tractor, replaced the MF 35 and apart from the squared-up bonnet, lights that were integrated into the grill and squared-off leading edge of the rear mudguards, the 135 retained many of the features of the MF 35X. The engine choice was, like its predecessor, the Continental 134 cubic inch, petrol unit or the 152

The 135 came in a variety of formats. This is a narrow-tread vineyard model.

cubic inch, Perkins diesel. Multi-Power transmission, hydraulic spool valves, weather cab, foot throttle, spring suspension seat and a cigarette lighter were optional for this model. Although this was the smallest of the series, an even smaller 300 version was offered by the French. At the other end of the scale was the new MF 165 tractor, which replaced the MF 65. Apart from the redesigned bodywork, the 165 was similar in many respects to its predecessor. Optional equipment included pressure control, which replaced the Multi-Pull hitch system, and as with its stable-mate, Multi-Power transmission, hydraulic spool valves, weather cab, foot throttle, spring suspension seat and a cigarette lighter were all listed as optional. The two larger tractors had a special front end so that they could accommodate row-crop equipment–essential for the US market–whereas the smaller tractor used the beam front axle of its predecessor. The 165 didn't remain the largest model for too long and was replaced by the MF 175. This used a larger Perkins engine but was also replaced in 1971 by the MF 178, which had an even larger 248 cubic inch Perkins diesel engine. Not wanting to stand still the whole range was updated soon after (now designated the 148, 168 and 188) and split into two versions. The budget series, or standard rig models, were stripped

Seen here is the Perkins, diesel engine of the model 148, presented in 1972.

of all their goodies and aimed at the farmer who was happy to buy a basic tractor without all the extras. Then there were the Super spec tractors, which were equipped with all the latest gadgetry, but the cost was obviously considerably more.

An advertisement for the biggest machine of the period, the M-F 1150, with V8 engine.

The DX 1000 range saw the introduction of the M-F 1100 (using a Perkins, 110hp, six-cylinder engine) and M-F 1130, which used the same engine but with a turbocharger and produced 120hp. These two new designs were introduced between 1965 and 1973. This year the 1100 was replaced by the 1105 which had a turbocharger added to boost the power and was produced mainly for the Canadian market. The 1130 was replaced also in this year by

the 1135, again the power output was raised to some 140hp.

For 1969 the new M-F 1080 was introduced; this was a derivative of the 180 model and used a Perkins diesel producing 81 PTO hp. This was replaced in 1973 by the M-F 1085. The biggest machine of this period, and only produced between 1970 to 1972, was the M-F 1150, which used a Perkins V8 diesel engine. For 1973 the M-F 1135 and M-F 1155 were introduced for the American and Canadian markets. These machines were assembled at the factory in Canada.

During the early 1970s, the model 1135 was introduced to replace the older 1130.

With the constant quest for bigger, more powerful machines, in particular in the USA, where farms sprawled for hundreds of thousands of acres, M-F always considered themselves major players. It was in 1969 though that their real involvement started, with their 1500 and 1800 four-wheel-drive models. Yes, there had been the earlier four-wheel-drive GP model but that wasn't made to satisfy the same requirements of the late 1960s onwards. Most of the other major tractor companies were supplying four-wheel-drive machines in the 1960s, but by 1969 this type of large machine became much more acceptable to the American farmer, who now was seeing the benefits it could give. At this time the biggest tractor that M-F were producing was the two-wheel-drive 1150, but farmers were looking for more power and so they produced the 1500 and 1800 models. These produced 153hp and 171hp respectively. Although this was on par with their rivals, it also had one extra benefit. It had a standard factory iso-mounted cab, which offered a quieter ride and extra room to move around and work in. This worked for a while but the competition was moving fast and for the early 1970s they came up with newer and bigger models. M-F were not about to fall behind, and as a starter they upgraded the 1000 series to the 1005 models.

The 1505 and 1805 offered more power, adjustable tread-width and an optional rear PTO. The 1970s was the era of big and powerful, and development of these vast machines moved at an alarming pace. M-F knew they would have to keep up with the rest, and so in 1978 their Brantford, Ontario plant started producing the new four-wheel-drive 4000 series machines–the 4800, 4840, 4880 and the 4900. These were the biggest machines they had ever produced with the smallest model rated at 225hp and the biggest at 375hp. They all used the Cummins 903 cubic inch, V8 engine with various ratings, and all had 18 forward and three reverse gears. These were a match for the competition. They were equipped with a rugged articulating frame, allowing them to make a turn in a 17 foot area. A fully independent, 1000 rpm PTO was included on all the models and the cabs were state of the art. The command module, as some would like to call them, had 7,000 square inches of tinted glass, an eight-way adjustable seat, two tool boxes, rear ice box, rear windshield wiper, dust penetrating amber lights, standard heating and air-conditioning, AM/FM radio and an eight-track player.

These machines were thoroughly modern, had plenty of standard components and were produced through to 1988, when once again they were upgraded. But the up-beat sales period of the 1970s was followed by a sudden reverse in fortunes during the 1980s. Much of the competition dropped out of the four-wheel-drive market and others sold off their interests. M-F too found the market hard going as sales started to dry up. In 1988 the M-F 4000 series were replaced by just one very large model. The 5200 was designed to take two sizes of engine, a 375 hp or 390hp unit. The four-wheel-drive market was now concentrating on a powerband from the 350 plus hp rather than the 400 to 500hp models of the 1970s. Although the 5200 was a great machine, M-F were running short of operating capital and in 1989 they sold the 5200 to McConnell Tractors Ltd. McConnell sold the Massey-Ferguson 5200 and its own yellow McConnell-Marc brand through to 1993. The design was well ahead of the pack but by 1995 McConnell decided it could no longer continue on its own and sold the line to AGCO, who had been formed in 1990. In 1993 AGCO acquired the rights to Massey-Ferguson and when in 1994 they needed a new four-wheel-drive, they took the McConnell/M-F designed tractor to the AGCO/White Cold Water, Ohio factory for production. Here they upgraded the machine and its bodywork and the new AGCO-Star was conceived, which had a choice of Detroit-Diesel or Cummins engine units. The M-F name disappeared from the big machines but special M-F red coloured versions could be ordered as an optional extra.

By 1973 the smaller series of tractors was due for an update too, and so were re-designated the 200 series,

The new 4000 series, made in Brantford, Ontario, made its debut in 1978. This is the big 4880.

Coping happily is the Massey-Ferguson 1250 tractor with four-wheel drive and articulated body.

which started off with the bottom of the range 230 model, a 34hp machine. The largest of these was an 82hp model 285; all were assembled at the Banner Lane works in England. By now the mid-range of tractors were being assembled in Beauvais, France and in their Detroit factory in the USA. The larger machines were produced in Canada and the USA.

By the mid 1970s there was a legal requirement for tractors to have not only cabs, but the cab also had to have a noise level restriction of no more than 90 decibels. Many of the other companies had designed and supplied cabs for their machines and M-F, not wanting to be left behind, decided to produce a new model with a new cab incorporated within the design. This new tractor was released from the Banner Lane factory in 1976 and designated the M-F 500. These models therefore were: the M-F 550, which replaced the M-F 148; the M-F 565, which replaced the M-F 165; the M-F 575 which replaced the M-F 168; the M-F 590, which replaced the M-F 185/188 and the M-F 595, which replaced the M-F 1080, which had been produced for the American market since 1973. Up to 1979, models of the 500 range were fitted with just the one side door which became very unpopular, and so after this date a second door was fitted. By mid 1980s, the cabs were

A Massey-Ferguson model 550, about to pull a boat from the water in France.

A new model, and equipped with a new cab, for the mid 1970s was the 500 series. This is the 595.

Although the agricultural economy was at a low ebb, M-F knew they would have to keep the momentum going, and so their next move was to work on the replacement for the 500 series tractors. The result of this was the 600 series, which consisted of the 66hp 675, the 77hp 690 and the 88hp 698, all of which were made at the Banner Lane factory in England. A model 699 joined the line-up in 1984, which was powered by a Perkins, 354 cubic inch, six-cylinder diesel engine and had twelve forward and four reverse gears.

The next to have a makeover was the 200 series, which basically became the 300 series in 1986. The 200 series had been much loved by farmers all over the world but it was now starting to show its age and so was updated with the 340, 350, 355, 360. The

The Massey-Ferguson 300 series was reliable and straight-forward. This is the 362 version.

painted all red to the roof and in 1981 a new grille was designed for some of the models, incorporating the headlamps. All used a Perkins engine, with the smallest of the models, the M-F 550, using the Perkins AD3.152. At the other end of the scale the M-F 595 used a Perkins AD4.318 unit.

The 1980s were a bad time for farmers in the USA, where there had been a huge slump in sales and M-F too were affected by the sudden downturn. Things got bad enough that they decided to close down their factory in Detroit, the one that Harry Ferguson had so hastily built so many years before, after having fallen out with the Ford Motor Company.

range was also increased at this stage with the model 399, which used a Perkins 365 cubic inch, six-cylinder engine which produced 110hp. The 300 series was a cheaper, simpler but more manageable tractor than the larger 600 series.

By the 1980s, the French arm of M-F in Beauvais were also making tractors in their own right, and were producing their new Topline 2000 models. These were medium-size machines and fitted nicely between the British-made smaller models and US and Canadian-made larger models. These were launched in 1979 and consisted of the 2640, 2680 and 2720, all of which used the Perkins six-cylinder,

The reliable 300 series tractors continued to serve through the 1980s; this is the 365.

The 3000 range was announced in 1986. Initially the 3090 topped that model range.

diesel engine in various capacity ratings. A 3000 tractor series was announced in 1986, which initially consisted of two models (3050, 3090) and a further 3095 model followed shortly afterwards as the top of the range model. When the 2000 series started looking a little jaded, a new 3600 series came along to take its place, which was basically a more powerful version of the 3000 series tractors. Just a few years later these too became part of the 3600 series. There was more power from the six-cylinder Perkins engine and by now models were being fitted with the new Autotronic system, a device giving the operator better control over the differential lock,

four-wheel-drive and PTO selection. Datatronic, a system that gave the operator direct information from his systems via a digital readout in the cab, was also available. All but the top-of-the-range model were fitted with the new Perkins 1000 series engine, which incorporated their new Quadram combustion system. Transmissions too were getting more sophisticated during this time and M-F had produced their Dynashift system, using electronics to multiply

The model 399, top of the smaller 300 series range, was a good workhorse for the company.

The 3000 series tractors were made in Beauvais in France. Pictured here is the 3080 model.

Part of the new 3000 series tractors, the 3670 used a six-cylinder, turbo-diesel engine.

Although part of the smaller 3000 range, the 3690 was a powerful six-cylinder tractor.

With its Perkins, three-cylinder, turbo-diesel, 354 cubic inch engine, this is the 3630 model.

the coverage of gears available for selection, in 1992. This development was also fitted to this range of tractors, helping to increase the amount of gears an operator had to play with. The usual eighteen transmission was now overtaken by the thirty-two gear version, not only forward but in reverse too. Tractors were playing a greater role on the farm and taking on a multitude of tasks and so a larger range of gears gave greater versatility to help complete these tasks better. Today, in 2005, this option has been advanced and is known as the Dyna-6 system. Based on the M-F Dynashift

This is the Dyna-6 transmission system, made available on the M-F 6400 tractor range.

transmission's heritage, Dyna-6 is a new advanced design, providing an additional transmission choice between the 32 forward and reverse Dynashift and Massey-Ferguson's continuously variable Dyna-VT transmissions.

With Dyna-6, operators can choose exactly the level of transmission automation they want at any time–either manual, semi-automatic or automatic. Simplicity is one of the system's main attributes with the automatic operation modes particularly easy to set up and use.

Massey-Ferguson was bought out by the AGCO Corporation, firstly their America section in 1991 and shortly after throughout the world in 1994.

The new parent company itself was only four years old at this time and was formed through a series of acquisitions and mergers. Once again the company went through a rationalisation period and large lines of tractors were slimmed down to make the company leaner and meaner. Two new series were introduced in 1995, the 6100 and 8100. In the USA they were classed as high-horsepower machines and were fitted with state of the art technology. The M-F 6100 series consisted of three models–the 86hp 6150; 97hp 6170 and 110hp 6180. These came with a variety of specifications including two- and four-wheel drive. The 6150 had a four-cylinder wastegate, turbocharged engine, whilst the 6170 and 6180 had six-cylinder Perkins Quadram engines.

Demonstrating how capable the 6280 was, this one has implements working at the front and rear.

The 6270 was a versatile tractor, with its Perkins diesel engine and four forward gears.

As far as the M-F 8100 series was concerned, there were four models–the 130hp 8120; 145hp 8140; 160hp 8150 and the 180hp 8160. Again the top three models were available in two- or four-wheel-drive.

With most of the attention being paid to the medium to large tractor sectors, Banner Lane in England felt like they were being left to one side. All this changed in 1997 when the old 300 series became the 4300 series. It received up-to-the-moment styling and the range went from the Perkins 52hp, three cylinder 4215 through to the big Perkins 110hp, six-cylinder 4270. In 2001, the workers at the Coventry Lane works received further good news when the model was up-rated once again, with a promise from AGCO of a £1.7 million investment in the site. The

This model is a post-AGCO buy-out M-F. It is the big 6270 model, with six-cylinder engine.

With a workload like this, the Perkins turbo-diesel and eight forward gears are invaluable.

The 8150, built from 1995, was a big tractor and had an engine displacement of 403 cubic inches.

The MF 9240 is powered by a wastegate turbocharged, 4.50 SBTII, 110hp engine.

company had dipped in and out of problems in the past months because of a slump in the world tractor market, and the 1,800-strong workforce at Banner Lane had already started working short time. The previous year, the spectre of closure at the plant was raised when AGCO executives warned that the company could pull out of Britain if it stayed out of the Euro. The M-F 4200 tractors were sold throughout the world, and more than 90 percent of Banner Lane's production was exported globally each year. An investment of this amount of money signalled fresh confidence and that the strength of the M-F range would lead the company to better times if the product was improved. Just as they had done before, the updating of a product whilst the market was going through a bad time, meant that when things turned around, the product would be ready to be sold in a healthy market. The 4200 series turned into the 4300, and not only was the updated machinery more versatile, it was also more comfortable with its newly redesigned cab and control console. They were still powered by the now familiar and rugged four- and six-cylinder Perkins engines. All 4300s also feature Fastram combustion where ultra high-speed air enters the combustion chamber for precisely controlled power production. There are up to eight different transmission configurations on the new tractors: the eight forward

The 1990s export 4240 model, just one of a vast selection of tractors from the 4200 series.

A sad day at Banner Lane, Coventry, England as the last tractors roll off the production line.

The advertisement clearly points the model 4200 tractor towards the haulage market.

Seen on a foggy day in France is this 4270. A six-cylinder, turbo-diesel machine.

Part of the 4300 series, which was moved to the Beauvais plant, this is the four-cylinder 4365.

A 4365, whose production is due for France. It is powered by a Perkins, four-cylinder, 95 hp engine.

No amount of mud was going to stop the 8270. It had an electronically-controlled 32 speed gearbox.

and two reverse manual box is an economical and reliable transmission. The top of the line twenty-four forward and twenty-four reverse PowerShuttle is equally reliable and also offers versatility in speeds with 11 gears in the three to eight mph range. Other 4300 series models include the MF 65hp 4335, MF 75hp 4345, MF 85hp 4355 and the MF 90hp 4360.

The bigger 8240, also well equipped, used a Perkins six-cylinder engine and 32 forward and reverse gears.

This 8260 model was a late 1990s update of the 8100 tractors, with Autotronic and Datatronic systems on-board.

This state-of-the-art seat would make sure that the operator was comfortable for his long spell in the cab.

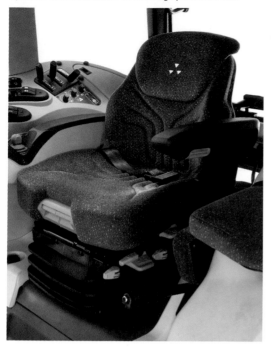

capacity add to the comfortable working conditions, and the standard instrument panel has also been upgraded. Other monitoring features are also available with an optional factory installed performance monitor. The Hydralock differential lock is standard on all four-wheel-drive models and a new factory installed supercreep option, on the 24/24 PowerShuttle transmissions, enables tractor speeds as slow as one mph at rated engine speed.

This farmer is all kitted up for the cold weather on his cabless 2005 model 400.

Operator convenience and comfort was improved during the re-design stages of the new high visibility cab. Side post mounted exhaust and relocated window wipers improve visibility, while the new right hand console is laid out for the natural movement of the operators arm and is home to all hydraulic and three-point lift controls. Improved temperature controls and heating and cooling

Neat and easy-to-use, the new 2005 range of M-F 2400 agricultural compacts will appeal to smaller farms.

A wonderful array of equipment and a great tractor without doubt, but it wasn't any longer down to the product. It could have been the best thing since sliced bread but if the price was wrong then it would not sell–and the price was wrong because the good old British Pound was just too strong. The strong UK currency was now damaging sales of tractors, whereas the Euro was not only giving a better exchange rate but was also a currency that was being used all over the continent. The decision was made to stop production at the Banner Lane works in England and the 4300 model became the last series to roll off the production line.

The announcement of the closure on Friday, July 25, 2002 of the Massey-Ferguson tractor factory in Coventry, with the loss of a thousand jobs, was a major blow to manufacturing and the economy both locally and nationally.

AGCO, as was threatened, had decided to consolidate production in France and Brazil; the manufacture of high specification vehicles was to go to Beauvais in France, while more basic units would be transferred to Canoas in low cost Brazil. In this move, the famous Banner Lane plant in Coventry was to close, marking the end of an era in agricultural machinery production. AGCO was the world's third largest manufacturer of farm machinery with sales of $2.5 billion in 2001. The Coventry office was to remain as the corporation's headquarters.

The 2005, M-F 2400 utility range, is ideal for agricultural, horticultural, groundscare and municipal markets.

With straightforward specification, the 4400 models fit neatly between the M-F 2400 and M-F 5400 Series.

The 4430 is a tough workhorse and ideal for a small to medium-sized livestock or mixed farm.

Excellent power-to-weight ratio makes the 2005 M-F 5400 Series ideal for a whole range of tasks.

Easy-to-use, 16 forward and 16 reverse speeds match every application on the latest 5400 range.

With restyled bodywork, the 6455 is just one-up from the smallest of the 6400 tractor range.

The 2005, 6455, uses a Perkins, four-cylinder diesel engine, which pumps out 100hp.

Still not the top tractor in its range, the 6495 model uses the six-cylinder Sisu engine.

The 6465 sits in the middle of the 6400 range and also benefits from most of the new equipment.

Front view of the 6455, with QuadLink suspended front axle, virtually eliminating fore and aft 'pitching.'

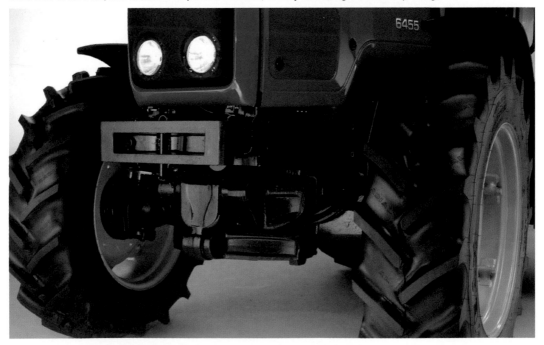

The cab of the 7480, provides a superb 140-degree view of side-mounted implements, a true multi-task machine.

Elsewhere tractors continue to be built and today in 2005 the model range starts with the neat, nimble and easy-to-use, M-F 2400 agricultural compacts, aimed at smaller farms looking for an all-round tractor, right through to municipalities requiring a durable general purpose machine. All models, 2405, 2410 and 2415, are equipped with emission-compliant Mitsubishi four-cylinder engines and are four-wheel drive. Robust, straightforward engineering in a cab-less package that meets stringent European noise legislation makes the MF 400 a great all-rounder–at home operating around the yard scraper as transporting feed to grazing livestock. Consisting of the 410 and 420 models, they use the latest generation, three-cylinder Perkins engine, which easily meets European noise legislation to produce some of the quietest tractors in their class. For agricultural, horticultural, groundscare and municipal markets, the multi-tasking four-wheel drive M-F 2400 utility range–2430, 2435, and 2440–will make the ideal mainstay tractors on small farms or a reliable runabout for larger operations. The emission-compliant, high-torque 800 Series Perkins engine for plenty of power, high in-field performance and fuel economy is fitted to all models.

Featuring minimal height and width, the M-F 3400 models–3435, 3445 and 3455, of which the last two are available in four-wheel drive only–are the pick of the bunch for work in vineyards, orchards, nurseries, greenhouse and municipal environments. If you run a small to medium-sized arable, livestock or mixed farm and are looking for a reliable tractor, capable of turning its hand to most tasks, then there is the new M-F 4400 series (4435, 4445, 4455) in both platform or cab format. With their straightforward specification, these tractors fit neatly into the range between the M-F 2400 Utility and the larger M-F 5400 Series.

The versatile MF 5400 series is ideally suited to a wide range of livestock and mixed farming duties. Designed to ensure timely, effective operation whilst meeting the needs of the most cost-sensitive farming enterprise, the MF 5400 is set to become a valued member of farming families throughout the world. Powered by the New Perkins 1100 series four- and six-cylinder engines, excellent power-to-weight ratio makes this series truly multi-purpose and ideally suited to a whole range of tasks. It has easy-to-use sixteen forward and sixteen reverse Speedshift transmission and a wide range of PTO options to suit all types of work and applications.

The biggest choice in power, the biggest choice in specification–real, useable power at your fingertips, high power-to-weight ratios and a choice of models to suit either heavy-duty deep soil operations or lighter, surface working gives the new MF 6400 series ultimate versatility. Fitted with the new Dyna-6, twenty-four speed transmission, six on-the-move clutchless gear changes within each of four ranges, provides a tremendous spread of powershift flexibility over a wide speed range for maximum field and transport performance. The M-F 7400 series tractors set new standards of operator control. They are fitted with Dyna-VT Continuously Variable Transmission, which enables precise selection of engine speed and ground speed. The new optional Datatronic III information, control and cost management system, greatly simplifies tractor operation and boosts productivity. It is operated via the new full-colour GTA console and complete with the new PC-based GTA100 Communicator software for accurate management of field, operator and tractor operating data. Last but by no means least, the new M-F flagship 8400 series featuring Dyna-VT continuously variable transmission and equipped to the highest specification; these are huge workhorses, capable of huge work rates. They use six-cylinder, turbo intercooled, Sisu Diesel engines with an Engine Speed Control function which memorises two engine rpm settings, that can be activated at the touch of a button. This makes it more convenient for operators to set, for example, working and headland turn speeds which can be recalled instantly.

In 2005 the Beauvais plant, the most modern tractor production centre in France, can boast that more than 800,000 tractors have been built there and nearly 70 percent of production is exported to over 100 different countries world-wide. The models produced here are the 8400, 7400, 6400 and 5400.

M-F tractors have been built at the Canoas manufacturing facility for over 40 years and today it is the largest tractor factory in Latin America, responsible for 70 percent of Brazil's tractor exports

A bird's-eye view of the operators cab showing the sophisticated controls required to work the 8400.

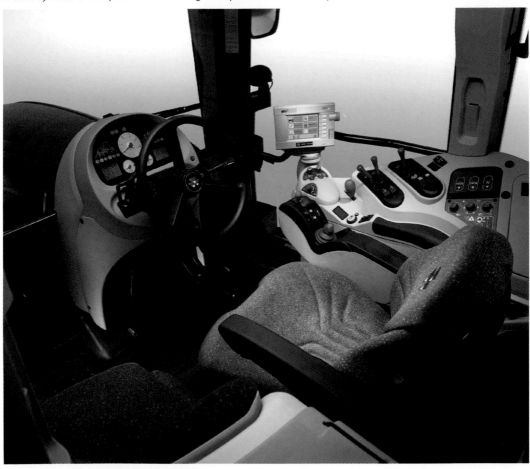

The M-F 600 Series. Strong, powerful machines engineered to handle heavy-duty operations.

and over half the country's total tractor output. Today the models built here are the 400, 600, 5300 and tractor kits.

Santa Rosa is the center for combine harvester production in Latin America. Opened in 1975, the plant builds a range of combines including specialist versions for rice harvesting. Agricultural machinery has been manufactured at Randers, Denmark for over 100 years. Its team of engineers is at the forefront of combine development and leads the field in the application of electronics in harvesting machinery.

The team also pioneered the concept of precision farming–hailed as one of the most important breakthroughs in modern crop production. Located in Kansas, the Hesston plant has a fifty-five year history manufacturing farm equipment. Hesston engineers pioneered the big baler concept in the 1970s and this has become one of the factory's best-selling products. Today the plant boasts 13 different production lines building a wide range of machines. The M-F product line-up offers machines to suit every type of agricultural operation in all parts of the world. Tractors, harvesting machinery, implements, municipal and garden machinery, quad bikes and materials handling equipment all bear the M-F hallmarks of top performance, reliability, durability, operator comfort and uncompromising build quality.

The company is truly international in its breadth of experience, selling its products in more than 140 countries around the world–from South Africa to America, from Indonesia to Uzbekistan and beyond––through a global network of over 5,000 dealers.

Matbro/Terex

1990s-present

 **TEREX** When introduced in the 1990s, the Matbro tractor was aimed at a particular market, that of the farm that needed a tractor to carry out particular yard duties. Generally known as a yard shunter it was capable, amongst many other duties, of shovelling large amounts of grain and lifting heavy bales of straw. Powered by a variety of Perkins, four-cylinder, diesel engines–for which turbocharging was available–they ran from the smallest in the range of 75hp, through to the biggest at 114hp. It used a Clark powershift system with torque converter, that had four forward and three reverse gears.

Matbro were based in Tetbury, in the south of England, and owned by Powerscreen. After the discovery of a major discrepancy in their accounts, the net result was that a once thriving company–the third largest manufacturer of telescopic handlers in Europe–was plunged into crisis. The impact was massive, the company being declared bankrupt and so production was ceased. The main rough terrain lift truck product line was eventually sold to John

This type of machine would not be seen in the field. It is purely for lifting and shoveling.

Deere and Powerscreen itself was bought by the Terex Corporation. The Tetbury site was retained as the main Matbro parts operation for the existing population of telescopic handlers, and after the acquisition of Powerscreen by Terex in 1998, the site became the headquarters for Terex Lifting. This was followed by a reintroduction of two telescopic rough-terrain lift-truck models, the T200 and T250, that had not been bought by John Deere. Production of these models began in 2000.

Production of the T200 and T250 models continued at Tetbury until the weekend before their move to

The Matbro took on a specialist roll, in a new sector, as a very maneuverable yard shunter.

The entry level of the new Terex machines is the T200, seen here supplying animal feed.

The heavy-duty front, extending arm of the T250 is ideal for moving and stacking hay.

Fermec's Manchester factory in November. There was plenty of capacity at the Manchester site, since mini excavator production ceased there at the end of 2000, when Case sold Fermec to Terex, and mini excavator production was transferred to the Case facility in Imola, Italy. The Manchester factory then became the centre for the Terex rough terrain lift truck operations in the UK. However, the company did not transfer the former Italmacchine, now Terex Lift Lifting, operation from Italy to the UK.

In 2005 the Terex T200 and T250 telehandlers continue to offer a pivot steer package and both machines use the latest Perkins tier II emission compliant engines. They use permanent four-wheel-drive, limited slip differentials and power brakes in both axles. Serviceability is made easier with good access to the engine compartment and the boom hoses are mounted externally for easy replacement. The T200 is the entry model and has a 100hp turbocharged engine, with a four forward and four reverse powershift transmission with kickdown function. The bigger T250 model has a 120hp turbocharged, intercooled engine, with four forward

The T250 model has a 120 hp, turbocharged, intercooled engine. There is good visibility from the large cab.

The T200 model uses a 100hp, turbocharged engine and has four forward and four reverse gears.

Terex acquired Powerscreen (Matbro) in 1998. Shown is the 2005, T250 model loading grain.

and three reverse speed, powershift transmission. Both have spacious and comfortable state of the art cabs, with easy access to all controls. Air conditioning, radial tires, pick-up hitch and air seat are just some of the options available on the larger model.

McCormick

2000-present

The McCormick company has a long and illustrious history. The company is named after the man who initially started this company, Cyrus Hall McCormick. The McCormick Company was one of several that amalgamated back in August 12 1902 to create the International Harvester Company. In late 1984, Tenneco, owner of the Case and David Brown brands, declared its intention to purchase certain assets of International Harvesters Agricultural Division. This deal was concluded in 1985 and International Harvester was placed under the control of Tenneco's Case division. From here onwards, all products from Case's agricultural division were rebranded Case International.

The story doesn't end there. In 1999 Case were looking for a merger with New Holland, and once the shareholders had agreed, the new company became Case New Holland Global N.V. (CNH). European Union regulatory authorities rubber-stamped the merger, providing that CNH divested themselves of the Doncaster Wheatley Hall Road plant and the 50 to 100hp C, CX and MXC tractors it produced, along with the MX Maxxum production and engineering know-how.

In 2000, after negotiations with various interested parties, the plant was purchased by ARGO S.p.a of Italy, and it announced that the Doncaster plant would become the global headquarters for McCormick Tractors International Ltd. It announced that products from Doncaster would be sold world wide under the McCormick brand name. Other sister companies under the ARGO name are Landini, Laverda, Valpadana and Pegoraro.

In January of the following year, the EU authorities gave their approval to the deal and McCormick Tractors International Ltd started trading. Within

The McCormick crawler is ideal for specialist farms that need crawler tractors in mountain areas, orchards or tough terrain.

The 2005 XTX range has three new models in the 173-228hp range. This XTX 200 is powered by the BetaPower engine.

days their first overseas distributor was signed up–Power Farming of Morrinsville–in New Zealand. During 2001 negotiations continued between ARGO S.p.a. and CNH Global for the purchase of the CNH transmission facility at St Dizier in France. This happened in April when CNH sold the plant to ARGO, and this now became McCormick France, and the headquarters for operations in that country. This now gave McCormick an operating base in France as well as control over the transmission build for the future, and with this the company grew to a total of 1,100 staff.

By 2002, McCormick distribution covered all Europe, Australia, New Zealand and South Africa. McCormick USA was also established to distribute McCormick products into the United States.

The name that pioneered a transformation in agricultural efficiency for more than a century and a half was truly reborn. Their manufacturing base is a plant which itself has a long and distinguished track record of tractor production.

In 2001 when trading commenced as McCormick Tractors International Limited, production began in January on the new McCormick range of CX and MC four-cylinder tractors. Four months later production began on the new McCormick range of MTX six-cylinder tractors. Later in the year a parts operation was opened at Doncaster to serve the UK and Irish markets, whilst in France another parts department was opened to serve the European market.

The line-up of tractors for the 2005 year included the C Series 73, 84, 90, and 102hp models. These tractors use a Perkins three- and four-cylinder diesel engine, designed to McCormick specifications with a choice of four fully synchronized transmissions. The CX Range (73, 84, 90 and 102hp models) are rugged four-wheel-drive machines with lean burn, high torque three- and four- cylinder diesel engines, synchromesh shuttle transmissions, and optional powershift and creep speeds.

The MC Power6 series (115 and 132hp, 6-cylinder models) is a new generation of tractors powered by

The CX range comprises 73, 84, 90 and 102 hp models, with four-wheel drive and a Perkins four-cylinder diesel engine.

The MC range is split into 90, 102 & 120hp four-cylinder models and 119 and 136hp six-cylinder models.

The Perkins 1106C, six-cylinder, air to air, after-cooled engine, meets all the latest emission standards.

The MTX BetaPower, is capable of taking on the toughest of jobs with its four-speed, powershift system.

Luxury cab, ergonomically positioned controls and climate control make life better for the operator.

The MTX can be fitted with a variety of hitches depending on the work being carried out.

the very latest electronically-managed engines providing outstanding performance and efficiency.

The MTX Range (118, 131, 152, 168, 197 and 204hp models) uses powerful, environmentally friendly engines, a slick powershift, power shuttle transmission and highly efficient hydraulics and PTO. A luxury cab provides outstanding visibility and ergonomically positioned controls; total comfort is guaranteed for those long working days.

There is a small crawler series too, the T series, which come in a platform model and two orchard models: standard track and large track option. There is also a V range tractor for vineyard work.

An all-new XTX range of tractors, comprising three new models in the 173-22 hp category are also available. The ZTX Range (230, 260 and 280hp) are powered by Cummins, six-cylinder, 24 valve engines; these three ZTX models now extend the McCormick product range up to an impressive 280hp. A new F Series of three- and four-cylinder models cover a power output of between 58-98hp and the C-Max Range (58, 68, 81, 91 and 98hp models) are positioned between the CX and the C series, offering enhanced features over and above the C series, yet economic and simplistic features in comparison to the CX.

All in all the new McCormick Tractors International Ltd. range is more than comprehensive and will cater for all the jobs that need to be covered on the farm.

The ZTX range, 230, 260 and 280hp models, all powered by the Cummins six-cylinder, twenty-four valve engine.

The New XtraSpeed transmission, with power-shuttle, offers thirty-two speeds, and up to eight on the go, for the XTX.

The XTX range offers a host of creature comforts in their latest cabs, making the operator feel very much in control.

Mercedes-Benz /Unimog

1926-1991

It was 1902 when Daimler was awarded a first prize by the German Agricultural Association for its locomobile. However, all-out suitability for fieldwork was not achieved until 1913, when Daimler introduced a motorized plow. This articulated plow weighed 6.6 tons and was not so far away from the principle of tractor-plus-trailing-plow, which was to prevail in the 1920s. In 1921, Daimler presented such a plough tractor, over five metres long and weighing four tons.

After Daimler merged with Benz in 1926, everything went in favour of the former competitor's model. The decisive criterion was the diesel engine, which had been installed in a three-wheeled tractor in 1922. Benz had developed this somewhat weird-looking tractor with a single, roller-type drive wheel with a diameter of 1.40 metres, immediately after World War I, together with Munich-based engine and tractor producer Sendling. Its heavy-oil engine was really only used to test the pre-chamber diesel in practical operation, one year before the latter was built into a truck for the first time. But the diesel-engined tractor became a complete success, too.

The prototype was sold on the spot, at the agricultural show in Königsberg in 1922. Two additional units followed before series production of the diesel-engined Benz-Sendling S6 tractor, with a single drive wheel, started one year later. Overall, Benz-Sendling was able to sell 1,188 units of the three-wheeled tractor up to the early 1930s.

The main reason for the plow's design with a single drive wheel, or that of Daimler's very similar plow tractor with two rear wheels–arranged very close to each other–was the fact that it did not require a differential. Very soon, however, it was realized that this advantage had been achieved at the

The early Benz-Sendling tractor, similar to current thinking that the plow is pulled by the tractor.

expense of stability–the tractor was prone to toppling over! For this reason, Benz-Sendling developed the four-wheeled diesel-engined BK tractor in 1923, also available as a road-going version with solid rubber tires. It was the direct predecessor of the OE model.

A poster for the Mercedes-Benz diesel tractor. Hard times prevented good sales.

Buyers do not always decide on the grounds of technical sensibility, however. While the three-wheelers sold extremely well, their four-wheeled brethren met with a good deal of reservation. It was to hand down this fate to its successor, the OE model, and to make things worse, the latter was introduced at an unfavorable period in time.

After the merger in 1926, Daimler and Benz were preoccupied with newly organizing their different business activities. During the later stages, Benz-Sendling had had its tractors built by Komnick in East Prussia, hence the designation BK–B as in Benz diesel engine and K as in Komnick chassis. The OE, by contrast, was to be produced in Stuttgart-Untertürkheim. By the time everything was ready for production, two years had passed and soon afterwards the world economic crisis would reduce customer purchasing power quite severely.

It wasn't exactly easy to achieve success with a new tractor in the German market of the 1920s: as many as 70 companies were competing. The Fordson tractor, built in large quantities and significantly cheaper, threatened to push all others out of the market. When import restrictions could no longer be maintained in 1924, the German government resorted to loans specifically granted to buyers of German products. However, the OE's design was far from an imitation of its American competitor. In Germany, two tractors were capable of holding their own against the Fordson, and these two were produced on assembly lines from the mid-1920s. One was the WD from Hanomag, a direct competitor in the lower weight category, low-priced and with technical improvements. The other was the OE from Mercedes-Benz, which was more like the Bulldog from Lanz.

However, the Bulldog was not powered by a diesel engine but by a hot-bulb heavy-oil engine. The OE largely corresponded to the Bulldog in terms of dimensions, weight, engine output, speed and reduction in the three-speed transmission. Laterally arranged flywheels, with one containing the clutch, as on the Lanz vehicle, also provided for similarity in terms of looks. The OE was far more than just a diesel-engined copy of the Lanz Bulldog. In quite a number of technical features, the tractor broke new ground, thereby contributing significantly toward making farm work easier. The diesel-engined, Benz-Sendling tractor with a single drive wheel–the worlds first diesel tractor–had been such a success that its successor, a much better vehicle in many respects, gave rise to great and perfectly justified hopes. Yet despite customers' positive response, the Mercedes-Benz tractor didn't sell well. Only 888 units of the three-wheeled S7 were sold between 1925 and 1931, and no more than 380 customers had by 1935 opted for the OE from Daimler-Benz. In 1933, when the OE's share in new tractor registrations had reached an all-time low, Daimler-Benz decided to discontinue production. It was after World War II that the company started producing farm tractors again.

The first drafts of an agricultural vehicle, made by Albert Friedrich who had previously been head of Aeroengine Design at Daimler-Benz, date back to the autumn of 1945. Friedrich assembled a committed team of development engineers and won over Messrs. Erhard & Sons in Göppingen, Germany, as development partners. Large-scale production of the Unimog began in 1948 at the mechanical engineering factory of Messrs. Boehringer in Schwäbisch Gmünd. Since high investments had to be made to reach economically viable production volumes, the project was taken over by Daimler-Benz in the autumn of 1950; production in the Gaggenau plant started in 1951.

The Unimog was an unconventional tractor, if you could call it that, but worked well.

An early Unimog poster declaring its multi-functional use as truck and tractor.

The Unimog was certainly adaptable; implements could be attached on the front and back.

A French advertising poster for the Unimog–tractor, transporter and industrial vehicle.

Quite clearly the Unimog is more a truck than a tractor but it was very versatile.

Specifically fitted with crop-spraying equipment, this is a special version Unimog.

The Mercedes-Benz star can clearly be seen. There were attachment points on the front too.

This is the 1600 turbo version of the MB trac, a big four-wheel drive machine.

From 1953, the Unimog was decorated with the Mercedes star and in the same year, a fully enclosed cab complemented the previous version with folding top. A rapid progress in model policy resulted in an anniversary production of the 100,000th Unimog in May 1966. But as successful as the Unimog may have been, it was only rarely used in agriculture. To cover this market segment, Daimler-Benz therefore launched an additional vehicle in 1972: the MB-trac. The new agricultural tractor combined Unimog engineering, including all-wheel drive and power transmission to four equal-sized wheels, with the looks of a tractor–a long and very narrow hood and behind it an angular, high-rising driver's cab. Unlike conventional tractors, however, the cab was located between the axles and fully enclosed– the MB-trac was the car among tractors. Within just a few years, the initial MB-trac 65 and MB-trac 70 (later 700) models developed into a broad series right up to the extremely powerful MB-trac 1500. In spite of this, the MB-trac failed to become a great hit. Daimler-Benz eventually integrated the MB-trac in a joint venture with the agricultural machinery unit of Deutz and production of the MB-trac was discontinued in 1991.

In 1973, the Mercedes-Benz name appeared on tractors again with the MB Trac.

The MB trac had three-point hitches at either end of the machine. The design was sold to Schluter.

Minneapolis-Moline

1926-1969

The Minneapolis-Moline tractor company was created in 1929 through the merger of three companies–the Moline Implement Company, the Minneapolis Threshing Machine Company and the Minneapolis Steel & Machinery Company. All three companies had been around for some time before the merger took place.

Around 1886, Midwest American farmers were calling John Deere plows 'Moline plows', a name that John Deere had used to describe his own implements. Unfortunately there was another local company with a similar name who also wanted to use that name for their product. An outfit by the name of Candee, Swan & Company produced a catalogue in which the non-John Deere products were almost mirrored, model for model and which also included the Deere trademark. This caused some rumblings and great confusion amongst local farmers, who could hardly make out which company's product they were purchasing. Deere took Candee, Swan & Co. to court in 1867, but in

mid 1868, due to financial difficulties, CS&C was bought out and renamed The Moline Plow Company. The case was concluded in November 1869 with a sweeping victory for Deere & Company. Unfortunately, the case was appealed to the Illinois State Supreme Court in 1871 and the initial decision was reversed, which caused Deere a temporary setback but gave The Moline Plow Company a big boost on its way to becoming a major manufacturer. This would not be the last time the two companies would clash; Deere would compete with his rivals in plow and tractor manufacturing also.

Initials and plaque identify this as the Minneapolis Threshing Machine Company tractor.

The 1920s, four-cylinder, Moline Universal, was a successful and very popular plow.

The Twin City model 16-30, a water-cooled, four-cylinder machine that could have been a car.

In 1915 the Moline Plow Company bought out the Universal Tractor Manufacturing Company of Columbus, Ohio with a view to entering the motorised tractor market. The production line for the Universal tractor was moved to Moline, a new building was erected and the tractor was then assembled at the new premises. The Moline Universal tractor, as it became known, was a two-wheel model that was used by the farmer and towed behind his horses. There was also a selection of implements to go with the machine. Most unusual for the period, it had a starter and electric lights and was credited as the first row-crop tractor.

In 1917 a larger tractor was also produced as the Model D, which used a four-cylinder engine supplied by the Root & VanDervoort Engineering Company of Moline. An advanced machine for its time, the company claimed that the Model D would take the place of six horses, but its purchase didn't require replacing every animal-drawn implement a farmer already owned.

After World War I the company was taken over by John N Willys, who continued to produce the Universal tractor into the 1920s. It was during this time that the tractor boom began to subside and Willys sold out to his partners, and the company changed its name to the Moline Implement Company. But times were hard and within a short time it sold the Universal Tractor concern to International Harvester. Now concentrating solely on the implement business the company merged with the Minneapolis Steel & Machinery Company and the Minneapolis Threshing Machine Company

in 1929 to form the Minneapolis-Moline Power Implement Company.

The Minneapolis Threshing Machine Company was founded in Hopkins, Minnesota, by John S McDonald. It was an extension of the Fond du Lac Threshing Machine Company. Initially, in 1887, the company was known for its threshing machines but it also ventured into manufacturing steam traction engines and soon built up a good reputation with the grain-growing farmers of America and Canada too. By 1911, steam traction engines were starting to lose favour to the smaller tractors of the period, and so it was that the company hired Walter I McVicar to design a new tractor for them–the Minneapolis 35-70. This was followed by their 15-30 model and later still came larger machines. But by 1928 the company could see that they couldn't remain competitive on their own and after hearing about the possible merger of the Minneapolis Steel and Machinery Co. with the Moline Implement Company, they decided to see if they too could join the merger. With the offer accepted by the other two, on March 30 1929 the Minneapolis-Moline Power Implement Company was formed.

The third outfit to merge was the Minneapolis Steel and Machinery Company, who were founded in Minneapolis in 1902 by J L Record and Otis Briggs. Their business was to manufacture steel components for the construction industry. It was in 1910 that they instructed the Joy-Wilson Company of Minneapolis to design a tractor for them and which became known as the Twin City 40 model. The largest tractor that Twin City built was the huge 60-90 model,

The logo on the radiator identifies this as a Twin City. It is a model 27-44 from 1928.

A close-up of the engine, showing the exhaust manifold, from a 1928, 27-44 model Twin City.

which weighed in at a staggering fourteen tons. This machine used a massive six-cylinder engine with a capacity of 2,230 cubic inches and was every bit up to the job when it came to working a threshing machine. Its top speed was 2 mph so it wasn't the fastest machine, but was certainly up to matching all the other large vehicles on the market at the time. It also had a smaller sister, the 40-65, which was in fact the second largest machine produced in the Twin City line. Whilst these huge engines were being produced Twin City found that they had a fair success with sales of their vehicles.

Replacing the JT model was the Z, which also acquired streamlining style.

This was the beginning of a successful venture into the tractor manufacturing business and led them to build tractors for other companies, such as the Case Threshing Machine Company and Bull Tractor Company. The company was quick to realise though that the huge machines that were being built were soon to become unpopular and therefore started building smaller, more economical machines, and so a new lightweight series of Twin City tractors was manufactured. Taking more of the traditional tractor shape and with enclosed bodywork, the 16-30 model was one of these machines. It came on the scene in 1917 and used a water-cooled, four-cylinder engine with a capacity of 588 cubic inches, somewhat smaller than the previous giants that were being produced.

Like many companies of this period though, they decided that going it alone was not viable and started negotiations with the Moline Implement Company, and later the Minneapolis Threshing Machine Company of Hopkins, Minnesota, regarding a merger. As we have already mentioned, this merger took place on March 30 1929, and so the Minneapolis-Moline Power Implement Company was now complete.

This was probably not the best time to be involved in farm machinery, in fact not a good time to be in business as the 1930s saw one of the greatest depressions of all time. The three companies had

done well though to amalgamate their strengths and even though things were not good in the agricultural manufacturing market, they still managed to produce some interesting new products. Most of the older tractors from the Minneapolis Threshing Machine Company and the Minneapolis Steel and Machinery Company were either phased out or only lasted for a few more years. The Twin City 17-28 for example,

You could be forgiven for thinking that this is just another truck but in fact it is the Minneapolis UDLX.

The UDLX had an enclosed engine compartment and comfortable cabin.

initially built by the Minneapolis Steel and Machinery Company, lasted until 1935, and the Minneapolis Threshing Machine Company's 17-30, introduced in 1920, managed to struggle through to 1934.

A Minneapolis-Moline Twin City KT (Kombination Tractor) model with four-cylinder engine unit was introduced in 1929, followed by an Orchard model a couple of years later–the main difference being the special wheel arches that covered almost all the rear wheels. For 1934 this model received an upgrade and became the KT-A. The company's first row-crop machine, the Universal 13-25, was introduced in 1931. This too used a four-cylinder engine and lasted until 1934 when the Universal model J was introduced, both being three-wheelers. The year 1935 saw the updating of the FT and MT models–all

received model J was replaced by the model Z, a four-cylinder, water-cooled machine with five-speed transmission, in itself a first. Much emphasis was put on the ability of the farmer to do his own maintenance and so mechanicals were kept as simple as possible and to make visibility better for the operator the top of the tractor bonnet was tapered towards the nose. This allowed better vision of any implements that were fitted to the front of the machine.

For 1938 M-M bought out an extraordinary machine, the UDLX (U-Deluxe) Comfortractor. This was like nothing before and looked more like an ordinary car than a tractor. The bodywork was all enclosed with the entry door at the rear of the cab. It had lights, heater, a radio and even a passenger seat. It used the standard model U, four-cylinder

This Minneapolis-Moline model U came as a conventional rowcrop or standard-tread tractor.

The big four-cylinder GTA was derived from the 1938 GT and remained a top tractor for the company.

The smallest M-M tractor of the late 1930s, this is a model R. It used a 2.7 liter engine.

The Minneapolis-Moline G models were extensive, sold well and lasted through to the 1960s.

of which used the Minneapolis-Moline four-cylinder engine unit – which received an extra A at the end of their designations to denote that. In 1936 the well-

engine and the five-speed transmission had an extra high top gear to allow it to reach a speed of 40 mph. One idea was that the farmer could take his family into the nearest town for a night out. Well, most farmers either didn't want to take their families to town or they just didn't have the money to buy one. Priced at around $2000, it was a huge layout for most farmers of the period, and it seems they just

During both world wars, tractor companies supplied military hardware. This machine was supplied to the US Navy.

couldn't justify that kind of money just to be tucked away in a cab. It was well ahead of its time but production was stopped one year later with only about 150 made.

At the same time that the model U was around, so was the GT, which was made between 1938 and 1941. This used the M-M model LE, four-cylinder engine and was a standard tread machine. With some slight changes this later became the GT-A (distinguishable by its yellow grille – the GT had a red grille) and continued in production through 1947. This same year the GTB was announced and an LPG model followed; the GTC was around between 1951 and 1953.

America entered World War II in 1941 and like all the other tractor concerns, M-M was required to do

Shown here is a Second World War specification model ZTX, used for hauling duties.

its bit for the war effort. It shipped tractor chassis abroad to the Allies, made ammunition, parts for tanks and ships and four different military tractors in two-, four- and six-wheel-drive.

After the war was over, the company introduced new and updated tractors. The U series for example – the UTS was presented in 1948 which had a four-cylinder engine; the much updated UTU row-crop was seen in the same year and lasted until 1955. A

This model UTS has ultra-high clearance, specifically needed for sugarcane cultivation.

Shown here is a standard-tread UTC, which had a water-cooled, four-cylinder engine.

UTC model version was presented in 1954, which was made specifically for sugar cane cultivation. This machine could be distinguished easily as it sat very high and had an arched front axle.

In 1951 M-M bought out the B F Avery Company of Louisville and continued to produce their BF tractor until the mid 1950s. This seemed to fill the small tractor slot for their product line and the Avery model V, a single plough model, helped even further as it was even smaller than the BF; both these tractors used a four-cylinder Hercules engine. Although it seemed like a sensible and good idea at the time, for some reason it didn't work and within a couple of years both models had been dropped.

During the Korean conflict, M-M returned to making military tractors and a new factory was established in Turkey for production of their U series

The smallest post-war Minneapolis-Moline, the model V, was originally an Avery.

No mistaking this tractor make. This is a model G, hitched up to a trailer.

Close-up of the model G engine. A four-cylinder unit designed by the company.

diesel machine. During this period, M-M also introduced their radically new machine known as the Uni-Tractor, a machine that would change the way farmers harvested their crops, or at least that was the idea. It was like an all-in-one tractor that a variety of implements could be attached to. Unfortunately the cost of having to buy all new implements to fit the tractor became a little expensive. The Uni-Tractor was a front wheel drive machine and the single rear wheel steered the vehicle. The operator sat high at the front of the vehicle and had a great view all round. Looking at it from the side it reminds you of the interior workings of a clock with all its belts and pulleys. The design was eventually sold to New Idea, who developed other larger machines from it. For the late 1950s and early 1960s, there were new ideas for everybody and more power was the name

A good view between the operator's seat, showing the controls of the model G.

This is the Minneapolis-Moline 4-Star Super model, which replaced the 445 in 1957.

and 700 range. The company seemed to be concentrating much more on the larger machines and the smaller tractors were being left behind. M-M were now also trading with Massey-Ferguson, who were selling some of the M-M range under their own brand name; the G-vi and G-705 and 6 were given the M-F name and colours. It also worked the other way–some M-F implements were marked with the M-M name.

During the Cold War, M-M returned again to supplying military tractors, aircraft tugs and electronic equipment.

The White Farm organisation, having taken Cockshutt and Oliver under their wing in the 1960s, now saw them also take over M-M.

The next few years were spent producing large

of the game. M-M joined in with power steering, torque amplifier, three-point hitch, live PTO and live multiple hydraulic outlets, which were no longer unusual. The 335, later renamed the Jet Star, and the 445, later renamed the Four Star, shared these additions when launched during this time. The quest for even more power saw ratings rise to the 100hp range, factory front-wheel assist came out in 1962 and a fully articulated four-wheel-drive tractor was presented in 1969. All these were denoted as the 500

Water-cooled, four-cylinder engine of 165 cubic inch capacity, this is the model 335.

All cogs, wheels and belts, this is the Uni-tractor. The need for dedicated implements didn't help sales.

A change of design came in the 1960s. This is the M5 model fitted with Ampli-Torc transmission.

tractors such as the G705 and 706, which eventually became the G1000 row-crop in the mid 1960s. Variations followed and much inter-company brand engineering was carried out. Dealers were even

given Fiat tractors to sell, which were fitted with the M-M name. The first M-M Super Tractor made its debut as the A4T in 1969 and used their own 504 cubic inch engine with ten-speed transmission.

The engine for the M5 was a 336 cubic inch, diesel, four-cylinder unit, producing 58hp.

The M series of tractors had started in 1960 with the M5. This is the M670, still with the same engine.

In the mid 1960s, the ageing Gvi was replaced by the G705 and the four-wheel drive G706.

These were assembled at the White factory and distributed by all three outlets, White, Oliver and M-M, and painted in their relevant colors. Even Fiat tractors were being re-badged and sold by M-M outlets as the G350 and G450 models.

By the mid 1970s, the only real M-M component worth a mention was its big six-cylinder engine, which White exploited as much as possible. It was uprated and uprated and fitted with a new drive-train

to cope with the extra power. By now the M-M name had been relegated to the also-rans. Only once more did it appear when the 1989 American 60 and 80 models were painted in the now dying colours of yellow and white.

After further corporate shuffles, M-M became part of the AGCO family. It is interesting to note that in a previous move, AGCO had purchased New Idea, so the Uni-Tractor system re-joined its parent company once more.

By the time the G900 had come along, Minneapolis-Moline were part of the White organisation.

Clearly an LPG-fuelled model, this is the Minneapolis-Moline 1050, introduced in 1969.

Muir-Hill

1920s-present

In the early 1920s Muir-Hill Service Equipment Ltd was created. In 1931 the name changed to E Boydell and Company Ltd and 1959 saw the company sold to Winget Ltd UK. In 1966 David J B Brown introduced the 101 tractor with its agricultural and industrial applications.

Babcock and Wilcox bought the company in 1968 and changed the name to Muir-Hill Ltd. During the following year the 101 tractor was fitted with a six-cylinder 6.354 litre Perkins engine and became the 110. This tractor was mainly for export but 1969 also saw the introduction of one of the country's most powerful tractors, the 161. Over the next ten years various changes were made incorporating larger engines, cab and fuel capacity modifications.

Finally in 1991 Lloyd Loaders (MH) Ltd UK acquired Muir-Hill from Aveling Barford, and the name still exists to the present day as part of this family-run business.

Following on from the late 1960s 161 model, the 171 was even more powerful.

New Holland

1895-present

The New Holland name has been around for many years but only in 1986 has it been seen on the side of a tractor, and subsequently grown into the brand leader that it is today. Through mergers and acquisitions this giant of a company is now part of the global CNH group.

New Holland has more than 5,000 dealerships and distributors throughout the world and is the leading international brand of agricultural machinery. They

The New Holland series TVT tractors are designed to be both easy to operate and highly productive.

In the cab, the AutoController joystick of the TVT takes just minutes for new users to master.

can offer farmers, anywhere in the world, exactly the right machine needed to cultivate, produce and grow, and along with it a full range of financial and after sales services.

The New Holland tractor range is more than comprehensive and caters for all requirements. It includes a selection of high, medium and low horsepower models, articulated frame tractors, bi-directional tractors, compact tractors for small-scale agriculture, special tractors for narrow, orchard and vineyard applications, crawlers and models created for home use and gardening. One tractor out of five now at work in the world is a New Holland.

Today for example, more than 10,000 New Holland grape harvesters are working in vineyards around the world. New Holland offers grape harvesters to suit any type of vineyard. Building on its great experience and constant research, the multi-purpose models of the SB and VN ranges reflect New Holland's leadership in grape harvesters. To meet the diverse needs of the specialist customer, New Holland also offers the TNN and TNV ranges of compact, narrow-width orchard and vineyard tractors.

New Holland also offers an industry-leading line-up of under 60hp tractors, ideal for homeowners and hobby farmers.

By offering a comprehensive and innovative range

Designed for use in demanding conditions, this is part of the all-purpose Series TKA.

Offering lift heights of 5.9, 6.8 and 8.9m, the LM-A Telehandler range has a model to suit most.

A six cylinder, 8.3 litre engine, powers all Series TG tractors, and features a wastegate turbocharger.

of products and services, to provide farmers with highly effective production tools, they are now the leading brand in the Latin American agricultural machinery market too.

When dealing with so many different crops, harvesting techniques and geographical differences, you have to be a specialist brand to serve all Europe-Africa-Asia region farmers and contractors, and with their extensive dealer network and a full line of products, covering the famous TM tractors, BB balers and CX combines, New Holland is at the forefront in the ever-changing world of agriculture.

Nicholas & Shepard

1848-1929

John Nicholas and David Shepard started building grain threshers in the early 1850s, even though the company had been around since 1848. They were based at Battle Creek, Michigan, USA. Besides threshing machines the company also manufactured steam traction engines, producing the Red River Special series around 1900. In 1911 they produced a prototype tractor and in 1912 the two-cylinder 35-70 was introduced. A model 25-50 was in production until 1927 and an 18-36, later modified to 20-46, was put on the market for 1918. The company supplemented their line of tractors with three others from the John Lauson Company of Wisconsin in 1927. Sadly, Nicholas and Shepard became part of the Oliver Farm Equipment Group in a 1929 merger.

Initially builders of grain threshers, Nicholas and Shepard also produced this 25-50 model tractor.

Normag

1930s-1940s

In the early 1930s, Prof. Dr Karl Glinz incorporated the manufacturing of the small Normag tractor into his Nordhausen hydraulic engineering company in Germany. After he died in 1937 his son Dr. Hans-Karl Glitz became chairman of the board. The Normag tractor business flourished and the company continued to grow until the beginning of World War II. After the war ended, Nordhausen restarted production by manufacturing spare parts for tractors and plant systems for the reconstruction of potash mining operations.

During the post-war years Normag continued to manufacture spare parts and also assemble a small number of tractors.

Normag were mostly involved with making parts for mining equipment but also made this tractor.

At the end of the 1940s the tractor market expanded and in 1952 the headquarters were moved to Velbert/Langenberg. In 1955 Normag returned to its roots by producing spare parts for mining equipment. Since then they have been bearing their old name Schmidt, Kranz & Co.

Nuffield

1945-1967

After World War II, the British Government approached the Nuffield organisation to see if would be interested in building a new wheeled tractor for both the British and world market.

Having moved the Wolseley car production to Cowley in Oxford from the Birmingham plant, space was now available and was soon given the go-ahead for tractor production. A team was gathered together and heading it up were Dr H E Merritt and Claude Culpin, who played a major role in the design of the tractor that would come out of the works–the Nuffield Universal.

It was May of 1946 when the prototype was put through its paces and a further selection of prototypes were made for evaluation in Britain and foreign markets. In December of 1948, after a delay of a year because of a steel shortage, the new tractor was rolled out to the public at the Smithfield show in London. Two versions were available initially, the rowcrop M3 and the M4 utility model.

A farmer seems very happy with his Nuffield Universal model, presented in 1948.

The Universal, as it was known, used a four-cylinder, side-valve TVO, commercial, Morris engine, which produced 38hp. There was a five-speed transmission and a top speed of about 17 mph. The initial price of just under £500 (about $880) was for the basic tractor with no fancy extras. If you wanted, for example, a hydraulic three-point lift and PTO, you would have been asked for an extra £60 (about $100).

Nuffield were not interested in producing their own accessories for their tractor, unlike many of the other

The Nuffield DM44, a tractor made to help feed the British people after World War II.

manufacturers, and so recommended other makes of implements to be used with their machines. These implements would first be tried and tested by the Nuffield technicians prior to recommendation.

Initial sales of the tractor were concentrated in Britain, mainly to help with the post-war shortage of food. Farmers could now acquire a machine that could tackle most farm duties and help with restoring food to people's tables, after the devastation poured on the country during the war. By 1949 though, tractors were also exported through the Morris Motors sales network to countries far and wide.

An Italian advertisement for the Nuffield 4DM, a four-wheel drive machine exported to Italy.

The Smithfield show of 1950 saw an increase of engine choice, with TVO, petrol and even a Perkins diesel version being presented. The Perkins P4 diesel engine was to be replaced in 1954 by a BMC (British Motor Corporation) diesel unit. The sales of tractors using diesel engines caught on rapidly and soon most tractors were being bought with diesel power–by 1955, 95 percent of tractors being bought in Britain were diesel powered.

A new, more economical and slightly more powerful TVO engine was presented in 1953 and the draw bar was repositioned in a more central position to help with better weight distribution. A year later the

Universal 4DN model was introduced with a new BMC four-cylinder diesel engine. During 1956–1957, a company by the name of Roadless Traction Limited, based in Hounslow, produced a half-track conversion of the tractor, known as the Roadless DG general purpose model.

Nuffield tractors used a mix of Perkins and BMC engines. Note the BMC badge on the front of this machine.

A new model, the Universal 3, was presented in 1957, which had a BMC, three-cylinder, diesel engine. By now the DM4 model had become the Universal 4, still available in petrol or TVO versions. By the end of the 1950s the Universal 4 was selling far more units than the 3, and from all the units produced, 80 percent were being exported to nearly 80 different countries around the world.

This is a German poster showing that the Bautz company also sold Nuffield tractors.

For 1961 two further models were introduced to replace the 3 and 4, the 4/60 and the 3/42. These numbers now had a meaning: the 4/60 for example, denoted that the tractor had a four-cylinder engine and produced 60hp, and so on. These were initially made in Birmingham but production was later transferred to a new factory in Bathgate, Scotland. For 1964 these were replaced by the 10/60 and 10/42 models (don't be confused, the ten denotes the new ten-gear transmission) and the following year

Nuffield introduced their new Mini model. This was not a popular machine and by 1968 the engine had been changed and the designation was now 4/24. Two new models, the 4/65 and 3/45 were presented in 1967, but these too were unpopular with farmers and press alike.

By now BMC had been bought out by British Leyland, who said they would keep the Nuffield tractor and name alive. When they introduced their three new tractors in 1969, they were in new two-tone blue colours and had the Leyland name on them; a sudden end had come for the Nuffield tractor.

The Nuffield 10/60 Diesel Tractor, first introduced in 1964 together with its smaller stable-mate the 10/42.

The 10/60 BMC diesel engine. It had four-cylinders and 230 cubic inch capacity.

The front radiator grille of the 10/60, with the BMC engine badge clearly positioned on it.

First produced in 1965, this is the BMC Mini, which was made to compete with the grey Fergie.

The Mini tractor was offered with either a BMC 950cc gasoline or diesel engine and put out a mere 15 bhp.

O

Oliver

1855-1976

It was in 1855 that James Oliver of Mishiwaka, Indiana, USA, patented his Chilled Plow. This was a plow that had a very hard outer skin, enabling it to tackle the hardest of terrain and giving it a longer working life. It wasn't long before this plow became popular with farmers, and manufacturing had to be increased to deal with the demand; Oliver was soon to gain the title of 'Plowmaker for the World'. By the 1920s Oliver started experimenting with his own tractor and produced a machine known as the Oliver Chilled Plow Tractor. About this same time Oliver agreed to a merger with the Hart Parr organisation, who already had a tractor line. So the two companies put their ideas together and started producing a range of new tractors.

The Hart Parr company was formed by Charles Hart and Charles Parr, their company initially known as the Hart-Parr Engine Works, based in Madison, Wisconsin, USA. They relocated to Charles City, Iowa in 1899, and in 1901 they produced their first traction engine. After the death of Charles Parr– Charles Hart had departed the company back in 1917 –the company merged with Oliver to become the Oliver Farm Equipment Company in 1929. Others also joined the group: Nicholas & Shepard and the American Seeding Company. The headquarters were established in Chicago whilst the separate factories remained where they were. This all spelled good news for the farmer as Oliver could now supply not only the tractors but the implements to go with them too. Then in 1944 the Oliver Farm Equipment Company changed its name to the Oliver Corporation.

In this same year they also purchased Cletrac, who had been around since 1916 as the Cleveland Motor Plow Company. It changed its name in 1918 to the Cleveland Tractor Company with Cletrac as the trademark name. The company produced crawlers for the world market and continued to do so until 1960, when Oliver was taken over by the White Motor Corporation.

After the merger of 1929, Oliver concentrated on producing new tractors, and what came out of this was the Oliver Hart-Parr 18-27hp rowcrop machine, in 1930. As with most rowcrop models it had a single front wheel, and the two rear wheels had adjustable track. This was followed by the 22-44hp model A, which was a standard four-wheel machine. With a boost in the power rating, this became the 28-44hp tractor, which was produced to 1937 and was the successor to the Hart-Parr 18-36. It used a four-cylinder, 443 CID, kerosene-burning, valve-in-head

The Oliver rowcrop was the first model to be produced after the amalgamation of the companies.

Another rowcrop machine, the model 70, with Oliver 'tip-toe' steel wheels. Rubber tires were an option.

This is the model 60. Essentially a smaller version of the 70 with a four-cylinder engine.

The Oliver 80 rowcrop tractor appeared in 1937, with a diesel version introduced in 1940.

engine, and was able to pull four or five bottom plows.

It was in 1935 that Oliver moved away from the four-cylinder engine unit, producing a six-cylinder Waukesha engine model 70. The machine sold on its power and speed and certainly looked the part with its long nose, accommodating the water-cooled, 202 cubic inch engine. Although the 70 initially came with a flat radiator at the front, it was given Fleetline styling in 1937 and the smoother rounder lines made it positively good looking. The 70 was produced up to 1948, with the row-crop configuration able to have either dual or single front wheels. The 70 was also available in standard, orchard and industrial configuration. In the USA they were also known as the Oliver 70, painted green with red wheels. In Canada they were painted red with cream coloured wheels and sold under the Cockshutt brand name as the 70.

For 1937 the older four-cylinder models were

The Oliver 90 model was a continuation of the earlier 28-44 series. It also had electric starting.

The Oliver 77 range was introduced in 1948 and this Standard model became very popular.

uprated and given new designations. The 18-28 became the 80 and the 28-44 became the 90. Although these were older models, they became thoroughly reliable workhorses for many farmers. The 80 Standard of 1940 was rated as a three plow machine and was available in both gasoline and kerosene fuelled versions. They used a four forward and one reverse speed transmission and had a top speed of over 5 mph. The model 90 used the familiar four-cylinder, 443 cubic inch engine, with a three-speed transmission. A more powerful model 99 was

A happy farmer on his model 77, depicted in the spring 1952 edition of the Oliver magazine.

introduced in 1937 and gained the distinction of having the longest production run of any Oliver tractor, being produced up to 1957.

For 1940 a miniature version of the 70 was produced, using a water-cooled, four-cylinder engine with four-speed transmission. The 60, as it was designated, was every bit as pretty as its larger stable-mate and filled a valuable model gap. By 1948 the 70 and 80 series tractors were starting to show their age and were replaced by the uprated 77 and 88 models. Although the 77 was uprated, the 88 was a new model, and fitted with the Waukesha six-

Clearly marked on the front of this rowcrop Oliver is the model number 66, introduced in 1949.

cylinder engine. A six-speed transmission was also new–it also had two reverse gears–and it was given the Fleetline styling. A year later, in 1949, the 60 was also given a power increase and was re-designated the 66, in line with the other models.

The biggest machine in the Oliver stable was the model 90 which, like its smaller stable mates, was upgraded to become the 99. Although it still had the

The Super 99, one of the most powerful tractors on the market in 1952. It used a two-stroke engine.

Continuing with the 90 line, this is the 99, which was in production through to 1957.

The Oliver Super 66, diesel version. Note the adjustable track set-up for the front wheels.

A rather drab, late 1960s advertisement for the Oliver tractor company.

The Super 77 came in many different versions. This is the rowcrop set-up with sun canopy.

old four-cylinder engine fitted through to 1952 and had not benefited from Fleetline styling, it did take a fairly major revamp in that year. The Waukesha, six-cylinder, 4.9 litre, diesel engine was fitted for starters and then in 1955 it was designated the Super 99. With this Oliver offered a choice of engines between the Waukesha six-cylinder unit or a General Motors, water-cooled, three-cylinder, supercharged, two-stroke engine.

During the 1950s the 66, 77, and 88 were once again upgraded to become the Super 66, 77 and 88. These

To a David Brown enthusiast, these may look familiar – in fact they are, just repainted in Oliver colours.

models were complemented by two further smaller models, the Super 44 and Super 55. Introduced in 1957,'the Super 44 was made at the Battle Creek plant in Michigan and featured an off-set seating position, therefore giving the operator better visibility of what he was doing. The Super 55 was produced from 1954 through to 1958 and featured a 3-point hitch and a 144 CID, four-cylinder, Oliver engine. As the 1950s came to an end, all these models were re-designated again, this time by adding a zero to the end of their respective numbers, so the 55 became the 550 and so on. There was extra power, slight changes in styling and dual-range transmission–named Power Booster by Oliver–on some models. The 1958 770 was one of these models and so its six forward speeds turned into twelve. The six-cylinder engine was still there but had had a power increase. The 550 had a more powerful engine

fitted and there was also a 100 series, which also had new colours and styling.

Numbers alone don't help with sales and as the late 1950s turned into the early 1960s, Oliver were taken over by White Motors. This wasn't the end of the company though, although actual Oliver tractors were to be few and far between. Now there would be other tractors painted in the Oliver colours; the first of these came from David-Brown, the 500 and 600 models, painted in Oliver green. Two home-made models were seen in the early 1960s, the 1800 and 1900, followed in 1967 by the 2050 and 2150 turbocharged models. The 1965 1250 was a Fiat tractor, badged White-Oliver from 1969. The 1970s saw the 55 series and many of the bigger machines were just repainted Minneapolis Molines. By 1974 the end had come when the last Oliver, a 2255, rolled off the Charles City production line.

This is an Oliver 1855 of the 1970s. It used a water-cooled, six-cylinder engine, producing 99hp.

More powerful than the 1855 was the 1955. Although it had the same engine it produced 108hp.

OTA

1949-1955

In 1949 the small OTA tractor arrived on the market. Weighing only thirteen hundredweight and fitted with the Ford 10 engine, it became one of the most popular small tractors around. The name OTA was derived from the company that manufactured it, Oaktree Appliances of Coventry, England. The small three-wheeler tractor had a high degree of manoeuvrability and was claimed to have a twelve-foot turning circle.

It also had a double reduction gearbox, with six forward ratios and two reverse, giving a top speed of up to 13.4 mph. Despite this, the need for a more powerful tractor became apparent and so the larger Monarch model was introduced in 1951. The Monarch was no match in price or performance against the other machines of the time and Oaktree Appliances withdrew from the market in 1955.

This is the little three-wheeler OTA, manufactured in Coventry, England.

P

Peterbro'

1919-early 1920s

pETERBRo

In the post–World War I years, Peter Brotherhood Ltd built water cooling towers, refrigeration units and ice making machinery. There were also horizontal oil engines and air compressors for fuel injection for marine diesel engines, as well as the famous Peterbro' Tractor.

The tractor was produced in Peterborough, England, in a factory covering sixteen acres. Alongside the production of tractors, the factory was equipped with its own pattern shops, foundries, steel working and heat treating plants. There were also machine tools of the greatest precision, numbering well over 1,000. The makers enjoyed worldwide reputation, extending over many years, for high class workmanship and robust design, resulting in the high degree of mechanical perfection which put the Peterbro' tractor in a class of its own.

It was designed to stand up to the hardest work on land cultivation or haulage, with the minimum of skilled attention and the least possible consumption of fuel and lubricating oil. In competitions open to

It's easy to see from the center-hub of this tractor, why it was called the Peterbro'.

The two main aims of this tractor was its robustness and least possible maintenance to the farmer.

the world, it was awarded the Bronze Medal at the Lincoln Trials in 1920; the Silver Medal at Christchurch, New Zealand in 1922; the First Order of Merit and Gold Medal, New Zealand and South Seas Exhibition in Dunedin 1925-6. It was reputed to be the highest grade tractor of its power band ever built.

Importantly it featured a British high-tension magneto with impulse starting device, that ensured an easy start in all weathers.

The fuel used was paraffin, with gasoline being used only for starting and accordingly it was fitted with a sixteen gallon paraffin tank and a two gallon gas tank.

The Peterbro' was reputed to be the highest grade tractor of its power-band ever built.

Pioneer

1909-1927

Initially called the Pioneer Tractor Company in 1909, it changed name in 1910 to the Pioneer Tractor Manufacturing Company of Winona, Minnesota, USA. They launched their first tractor, the Pioneer 30, that same year. Featuring a four-cylinder, horizontally opposed engine, this machine had removable windows from its enclosed cab.

During 1912 the six-cylinder 45 model was presented, which had three forward gears and speeds ranging from 2 to 6 mph. Following the success of the earlier tractors, Pioneer manufactured the four-cylinder Pioneer Junior, followed by the Pioneer Pony which had a 15-30 horsepower rating.

During 1917 the Pioneer Special, also known as the Winona Special, was manufactured, which was later replaced by the 18-36 model. This model remained in service until the company ceased the tractor business in 1927.

This is the 20-60 model Pioneer. The company ceased trading in tractors in 1927.

Platypus

1950s

British-built in Basildon, Essex, England, in the 1950s, Platypus produced a range of small crawler-tractors. These were mainly powered by diesel engines, although there was also a petrol option. Compact, powerful, rugged build with economical maintenance, was the claim by the manufacturers Rotary Hoes Ltd. With easy maintenance of the steel track by on-site re-pinning and bushing, without special tools, it proved to be very inexpensive to maintain. Track pins and bushes were reversible to give extra life, and the tracks could be disconnected at any link. Thanks to the bellows-type dirt seals, isolation chamber and axial oil seal to the sprocket drive shaft, there was near perfect sealing under all conditions.

Platypus offered several different track options–narrow gauge: 31 inches between track centres with 7 or 8 inch tracks; wide gauge: 46 inch width with 9 or 12 inch tracks; extra wide gauge: 54 inch width with 9 or 12 inch tracks; super extra wide gauge: 54 inch width, 24 inch track. The last of these was given the name Bogmaster, and was adapted specifically for soft ground work–Platypus claiming

A close-up view of the Platypus 30 engine. There was a choice of Perkins diesel or gas.

that it exerted less than 1.3 pounds of ground pressure per square inch. The Platypus machines were mostly powered by Perkins diesel engines, although there was also a gasoline option on the smaller 28 and 30 models, and they used six-speed transmission units. Although the costs of these machines were said to be a lot less than comparable tractors, the crawlers ceased production in 1956.

This Platypus model 30 was one of the smaller crawlers and was available during the 1950s.

R

Ransome

1903-1966

Ransome was among the leaders when tractor development was in its early stages in Great Britain. A prototype tractor with a 20hp engine was built in Ipswich, England, in 1903. It was equipped with a three-ratio gearbox, providing three forward speeds, three in reverse and three speeds on the pulley.

The first commercially successful Ransome tractor was the MG2, announced in 1936, the first of a series

This is the small single-cylinder engine of the Ransome crawler. It didn't need a great deal of power.

Ransome offered a gasoline tractor as early as 1902 but their first dedicated tractor was the MG2 crawler.

of MG mini crawlers which held a small specialised share of the market for some thirty years. These miniature crawler machines were aimed at the market gardener, hence the MG designation. Total production of MG tractors amounted to approximately 15,000, or an average of 500 a year, which included the war years and the post-war period when Ransome made 1,000 tractors a year, at the peak of the MG's popularity.

This Ransome crawler is very small, and was aimed mainly at small farms and market gardeners.

The little tractors were highly unconventional in design—for example, the flywheel incorporated a centrifugal clutch which disengaged when the engine fell below 500 rpm. The drive from the clutch was taken through reduction gears to the two crown-wheels and differential gearing. One crown-wheel produced a forward gear, while the second gave a reverse gear.

In 1949 Ransome produced the MG5 tractor which replaced the MG2 and finally in 1959, the MG6 and MG40.

Ransome of England ceased production of tractors in 1966 and more recently have concentrated on lawn care machinery.

In 1977, Jacobsen, the American mower manufacturer, took over Ransome, and today the name appears on a wide range of mowers, sweepers and compact tractors.

Renault

1898-present

RENAULT Louis Renault was born into a typically bourgeois Parisian family in February 1877. The youngest of five children, he had two sisters and two brothers. His father, Alfred, had built up a comfortable fortune through the sale of fabrics and buttons. At an early age Louis developed an enthusiasm for all things mechanical, including engines and electricity. The Renault family had a second home in Billancourt, very near to Paris, and it was in a garden shed there that the young Louis set up his first workshop.

Renault started making tractors by modifying their World War I FT17 tank. This is the model H1.

At the age of 20 he converted his De Dion-Bouton tricycle into a small, four-wheeled vehicle and added another of his inventions that would soon propel the motor car into a new era–the 'direct drive'–the first gearbox.

It wasn't long before the armor-plating had gone and the first tractor started to take shape. This is the model PE.

On December 24, 1898 Louis made a bet with friends that his vehicle could climb the 13-degree slope of the Rue Lepic in Montmartre. Not only did Louis win his bet, he also pocketed his first 12 firm orders. His career was under way, and a few months later he filed the patent for the direct drive system. It was through racing though that Renault Brothers became known, with Louis and Marcel at the wheel of their vehicles.

In 1909 Fernand died after a long illness and so now Louis was alone, having lost Marcel in a tragic racing accident some years earlier. It was now that

Seen here is a Renault model 781, from the 1980s. The standard engine model produced 75hp.

Another tractor from Renault was this model 421 M from the late 1970s

This is the engine of the 421M. By late 1970, Renault tractors offered a choice of engine ranging from 30-115 hp.

the company was renamed the Louis Renault Automobile Company.

War broke out in 1914 and Renault factories switched from making cars to helping the war effort, producing all kinds of equipment: trucks, ambulances, stretchers and more than 8 million shells.

In 1917, Louis Renault designed the first light armoured tank, the famous FT 17, and it was only a couple of years after this, in 1919, that Renault produced their first tractor; basically this was derived from the FT 17 tank but used for agricultural work. This was followed by a machine which did away with the armour plating, with much reduced weight and increased field maneuvrability. The type HI was shortly followed by the HO type, which was a wheeled version and much more advanced than its predecessors. It weighed 2.1 tons and produced 20hp from its four-cylinder gasoline engine.

Then in 1926 the PE model was presented, which was Renault's first purpose-built wheeled tractor. It used a more efficient 20hp gasoline engine and featured a spring-damped towing hitch. Further improvements were added as the years went on and it was converted to run on air gas, as gasoline prices became more expensive in the 1930s.

Renault had been experimenting with diesel engines since 1929 and in 1933 they introduced the YL tractor. This used a 30 hp diesel engine and featured rubber, agricultural tires. An alternative gasoline engine version was also available, the VY.

At the start of World War II, the company was once again obliged to produce materials for the war effort and although they ceased making tractors, development continued. For 1941 the 301 model was presented with diesel and air gas models soon

Out in the Italian countryside, collecting hay is a Renault 65-34 model of the 1990s.

to follow. The 306 and 307 diesel and gasoline models came next and had an output of 70hp.

In 1947, the company launched the R3040 series, of which a narrow and vineyard version were included. This was the first production tractor to feature a complete electrical system and was the first machine painted in the familiar Renault tractor orange livery. It came with hydraulic lift, position control, second PTO, and variable-track wheels.

The old Renault factory at Billancourt was on an island in the middle of the river Seine where expansion was impossible. So as the 1950s kicked in, Regie Renault, as they were now known, and under state ownership, invested in a factory at Le Mans, with a view to increasing production capacity. The new factory would be well served by rail and would include a foundry, transmission machining and assembly department and final assembly line.

For 1956 a new tractor was introduced, the series D.

Pictured here is a late 1990s Renault model 106-54, which had a 100 hp engine and four-wheel drive.

These had a choice of water or air-cooled diesel engines, differential lock, 540 PTO, hydraulic lift and down-swept exhaust pipe. Development continued with vigour, with the three-point linkage of the N series, whilst at the same time power was steadily increased also. In 1963 the company presented a 55 hp model which featured, for the first time, a twelve-speed gearbox. Just two years later the Super D series was introduced which incorporated all these features along with tracto-control and direct-injection diesel engines. 1967 saw

The Renault Herdsman, with its four-wheel drive is a versatile machine. Originally it used a Deutz engine.

the introduction of the first four-wheel drive tractor, with body-styling made more angular, along with further refinements to the hydraulic system. A year later Renault introduced a specialist vineyard and orchard model for the first time. Great emphasis was now put on improvements for safety and comfort,

The late 1990s also presented the Renault 155.54 tractor model, which used a turbocharged engine.

The Renault Ceres 340X is deep in the mud but the driver is comfortable in his TZ style cab.

for example hydraulic braking and lifting systems, anti-vibration platform and cabin heating. The Renault tractor division was also given its own identity in 1969 when it became Renault Motoculture.

In 1974 they introduced forty new tractors rated between 30 and 115hp. These were equipped with many technological advances such as a shuttle transmission, for easier direction changes, and came in a choice of two- and four-wheel drive versions using MWM series engines. As the 1970s progressed the tractors became more sophisticated. For 1980 Renault Motoculture became Renault Agriculture, with their own unique logo. In 1981 there was not

This is a bird's-eye view inside a 1987 TZ cab. One of the most up-to-date of its time.

only a color change, but speeds were increased and a fully synchronised shuttle reverser was introduced. The new TX style cab was also presented for models between 83 and 135hp, which gave the operator more comfort and better visibility. A passenger seat and roof hatch were also included. For the economy conscious farmer, the TS cab was available which was a basic model cab with no frills.

The Fructus 140 model, designed for farmers working in orchards. It was small and maneuverable.

Designers became more aware of the need for efficiency during the 1980s and so Renault introduced the Eco-Control device. This was a sensor that measured the exhaust gas temperature to determine how well the tractor was performing.

For 1987 all the lower rated tractors were given a facelift and renamed the LS series, whilst the 65 and 75hp models, using Perkins engines, became the SP models. These were followed by the MX and PX tractors, which had revised cab controls and featured a new gearbox and improved steering. From here Renault continued to improve its cabs and cab

The late 1990s saw the Ares series presented, and this one is top of the range, the 935 RZ

Next to the engine, probably the next most important part of the modern tractor is the connection point.

In the spring of 2003, Claas acquired a controlling interest in Renault Agriculture, with a view to increasing that interest in the near future. Tractors now wear the Claas badge and colours, with new machines on the drawing board for the future.

A monster tractor, and it has to be to pull this lot. The Atles is a powerful, top of the range tractor.

controls, making them more user-friendly and giving a smoother ride for the operator.

It was during 1993 that Renault introduced their Ceres tractors, with sloping hoods and a choice of two cabs. The following year an agreement was signed with John Deere for Renault engines to be sold by them and for John Deere to sell Renault tractors. An agreement was also signed with Massey-Ferguson for a joint venture for the design, development and manufacture of drive lines. 1n 1997 the Ares and Cergos tractors made their debut and by 1998 Renault were producing 9,000 tractors per year.

This is the mid-range Renault Cergos 340 model. The modern shape of the nose is evident here.

Equally at home in the fields or around the farmyard, the Temis model has exceptional grip.

The Temis is a mid-size tractor from Renault. Seen here is the 650X used for road haulage duties.

Rock Island

1855-1937

The Rock Island Plow Company of Illinois, USA, was started back in 1855 and made tillage equipment very successfully. In 1914 the successful Rock Island Plow Company arranged to sell Heider tractors, a company based in Carroll, Iowa. Demand was so great that the small Heider factory was overwhelmed, so in 1916 Rock Island bought the whole concern and transferred production to its own plant. They continued to produce Heider tractors but also manufactured the Rock Island F 18-35 model in 1927, which used a Buda, four-cylinder engine. There was also a model G-2, 15-25, which used a Waukesha, four-cylinder engine, which was introduced in 1929. The company continued to produce tractors until 1937 when it was taken over by J I Case.

Rock Island started by making tillage equipment but then sold and made the Heider tractor.

Rushton

1926-1932

The Rushton agricultural tractor was built by Associated Equipment Company (AEC), at their Walthamstow factory, England. George Rushton was determined his tractor would compete with Fordson, and after an unsuccessful prototype, bought a Fordson and proceeded to copy it. Sadly, when the Rushton was made it was heavier and more expensive. The Rushton was one of several tractors that Ferguson considered using for a version of his hydraulic system; this didn't happen though. Both wheeled and crawler types were produced, but unfortunately within a couple of years the project was doomed, partly due to the Great Depression, and in 1932 the company went into receivership. Tractors (London) Ltd did try to revive it for a period, producing Rushtons in small numbers.

George Rushton had hoped he could beat Ford at his own game. Unfortunately he didn't!

S

SAME

1942-present

The SAME (Società Accomandita Motori Endotermici) company was founded in Treviglio, Bergamo, Italy, by Eugenio and Francesco Cassani in 1942. This just happened to be right in the middle of World War II, with hostilities in full swing, during a time when there was an obvious lack of raw materials and very few production facilities available.

By the end of the 1920s Francesco Cassani, with help from his brother Eugenio, huge support from his mother Luigia and many frustrating and sleepless nights, had designed a tractor that was equipped with a diesel oil engine. Unfortunately due to problems with distribution and manufacture, Francesco was beaten to the line by the Americans, who produced their own Caterpillar model 65, the first commercial fuel-oil tractor.

At this time, the tractor market had taken off in Italy and the Italian government, with its fascist regime, launched a competition to find the best Italian tractor. With such illustrious names as Fiat, Landini and Motomeccanica taking part, it was surprising that the little Cassani came out on top. With this a search was started to see who could help to manufacture the machine. One approach came from Breda, but Francesco refused and decided to go with the Barbieri company. Barbieri seemed like a good reliable company, but unfortunately this was not the case. They were already having financial problems and were hoping that the Cassani deal would help to get them out of trouble. Things went from bad to worse and finally after surrendering his share, designs and patents, S A Cassani was saved from going bankrupt, but was dissolved by agreement of the partners.

Francesco was not one to give up and through the 1930s he also designed diesel oil engines for trucks, for boats and for aeroplanes. During this same period, due to the lack of availability, he designed his own injection pump and founded Spica–Società pompe iniezione Cassani–a company that specialized in the manufacture of injection apparatus for diesel engines.

World War II left Italy devastated; both the Allies and the Germans had left behind a country that was so ravaged it struggled to survive. At some stage though, agriculture had to revive itself and Francesco had decided to lend a helping hand. He

The first tractor in the world with a diesel engine. Designed and built by engineer Francesco Cassani.

The SAME DA25 was a modern tractor for its time, it had four-wheel drive and seven gears.

The engine of the DA25, a two-cylinder diesel unit that produced 25 hp.

Seen here in the SAME museum in Italy, is the 240 DT of 1958. A small universal 10 hp tractor.

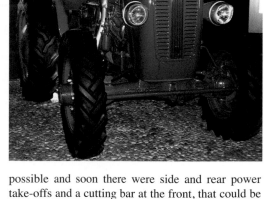

designed a motor-reaper, a sort of tricycle with an 8hp engine. Seen as better than a horse but smaller than a tractor, Cassani had viewed this as a tractor that could be coupled with many different agricultural implements.

After a brief visit to England, Francesco was convinced that the agricultural mechanisation he had seen there should also be happening in Italy. He therefore went about designing a new, economical tractor. So the new machine that bore the name SAME was a 10hp, three-wheel, rather ugly contraption that had a reversible seat, allowing the operator to check the work he was carrying out. Cassani was keen to help the farmer in any way

possible and soon there were side and rear power take-offs and a cutting bar at the front, that could be removed with ease. This became known as the Trattorino universale–an all-purpose small tractor.

Times were hard in Italy though and not too many farmers had the money to spend on new tractors. When they did they would probably buy a machine with a reputable name–Ford, Ferguson, possibly even a Fiat. They were unlikely to go for a home-made tractor of unknown make. Still, Cassani worked hard and used all his cunning and intuition to increase sales.

There was one feature that he saw as a must for his tractor and that was four-wheel drive. He had seen the four-wheel drive American jeeps during the war, tackling the mountainous terrain found in parts of Italy. Now he wanted to adapt his tractor so that it too had four-wheel drive. He felt this would surely put him ahead of his rivals and secure sales of his machines. It was in 1952 that this dream came true in the DA25, and the first diesel four-wheel drive tractor was put on sale. Sales started to pick up when farmers realized how economical and stable these tractors were. Although the factory–based in Via Madreperla–was small, it grew quickly and by 1955 it was selling 1,750 units.

As production increased more space was needed and after an offer from the Caproni company for their factory, Cassani took that over for his new models–the twin-cylinder DA38 and three-cylinder DA47 Supercassani. The Sametto was to follow shortly. Aimed at the farmer who needed an orchard tractor, this machine was the parent of a long and illustrious family.

Produced in 1969, the Minitauro model used a SAME, three-cylinder, 45 hp engine.

A side view of the Minitauro. These machines came in two and four-wheel drive. Production ceased in 1979.

By now SAME were becoming known around the world and the first SAME outlet with the ability to assemble the four-wheel drive tractors was opened in Albertville, France. With this success, Francesco wanted to open a factory in South America but was scuppered at the last moment. On his return journey to Italy he started the designs for his new factory. By 1957, with the factory all finished, production reached 3,000 units, but Francesco wanted more. Another trip to South America in 1959, this time Argentina, was short lived when he received an urgent message that Eugenio had died; he returned to Italy immediately.

With the new factory came further new ideas. New engines were to be designed with more power but

without becoming too large. A compact 'V' configuration engine was developed from existing production line modules. In 1958 the Automatic Linkage Control Unit was fitted to the twin-cylinder 240, soon to be followed by the 360 three-cylinder models.

On March 3 1961, the new Samecar was presented

The SAME Drago, as seen here, was produced in 1972. It used an in-line, six-cylinder engine, producing 98 hp.

and demonstrated to the Agriculture Minister, Mariano Rumor. A kind of dual-purpose machine, it was a tractor with a truck-like cabin at the front. Both narrow versions for the French market and larger versions were designed and manufactured. It was presented with great fanfare and received great publicity. But even with all this it didn't create the sales needed and the vehicles started to pile up in the factory. The idea was sound but the time was wrong. The production line was stopped and the Samecar was forgotten.

As 1965 came around a new machine was born, a 60hp tractor by the name of Centauro. Using a SAME four-cylinder, 3400 cc, air-cooled turbo engine, it had a a maximum output of 55 hp. The transmission had eight forward gears and four reverse. From this tractor came the LEONE 70 and Minotauro 55, two tractors that established the SAME name throughout the world. In 1968 the company launched the Drago 80hp tractor, which used an 'L' series, in-line, six-cylinder engine.

The company was now expanding into Europe, Africa and Australia too. Soon Chinese, Japanese and Cuban representatives were visiting the SAME factory with a view to making purchases. Whilst on his travels in Bolivia, Francesco got his ideas for the new Dinosaur model, which was to use a V8 engine and large proportions. Unfortunately it would never get on the road; after the first ten pre-production

The Delfino model was a small tractor, ideal for working in the mountainous areas of Italy.

The original Explorer 70 model was presented in 1984. Seen here is a more recent, updated model 70.

examples were made, it was abandoned.

It wasn't long after this that Francesco fell ill and it would only be a matter of time before he would no longer head the company. One of his last duties was to see the acquisition of the Lamborghini tractor

concern. After his death a further acquisition was made, when Hurlimann of Switzerland were taken on board. But the good times came to a crushing end with a world agricultural recession between 1973 and 1986. Demand fell and the company started to feel the pinch. There was now a period of managerial change and change again. New working methods, stricter work practice and modernization all helped to keep the company ahead and in good stead for the future. During this period, production did not stop: the Panther model was launched in 1973, which used a five-cylinder engine along with synchronized transmission and hydrostatic steering. Just two years later the Tiger 100 was launched and given 'best tractor in Europe' tag. For 1983 the Laser and Explorer families were launched with their 1000 series engines. The end of the 1980s saw the electronic era begin for SAME, with electronic injection adjustment on 1000 series engines and new electronic control units for the various functions installed on the tractor. The Titan series was launched in 1991 and by 1993 a smaller series of tractors was designed with low power for traditional applications.

The 2005 Argon Classic is a specialist range, which is particularly suitable for row-crop work.

Once rumour was out that Deutz-Fahr was looking for a buyer, SAME, or SLH Group as they were now known, attacked the problem with vigor. After some time an agreement was made and the failing Deutz-Fahr, now a part of the SLH group too, went back into profit in 1998, just two years after its purchase. Today the SAME-Deutz-Fahr group have a selection of tractors to match any company. If the competition that was held by Italy's fascist ministers so many years ago were held again today, SAME would once again be amongst the finalists.

The slimline Dorado S range is intended primarily for use in the narrow rows of vineyards and orchards.

Conceived to keep pace with a rapidly changing farming industry this is the new Krypton F crawler.

The 2005 Silver 85. The engine bonnet tapers down to provide excellent forward visibility in all field and road work.

The SAME Explorer Classic models are a medium-high power range of tractors, ideal on small and medium farms.

The sturdy yet harmonious lines of this Silver model are expressed by none other than Giugiaro.

Aimed at agricultural professionals and contractors, the new Diamond offers high performance and reliability.

The combination of the new Deutz Euro II engine with electronic management makes the Iron very attractive.

Saunderson

1903-1920s

As a youngster, Herbert Saunderson spent time in Canada before returning home and starting an engineering company in Bedfordshire, England. He also acted as an agent for Massey-Harris farm implements.

The first Saunderson tractor was built just after the turn of the century and soon a succession of designs followed. With its 30hp, single-cylinder engine, positioned directly behind the driver, the Saunderson Universal became a popular machine and could carry a two-ton load on its platform and another two tons on its trailer. The 25hp Model G, introduced in 1916 became Britain's best selling tractor. At this time Saunderson was the biggest British tractor manufacturer. The model G was followed by a lightweight model in 1922, which received good reviews. Unfortunately, much like many other companies of the period, Saunderson were not big enough to compete with the likes of Fordson and by 1924 production was stopped and the company ceased manufacturing tractors.

The Saunderson machine was as much a load carrier as a tractor and therefore used for forestry work.

Sawyer Massey

1835-1940s

What became the Sawyer Massey company was founded in Hamilton by John Fisher of New York State, USA, in 1835. Just one year later he produced the first threshing machine in Canada. The company prospered with financial backing from a cousin, who also became a partner in the business, which now took the name Hamilton Agricultural Works. L D Sawyer and his brother Payson, who were expert machinists, joined the company and ended up taking control. When John Fisher died in 1856, the company took the new name of L D Sawyer and Company.

By 1869 the company was selling a multitude of agricultural equipment, from separators and treadmills to mowers, threshing machines and much more.

It was in 1889 that Hart Massey–president of the Massey Harris Company of Toronto–Walter Massey and Chester Massey purchased a 40 percent interest in the company. There was a reorganisation and the company became Sawyer & Massey Company Ltd. All went well for a while but by 1910 differences started to show in choice of product. The Hamilton part of the company were interested in progressing with steam traction, whereas the Masseys were more interested in gas tractors. The Massey contingent withdrew their interests in the company and after another reorganisation it became known as the Sawyer-Massey Company Ltd., with the now familiar circular trademark evident on their machines. Over the next few years different types and sizes of engines appeared with various modifications to their machines.

Just prior to the First World War, Sawyer-Massey put

By 1910 Sawyer-Massey had become one of the biggest steam engine manufacturers in Canada.

The Sawyer-Massey company was based in Hamilton, Canada. This is their 1918 20-40 model.

their hand to producing a gasoline engine tractor. The machine used a steam traction engine, wheels and gearing, on which a four-cylinder engine was mounted, well to the rear of the tractor and rated at 22-45hp. This was soon to be followed by the 30-60 model.

Smaller tractors were also made after the war of 11-22hp and 17-34hp, along with a limited number of 17 and 20hp models. By the mid 1920s gasoline and steam engine tractor production ceased. Construction machinery was taken up, after which the company was bought out by T. A. Russell, President of Willys Overland of Canada. Things went from bad to worse and a small spell making trucks ended with the company closing after World War II.

Sawyer-Massey were a well established producer of steam machinery but also built tractors later.

The Sawyer-Massey 20-40 tractor offered 20hp on the drawbar and 40 hp on the Pulley.

Schluter

1937-1993

It was in the upper Bavarian cathedral city of Freesing, Germany, that the Schluter tractor was born. The initial product of Anton Schluter, the series of DZM tractors were developed through three generations of the Schluter family. Although tractor production started in 1937, the company had been around since 1899, when it was established by Anton Schluter as an independent builder of gasoline and dual-fuel engines. By 1921 they were supplying Schluter diesel engines of between 5 and 300hp, all around the world. It was in 1937 that the first of many tractors were presented. These were 14 and 25hp models. During World War II they produced wood-gas-fired tractors and supplied wood-gas

As time progressed, the little Schluter company attempted to keep up and started producing ever bigger engines.

The Schluter tractor was a product of Anton Schluter, based in Freesing, in Bavaria, Germany.

Powerful little tractors, they were ideal for the small farms scattered around the Bavarian countryside.

electric generator sets of 25 and 50hp. After the war and into the 1950s the range was extended with 30, 45 and 60hp models and by the mid 1960s they were producing machines of 100hp, complete with safety cab. By the late 1960s, even bigger machines were presented and in 1974 the huge 240hp, Trac 2500 TVL and 320hp, Trac 3500 models made their appearance. Four years later the one and only 500hp tractor with a turbocharger and twelve-cylinder engine was introduced.

The 1980s saw a change of direction. There was a need to save energy, and so the machines were scaled down a little.

For 1982 a new series of compact machines were

presented and a new 180hp model with air-cooling and turbo was added, the most modern diesel yet produced by the company. Four-wheel steering and engine management was introduced and a large order of 70 machines was dispatched to Saudi Arabia.

By the end of the 1980s more new Trac models of 140, 170 and 200hp were being introduced, but now with a speed restriction of 50 kp/h, which had been introduced in 1986. Even this did not help the company, who by now were in financial trouble. In

A well-worn Schluter, still in use today. Note the make-shift roll-over protection bars.

1991 the company closed its foundry gates and in 1993 was taken over by the agricultural machinery company of Schoenebeck AG. Schluter was finally closed with spare parts for older models being distributed by Kraus AG.

The Schluter company produced high-powered super tractors in the 1970s and 1980s. This is a diesel model.

SFV/Vierzon

1930s-1960s

Société Française de Matériel Agricole et Industriel, of Vierzon, France, started life back in 1847 making farm machinery; in 1861 they started making steam engines. It was during the 1930s that they built their first tractor, which was powered by a 50-55hp, semi-diesel, hot-bulb engine.

After World War II, the styling was changed slightly and a new model, the 19hp 201, was introduced, again a semi-diesel. There were larger versions too like the 551, which had a massive 991 cubic inch engine capacity, but although these tractors were very reliable, they soon started to look dated and were falling behind the new generation of multi-cylinder machines of the period.

By the late 1950s, J I Case had bought the company and by the early 1960s it had ceased all production of tractors.

Along with several others, SFV also built their own version of the big, single-cylinder diesel tractor.

SOMECA

1952-1960s

The Société de Mecanique de la Seine, was a part of the Simca group and ran their tractor manufacturing section. Simca had started by building Fiat cars under licence, but with their tractor division they decided to buy out a company to join in the now flourishing tractor-market. So in 1952 they purchased the MAP–Manufacture d'Armes de Paris– an existing French tractor maker, to whom they already supplied parts. The first model was the DA50, which used an OM–now part of the Fiat group–diesel, four-cylinder, engine. Further models followed, for example the 55 and the 617/715, all with the Fiat/OM influence. The range was further expanded in the mid 1960s, but it wasn't long before SOMECA was swallowed up by New Holland and Simca was taken over by the Chrysler group.

A pretty little SOMECA tractor. Most of these used the Fiat owned OM diesel engine.

Steiger

1960-present

With over 4,000 acres of farmland to tend to, you need some pretty big machinery and it was this that concerned the Steiger family from Red Lake Falls, Minnesota, USA, when they decided to design a new tractor to cope with this large mass of land.

The Steiger Tractor Company was born in 1957 when John Steiger, along with his two sons Douglas and Maurice, built a tractor in their dairy barn. It was a monster compared to other machines and weighed 15,000 pounds and was powered by a 238hp Detroit Diesel engine; no major manufacturer had anything like this to offer. The machine turned out to be reliable and clocked up many hours of work on the farm, and it wasn't too long before neighbours and friends began to take an interest and want one. The first Steigers made for customers were slightly smaller than the original prototype and had tiller steering. Steiger number 2 was a little more sophisticated and used a modest 100hp Detroit Diesel power unit. A proper steering wheel was added for better control on the 118 hp, 1200 model, launched in 1963. These all had four-wheel drive and used the Steiger patented power splitter, which allowed the chassis to articulate and therefore turn in a much tighter circle. By 1969, 126 tractor units had been made on the Steiger farm.

A consortium of businessmen decided to invest in the concern and soon the company moved from the farm to a disused tank factory in Fargo, North Dakota. This site too soon became too small and new premises were located, where some twenty units were being made every shift. The 1970s would prove to be a boom-time for tractor manufacturers and the Steiger machine was no exception. The Bearcat model was released, using a Caterpillar V8

Seen here at a presentation is the first Steiger, which was built in the Steiger family dairy barn in 1957.

Again in lime green, this is the Steiger Panther 1360 model. It had four-wheel drive, through equal size wheels.

engine and a ten-speed transmission. Then came bigger machines like the Panther ST310 in the late 1970s which used a six-cylinder Cummins diesel, followed by the Panther 3300 with its Detroit Diesel V8, 350hp power unit. The year 1978 saw the Tiger III ST450, with a huge Cummins six-cylinder, turbocharged engine. Steiger were also providing machines to the bigger companies of the day. For example, the Allis Chalmers 440 was a disguised Bearcat and the International Harvester 4366 was also built by Steiger. Back in 1972, IH had bought shares in the Steiger concern and so already had a connection with the company.

From the side it is easy to see how big this machine is. It has an articulated chassis and front mounted diesel engine.

The lime green colour is a regular Steiger colour. This is the Puma 1000 model.

The Panther model – the cab is so high up that special steps had to be incorporated down the side.

The Steiger company grew during the prosperous 1970s but the 1980s were hard for the struggling farm community, and the company fell into financial difficulties. So it was that in 1986, the Tenneco concern, who also owned Case International, took the company over. Steiger built tractors under both brands, and both red and green paint schemes, until 1990 when the green Steiger brand was dropped, although it returned in 1995 on red Case-IH tractors. Today, Steiger lives on in the STX series four-wheel drive tractors from Case IH.

In 1986, Tenneco, who own Case IH, took the Steiger concern over. This is the latest STX model.

The STX model can be supplied in either tracked format or with conventional wheels as seen here.

Steyr

1864-present

Steyr was established in 1864 when Josef Werndl launched his arms factory in Steyr, Austria. It was 1947 when the company moved into serious tractor production with the model 180, which was a water-cooled, two-cylinder, diesel machine producing 26hp. Produced up to 1962, this machine was constructed using common components from the parent company's truck division and went on to sell some 45,000 units. Two years later in 1949 the Steyr 15hp model 80 was introduced, which was a single-cylinder machine. This too sold extremely well with around 65,000 units being bought up to 1966. By now Austrian farmers were demanding more from their tractors and Steyr responded by introducing their Jubilee series in 1964. These had hydraulic draft control, dual speed PTOs, four-wheel drive and were the first to be specifically designed for front loader operation. In 1967 the Plus series came with a choice of two, three and four-cylinder models–the 34hp 430, 40hp 540 and 52hp 650. This family of tractors would go onto sell 110,000 units before being phased out in the 1980s.

The Steyr philosophy was to develop constantly, and in 1972 the Austrian farmer was presented with a transmission that had sixteen forward and six reverse gears. In 1974 the series 80 range of machines was introduced, which ranged from 48 to 165hp and had a unique flat-floor cab allowing the operator to sit more comfortably and for the hand-operated controls

The Steyr 8080 turbo, bio-diesel tractor, which uses a fuel derived from rapeseed oil.

Steyr Profi tractors present a new range of engines to meet specific farming requirements.

to be better positioned. Then in 1975 the Steyr 1400a was introduced, which produced 140hp and was fitted with a turbocharger, powershift transmission, four-wheel drive and fully soundproof cab.

For 1980 Steyr was offering their bi-directional,

An advertisement for the 900 series Steyr tractors. The company was taken over in 1996 by Case.

260hp, 8300 model, whilst their 48hp, three-cylinder, 8055 model and their two four-cylinder models–the 8075 and the 8090–were selling well in their home market.

Two new pieces of gadgetry were added in 1986: SHR–an adjustable electronic hitch control system, and Informat–an electronic management system. 1992 saw the introduction of the 900 series: tractors that offered high PTO outputs and were specifically designed to negotiate the slopes encountered by the Austrian hill farmers. For 1993 the 9100 series and 9000 series tractors were launched and a year later the Miltitrac upgrades took place. These featured sophisticated, multi-speed, PTO controls and state of the art front linkage and PTO mechanisms. The M900 series, when introduced, went from 65 to 75hp, whilst the larger M9000 series was also launched, expanding in 1995 to include 110 to 150hp tractors.

To everyone's surprise, 1996 saw Case IH purchase a controlling interest in Steyr, and with it a huge presence in the Austrian agricultural market. The bonus was the development work that Steyr had been carrying out on their front axle and transmission technology. Case developed a Steyr-designed prototype transmission, which was used in the Steyr CVT and Case IH CVX models, which were made commercially available in 2000. Steyr have always been an advanced and forward-looking company and with Case behind them, they now have stability and a good range of modern tractors.

Every Steyr CVT is powered by a 6.6 litre turbocharged, intercooled, low-emission diesel engine.

Take a seat in the CVT and see the new interior equipment and fittings that offer passenger car standards.

The CVT front axle has independent, single-wheel suspension, offering more safety and driving comfort.

T

TAFE

1961-present

Tractors and Farm Equipment Ltd (TAFE) was established in 1961, in collaboration with Massey Ferguson UK. TAFE's objective was to empower farmers through total farm mechanization by manufacturing a complete range of tractors, implements and accessories. The TAFE range has been developed and improved using the very best in world tractor design and modern technology. TAFE now manufactures over 35,000 tractors per year in the 25-45hp range, in addition to a wide range of accessories. Exports are an important facet of TAFE, with successful forays into the USA, Canada, Sri Lanka, Bangladesh, Turkey and Africa.

The TAFE 35 D1 is an ideal small tractor that can be used by small landowners and market gardeners.

Originally designed for heavy duty farmwork, TAFE tractors are reliable, economical and able to cope with the rigors of the toughest agricultural or horticultural applications. The TAFE range is also ideal for use on smallholdings, golf courses, equestrian centers, forestry, nurseries and caravan parks.

TERRA-GATOR

1963-present

In 1963 the Ag-Chem Equipment Co. Inc., was founded by A E McQuinn. The company began as a distributor of specialised spray equipment and by 1967 had produced their first machine, the HAB-8 hydraulic adjustable bander and broadcast boom. In 1970 a new manufacturing facility opened in Jackson, Minnesota, USA. 1973 saw the first three-wheel applicator with high floating tires—TERRA-GATOR model 1253. The model 2505 followed in 1976, a five-wheel applicator nearly twice the size of the previous model. In 1979 the model 1603 replaced the 1253 and in 1984 their first four-wheel flotation unit, the 1664, was presented.

A close look at the engine tells us that it is a Caterpillar, but exact specifications vary according to requirement.

The 1800 series was introduced in 1989, and just two years later the 400hp 1903 became the biggest and most powerful chassis in their agricultural line. 1987 saw the new generation 8103 model with the Terra-Shift transmission and newly designed cab and 1998 saw the introduction of the four-wheel 8104. The 3104, a severe service, four-wheel machine, with articulated steering, the 10,000th TERRA-GATOR was delivered in September of this year. In 2001 AGCO Corporation purchased Ag-Chem Equipment

Since being taken over by AGCO, the Terra-Gator name has not completely disappeared.

Company, Inc. The 275hp 6103, 300hp 8103 and 400hp 9103 introduced a new level of operator comfort to three-wheel applicators. The four-wheel, two-wheel drive 8104 and four-wheel drive 8144 feature 300hp engines. In 2004 AGCO Application Equipment presented the TerraGator 9203, three-wheeler with 425hp and a 27 ton load-rating, the highest performance applicator on the market.

Is it a truck or is it a tractor? The 1664T was produced by Ag Chem of Holland using many John Deere parts.

Turner

1940s-1957

After World War II, with a great deal of spare capacity around, Turner Manufacturing of Wolverhampton, England, looked towards engine and motor vehicle manufacture.

They produced two engines in 1946, a single cylinder stationary engine and a V twin-cylinder 15hp unit. Two years later they introduced a four-cylinder unit, initially rated at 30hp but increased to 36hp in 1949. During this period there was a lot of interest in agricultural machinery, in particular tractors, and so it was that in 1948 the company developed an agricultural tractor called the Yeoman of England. It used the 60 degree V4 cylinder, 3271cc, 40hp diesel engine, which was built in-house and designed by Freeman Sanders. A large range of accessories was also made available, including ploughs, cultivators, harrows and mowers and a company by the name of Scottish Aviation also manufactured a cab for the tractor.

In 1950 the machine was sent for tests by the NIAE, where several faults became apparent. The radiator was too small to cope with the heat generated when under belt test and overheated. There were also problems with the transmission and steering equipment. These were rectified by the company but when it was put on sale it was more expensive than the Fordson and other similar machines of the period. The tractor gained a seriously bad reputation

and never took off, even though there was a modified series III version. By 1957 Turner had ceased tractor production and later became part of Caterpillar.

Better known for its car production, Turner dabbled in making tractors too. This is the Yeoman of England model.

The Yeoman of England engine, a V4 configuration, 3271cc, producing some 40hp.

Barely making it to production due to so many faults, the Yeoman of England got a bad reputation.

U

Universal

1960s-present

Long Manufacturing Company in Tarboro, North Carolina, USA produced their own first tractor in 1948, the model A, which used a Continental, four-cylinder engine. The Universal tractor that they were associated with was in fact made by Uzina Tractorul Brasov (UTB), in Romania, in Eastern Europe. The semi-complete units were shipped to Long Manufacturing, where final assembly was carried out for the US market. Between the 1960s and 1990s this allowed Long to distribute low-cost Long/Universal tractors with more than a little success. Unfortunately Long didn't survive the agricultural downturn of the 1980s and filed for bankruptcy after running into financial problems. Today Long is back and so are others who are distributing the Universal tractor, in the USA and elsewhere.

The Universal 600, which was made in Romania, then shipped to the USA and assembled there.

Universal Tractors provide a reliable alternative in today's marketplace–all models are powered by water-cooled, direct injection engines, using CAV

licensed fuel systems. The constant mesh, synchronized transmission, provides twelve forward and three reverse speeds, with overlap in the popular work ranges. An optional 8 plus 8 shuttle shift is available for high loader usage. All Universal tractors have pedal-operated differential lock with automatic return to off position, and hydrostatic power-steering provides effortless and precise control at all engine and travel speeds. The independent power take off provides 540 rpm and a category one and two, three-point hitch uses high capacity hydraulic pumps and remote valves as standard. A roll-over protection system, with seat belt, is standard equipment.

The Universal 320 DT is the smallest model in the line and uses a two-cylinder, 32hp, direct fuel injection, diesel engine. The Universal 453 DTP is an ideal machine for small yard work and is equipped with a three-cylinder, 45hp, direct fuel injection diesel engine. This comes in two or four-

This is a 1980s, mid-range Universal 533 DT model, which uses a three-cylinder engine.

wheel drive. At the top end of the line is the Universal 783 DT, a powerful tractor that will tackle lots of jobs around the farm and which uses a four-cylinder, 82hp, turbo charged, direct fuel injection, diesel unit. Again this comes in two- and four-wheel drive and in addition has a cab. Not a staggering selection, but keenly-priced machines that will carry out most duties on a farm.

Ursus

1922-present

Although Zakkladow Mechanicznych (Ursus) did not start building tractors until 1922, it had long been established as a builder of equipment for the food industry. From its Warsaw base in Poland it started producing internal combustion engines and by 1913 this was its core product.

Ursus had been working with a prototype engine for some years before they fitted it to a production tractor in 1922. However this tractor was never produced in any large numbers–in fact only a hundred of these Ursus tractors were made over the next five years, with the company concentrating mainly on producing trucks and buses.

Unfortunately the company went out of business in 1930 but it was then rescued by the Polish government. During the next few years the company made a variety of vehicles and when World War II came around they produced some 700 military tractors. Not until the war was over in 1947 did Ursus start to produce tractors in a big way, initially copying the German Lanz Bulldog, then turning to Zetor of Czechoslovakia for inspiration. This was an alliance that would last over the next decade or so with the two companies sharing many components, although Zetor was the more advanced of the two companies and therefore many more of the main components came out of Czechoslovakia.

The post-Lanz Ursus range of tractors began with the twin-cylinder C325, in 1961, powered by a 111 cubic inch diesel engine that produced 21.7hp at the drawbar and 24.6 PTO hp at the rated 2,000rpm. This machine was later uprated to the 120 cubic inch C335.

In the 1970s Ursus set up a deal with Massey-Ferguson: they would build a series of 38-72hp tractors based on Massey-Ferguson machines. This was a successful partnership partly due to the

The big Ursus 385 was a heavy-duty tractor and was basic but could cope with most loads.

The 1960s C335, took over from where the 1.8 litre, diesel engined C325 left off.

low price of Eastern European tractors, which was always a key selling point. However following the collapse of the Eastern Bloc, Ursus was privatized in 1998.

The year 2005 saw Ursus producing tractors for many different uses, starting with the 3514 model fitted with a three-cylinder engine producing 47hp,

through to the 6014, four-cylinder model that produces 83hp. All these modern tractors are well equipped and can receive a variety of attachments.

Also part of the new model range is this Ursus orchard model. It is slim and has a comfortable cab.

The new generation of Ursus tractors includes this 3514, three-cylinder, 47hp model.

Valmet-Valtra

1951-present

The Valmet 15A was introduced at a time when small tractors were replacing horses as the principal means of power on the farm. The 15A weighed 780 kilograms and was powered by a 15hp, 1.5 litre, four-cylinder gasoline engine, manufactured by the Linnavuori engine factory. Sales got off to a good, profitable start, and September 1954 saw the delivery of the 2000th Valmet tractor. Just as today, users continually requested more power, so the Valmet 20 was introduced in May 1955. Also powered by a gasoline engine, but now producing 22hp, this new model could be fitted with a hydraulic lift linkage. It rapidly became clear, however, that farmers were in need of a medium-heavy diesel tractor. Gustaf av Wrede, Director General of Valmet Oy, initiated the development of what was later known as the Valmet 33. This tractor was designed at the Tourula factories in Jyväskylä under the leadership of Olavi Sipilä, who had also contributed to the design of the smaller Valmet tractors. The new tractor was again powered by an engine from the Linnavuori factory. The impressive diesel-powered Valmet 33 was launched at the Helsinki Messuhalli Fair in November 1956 and in 1958 Valmet began exporting tractors, with 1250 machines going to Brazil and a further 250 to China. Exports to Brazil started promisingly, but almost

Shown here is the popular model 361D, 46 hp model, which was launched in Finland in 1961.

immediately the Brazilian government decided to commence domestic tractor production. Competitive bids were invited and of the ten applicants, six, including Valmet, ultimately commenced production. So in 1960 Valmet established a factory in the town of Mogi das Cruzes, near São Paulo and the first 40hp Valmet 360D tractors were completed

This is the Valmet 565 model with synchromesh transmission. It had a 52hp engine and was launched in 1954.

in December of that year. Initially Valmet did not receive a permit to use its own diesel engines, and as a result early tractors were fitted with MWM power units.

Back in Finland, contractors were demanding tractors with yet more power. Valmet responded in 1964 by launching its largest tractor so far, the 864, fitted with an American power transmission. In the same year Valmet also introduced a pivot steered forestry tractor, which was mostly constructed from Valmet 361D farm tractor components. Owing to a shortage of capacity in the Tourula factories, forest machinery manufacturing was transferred to Tampere.

Olavi Sipilä moved to Tampere at the same time, and Rauno Bergius was assigned product development manager at the Tourula unit. His first design was the Valmet 565, featuring a synchronised transmission. The next issue to be addressed was the tractor cab–a protective frame was soon to become an obligatory feature by law. Introduced in 1967, the Valmet 900 represented a new line of thinking. It was the first tractor with an

The 1967 Valmet 900, had a 90hp engine, an integral cab as standard, and hydrostatic steering system.

integrated safety cab as standard, making the operator's life not only more comfortable but safer too. The gear levers of the synchronised 8F/2R transmission were now located more comfortably on the driver's right side. With tractors now having cabs, a higher assembly area than was available in the Tourula plant was necessary–a new factory would be required. Initially this was to be located near Jyväskylä, but an alternative location was

found 45 kilometres away in Suolahti, where production commenced in September 1969.

In this same year Valmet introduced the turbocharged, 115hp, four-wheel drive 1100. Ergonomic features were further developed and in 1971 the company introduced the Valmet 502, which claimed to have the quietest cab in the world. The

The Valmet 702 S was produced in 1975. It had a 90hp engine and sold extremely well due to its cab.

The odd-looking Valmet synchro used twin clutches: one for the drivetrain and one for the PTO.

This Volvo BM Valmet model was presented in 1985, and soon the company had 25 percent of the Nordic market.

Shown here is the 2005 Valtra HiTech S series tractor taking on plowing duties.

range of ergonomic tractors was complemented with the introduction of the 75hp, 702 and 115hp, 1102. In 1973 Valmet became market leader in Finland and in 1975 introduced the six-wheel, 136hp, 1502. This was not produced in large numbers but it did provide inspiration for a number of other products, including a 3.3 litre engine developed from half of the 6.6 litre power unit. This in turn led to a series of engines with a displacement of 1.1 litres per cylinder.

In 1978 Valmet introduced the four-wheel drive 702-4 and 702S-4, featuring a propeller shaft located within the tractor frame. As a result, the ground clearance was an impressive 47 cm (18 inches).

The Valtra name had been registered back in 1963, and in 1970 it was used to brand a range of implements engineered specifically for operation with Valmet tractors: front loaders, timber cranes and other special machinery. Following negotiations with Valmet, Volvo BM made a strategic decision to cease manufacturing tractors and farm machinery. However, the company wished to remain a component supplier in order to reduce the impact on

For 2005, Valtra has a surprising array of tractor models like this Valtra S model with snow plow and blower.

In 2004 Valtra introduced the Valtra XM series of tractors. This one has a front loader fitted.

employment in Eskilstuna, Sweden. The tractor operations of Volvo BM were transferred to a company called Scantrac, 50 percent of which was owned by Valmet. The design of a new range of tractors designated Volvo BM Valmet had already commenced by the time contracts were signed in September 1979. Valmet was later to become the outright owner of Scantrac.

This is a Valtra from the 2003 season. An M series tractor is seen here using a harrow to make silage.

In May 1982 Valmet introduced the red 04 models, ranging from 49 to 67hp and in June, a completely new 05 line of 65 to 95hp tractors was produced. Production of the new line commenced in Brazil in the mid 1980s and continues today.

in 1983 Volvo BM Valmet tractors became market leaders not only in Finland and Sweden but in all the Nordic countries.

Again for 2004, Valtra were selling the series C tractors, seen here in action with a front loader.

In 1986 Valmet and Steyr-Daimler-Puch AG signed a letter of intent to co-operate on the design and manufacture of a range of engines, and a series of tractors from 90 to 140hp. The project started out well but in 1989, Deutsche Bank, owners of Deutz, and Steyr's owners, Kreditanstalt, required Deutz and Steyr to instigate a co-operative venture, causing Valmet to withdraw. Based on knowledge gained from working with Steyr, Valmet proceeded to develop the Mezzo and Mega ranges. Co-operation with Steyr had produced a number of advanced features and sales of four-cylinder Mezzo tractors, introduced in 1991, and the later 6-cylinder Mega models grew rapidly.

The recession of 1991 and 1992 also hit the world tractor industry. At Valmet, the Brazilian tractor operations and the diesel engine factory located at Nokia, Finland, were merged with their European tractor operations.

In 1993 Valmet became the first tractor manufacturer in the world to obtain ISO 9001 certification. In 1999 the company also received the Finnish quality award. During this turbulent decade ownership

Plenty of clear vision and uncluttered instrumentation, this is the interior of the S series cab.

Sophisticated and high-tech, this is the interior of the cab used by the T and M series tractors.

changed twice. Valmet Oy wished to concentrate on paper manufacturing machinery and general factory automation–and as a result, in 1994 Sisu acquired the tractor division. In 1997 Valmet, as a division of Sisu, became part of the Partek Group.

New millennium models were seen at the Agritechnica exhibition in Hanover in 1999. The introduction of the S series spearheaded future development, incorporating increasingly high levels of information technology.

50th anniversary celebrations were held in 2001 and from the beginning of that year, all tractors carried the Valtra brand name.

The new T series was launched in 2002, the M, XM and C series were introduced in Europe in 2003 and the BF/BL series in Brazil.

The Kone Corporation acquired Partek in 2002, and Valtra Inc became part of the Kone Corporation. Although a temporary arrangement, Valtra was able to enlarge the factory premises in Suolahti during this period. Kone sold Valtra Inc. in June 2003, to the AGCO Corporation and as of January 5 2004, Valtra became part of the AGCO Corporation.

Valtra also have a presence in Brazil. This is the big 8550 model shot during the sugar beet harvest in 2004.

A huge machine, the 2005 Valtra T series tractor with its eight large wheels carries out its seeding duties.

In contrast, this is the little Valtra 3500 vineyard tractor from 1999, seen on its way to the vineyard.

Versatile

1945-present

Peter Pakosh was working at the Massey-Harris works in Canada when he became disenchanted with ideas that were not being taken up by the company and so decided to go his own way. He started a business by the name of Hydraulic Engineering Company, which was started in Toronto, Canada in 1945. Soon after this he invited his brother-in-law, Roy Robinson, to join him as a partner, which he did. The first grain auger to be produced was built in 1946, in the basement of where Peter Pakosh lived and it became successful enough for the new company to start working on a sprayer. The machine they came up with was a very simple design and the local farmers took an instant liking to it, not just because it was a good machine but because it could be repaired with ease, or as they would say with 'bailing wire and spit.' Repairs were costly and time-consuming and to be able to do the work yourself was a bonus. It was this machine that was given the name Versatile.

Following this success came swathers, which were also a great success, and in 1963 the Versatile Manufacturing Company was formed–by now they had made a move to new premises in Winnipeg. Just three years later in 1966 the company presented its first four-wheel drive machine, the D-100, which was powered by a Ford, six-cylinder, diesel engine, which produced 125hp. One hundred of these machines were made before the model was then replaced by the D-145.

The 875 versatile super-tractor had four-wheel drive and articulated chassis. The engine is a 280 hp Cummins unit.

By the late 1960s and early 1970s, Versatile had become the most successful farm equipment manufacturing company in Canada's history, and its explosive growth in the United States would soon propel it into a multi-national player. In 1976 it had four models on show, the 700, 800, 850 and 900, all marked as a Series Two. By 1981 a multi-million dollar plant expansion allowed the company to present nine models, ranging from 71hp through to a huge 470hp. The following year they introduced the bi-directional model, which was shortly followed by

This is a machine that belongs on the huge sprawling farms of Midwest America. This is the huge Versatile 876.

This model 846 Versatile has a Ford badge on the front. They bought the company out in 1986.

Five models make up the new Buhler Versatile four-wheel drive 2000 series.

the D6 tractor. It was now that the Ford tractor division stepped in and bought not only the Sperry New Holland company of Pennsylvania but also Versatile Manufacturing. With this the company became Ford-New Holland. As things progressed, the following years saw more name changes as Fiat bought out the Ford-New Holland outfit, which was cause for further name changes. In the late 1990s, John Buhler, of Buhler Industries, showed a great interest in buying out Versatile from Ford, and after a series of legal encounters of various kinds, he finally acquired the company. It wasn't too long after this that machines were again being made at the plant, in fact in 2001. Initial tractors made were the four-wheel drive machines of 240 and 245hp and the Genesis two-wheel drive tractors of 145 and 210hp, painted in the traditional red and yellow paint scheme.

New Holland TV140 Bi-directional tractor, a productive and versatile 105-PTO horsepower tractor.

The new 2000 series have power ratings from 290 to 425hp and they are all four-wheel drive.

There are four models in the new Versatile Genesis line-up, and all use the Genesis engine in various hp ratings.

Volgograd

1930-present

The first tractor to come off the production line from the Volgograd company was in 1930, and by the time the company was ten years old they had produced 200,000 tractors–over half the tractors sold in the USSR during that period. The company was still known as the Stalingrad Tractor Factory at this time. During World War II, the tractor factory was converted from making tractors to making T34 Russian tanks. It is said that the workers were given basic military training and used to drive the tanks straight off the production line and into battle on the front lines. Tank production continued until the factory was overwhelmed.

After hostilities were ended the factory returned to making tractors and during the Soviet period produced 2.5 million tractors for agricultural use. In post-Soviet times production decreased and hard times hit the factory. Today it still makes tractors and some military equipment too.

Making plenty of dust but not sales, this is a Volgograd tracked vehicle rolling a dusty field.

Volvo

1927-1984

BM·VOLVO Like the Munktell company, Bolinders also devoted time and effort into making a farm tractor very early on. Bolinder only produced one tractor model by themselves before the successful collaboration between them and the Eskilstuna-based Munktells began. Because of the exceptional engines Bolinder had produced over the years, it was natural to incorporate that knowledge and experience into the new company and its products when the two companies merged in 1932.

In the beginning of the 1940s the Volvo product range had extended to include a small agricultural tractor, which was destined to bring Volvo tremendous success in this area. The production of tractors, which took place alongside the car production in Göteborg, went on to expand at such a rate that it completely overshadowed the car sector during 1946.

After World War II, the demand for tractors in farming, in forestry as well as in other applications grew rapidly.

Volvo and Bolinder-Munktell began to collaborate and, eventually, Bolinder-Munktell was acquired by Volvo in 1950 and all production of tractors was transferred to Eskilstuna.

With the development of diesel engines, however, the crude-oil engine went out of date. AB Bolinder-Munktell, the AB Avancemotor company made a

This is the Bolinder-Munktell T55, ploughing in Sweden. It was also marketed in red as the Volvo T55.

By the 1970s, Bolinder-Munktell had joined Volvo and the tractors had new badges.This is the Volvo BM 700.

great many things including one tractor model, and just before that a sort of predecessor to the tractor, which was a motorized plow. After the company was bought by Munktell, tractor production was phased out gradually and halted in 1932, when they concentrated on a diesel engine series of their own. In 1952, a new line of diesel engines was presented consisting of one- two- three- and four-cylinder direct-injection units.

Now with a rapidly growing Volvo as owner, BM took major steps towards becoming a highly industrialized, efficient producer of agriculture, forestry and construction equipment. In 1973 the company changed its name to Volvo BM AB and the products were branded Volvo BM. As a result of declining profitability, the Board decided to phase out tractor manufacture in 1979 and the last agricultural tractor left the company in 1984.

Seen here with its all new, up-to-the-moment cab, is the BM Volvo 650 model from the late 1950s.

The joint venture tractor that bought Volvo and Valment together, this is the 2105 of the mid 1980s.

W

Wagner

1950s-1960s

Wagner Tractor Inc of Portland, Oregon, USA, was conceived in the early 1950s and produced big, four-wheel drive machines. In 1955 three models were presented: the TR6 model used a 302 cubic inch diesel engine, the TR9 had a larger diesel unit of 495 cubic inches and there was a TR-14 model too–again, the diesel engine was even bigger at 672 cubic inches. These were big machines with articulated bodies.

In 1959 John Deere had introduced a four-wheel drive, supertractor, the 8010, which pushed out some 215hp. This was in fact bought in from Wagner but was not a success and many were recalled to the factory after problems with the drive-train. Even after it was updated to the 8020, and modifications made, sales remained poor.

Although the markings on this big machine are that of John Deere, it was in fact a Wagner WA 17.

Wallis

1912-1928

 The Wallis Tractor Company was created in Cleveland, Ohio, USA in 1912 by HM Wallis and friends. As the son-in-law of JI Case he had been involved with the JI Case Plow Works in Racine. The first machine to be produced was the Wallis Bear, which had a rating of 60hp at the belt. Then in 1913 the Wallis company moved to Racine and settled into the JI Case Plow Works premises and within a short time they announced the Wallis Cub, noted to be the first farm tractor with a unit frame design. After the failure of their first tractor, Massey-Harris also distributed this machine. In 1915 the Cub Junior was presented–also designated model J–which used a four-cylinder engine and had a 13-25hp rating. For 1919 Wallis introduced their model K, which was made up to 1922. Again this used a four-cylinder engine and was rated at 15-25hp. This was followed in 1922 by the OK model, which

The oddest looking machine, this is the company's first attempt at making a tractor, named the Wallis Bear.

initially differed little from the K. An orchard model was presented in the early 1920s, which had covered rear wheels, dished front wheels and a re-routed exhaust pipe. More changes took place in 1927, which was when the Wallis 20-30 model was also introduced. The following year the JI Case Plow Works sold out to the Massey-Harris company, which continued to sell tractors with the Wallis name for some time before retiring it to the history books.

White/New Idea

1960s-2002

Of all the Cleveland-based auto manufacturers, the longest-lived company was White Motor, which got its start with steam-powered cars, but became one of the main truck manufacturers in America. In fact the company didn't even start with automobiles, it goes further back still and started in business as a sewing machine maker. It was Thomas White of Massachusetts, USA, who founded the company and moved to Cleveland in 1876. Although better known for their trucks, they decided to enter the tractor business by buying up companies that were struggling to stay afloat in the 1960s. There was no shortage of ailing companies and in 1960 they bought Oliver, but continued to produce the successful and popular Oliver 55 models throughout the decade. Oliver had been in business since 1929 when it too had come about as a result of combining

Seen here is the front-end of the Wallis 23-30 of 1927, which was an uprated model 20-30.

This is the Wallis 20-30 model. Not long after this was introduced, the company sold out to Massey-Harris.

several small companies. White purchased the Cockshutt Farm Equipment Company in 1962; this company's history stretched back to 1839. In more recent times Cockshutt manufactured tractors such as the model 20, introduced in 1952 and which used a Continental L-head 140 cubic inch, four-cylinder engine with a four-speed transmission. There was also the model 40, a six-cylinder, six-speed tractor. Following these acquisitions, White acquired Minneapolis-Moline a year later. The brand names of all three companies were retained by White until as late as 1969, when the entire company was restructured as the White Farm Equipment Company with headquarters in Oak Brook, Illinois. The parent company, White Motor Corporation's headquarters remained in Cleveland, Ohio.

By now the merged companies were mixing and matching components, which obviously made economic sense but aggravated tractor enthusiasts. It was in 1974 that finally all machines used the White name although most were still being produced in their respective factories and still using their own components.

This is the four-wheel drive Plainsman. Sold as a White in Canada but as a Minneapolis-Moline in the USA.

When White took over Minneapolis-Moline, things started to get confusing, as can be seen on the badges here.

The big 2-70 Field Boss was a six-cylinder tractor. This gasoline model was now losing out to all the diesel models.

The White replacement for the mid-range Oliver tractor was the 2-60. This though, was only a Fiat in disguise.

The White 2-60 was produced in 1974 and had a water-cooled, four-cylinder engine.

The first articulated, four-wheel drive tractors of the White brand name were presented in 1969. This new 139hp machine, shared by all three companies, was known as the Oliver 2455, the Minneapolis-Moline A4T-1400 and the White Plainsman A4T-1600. The following year the company introduced the 6 series Oliver 2655 and Minneapolis-Moline A4T-1600: all used a 585 cubic inch engine, rated at 169hp.

In 1974 White consolidated Oliver, Minneapolis-Moline and Plainsman into a newly designed 150hp, four-wheel drive machine. The White advertising stated 'like nothing you've ever seen before.' The new White 4-150 Field Boss was powered by a

The White 4-150 was introduced in 1974. The 4 denotes the number of wheels, and the 150 relates to the horsepower.

Another view of the 4-150. The long nose houses a water-cooled, V8, 636 cubic inch engine.

Caterpillar V8 engine and was improved to allow for a tighter turning circle. The White 'Boss' line styling and silver charcoal gray color replaced the clover green, prairie gold and white sumac red of the older models. In 1975 it was joined by the 180hp 4-180 Field Boss, a new powerful four-wheel drive machine that offered air conditioning, heater, and a protective roll-over cab. In 1978, the 210hp, 4-210 joined the Boss line and its cab included the latest improvements such as reduced sound level. The dashboard had a 14 channel monitoring display and night visibility was improved with the addition of two headlights placed on top of the grille.

As all this progress was being made, the company found itself sinking deeper into financial problems and in 1976 White Motor Corporation and Consolidated Industries planned to merge. Unfortunately the plans didn't work out and the future of White Motors was left in doubt, with speculation running high that they would sell off

their farm equipment division. In 1977, Consolidated Freightways Incorporated took on the distribution of the Freightliner trucks and White lost forty percent of its truck sales. By 1980 White had run out of cash and was obliged to file for bankruptcy. Then in the November, they announced that they were going to sell the farm equipment line to TIC Investment Corporation of Dallas, Texas, who resumed production the following year under the name of WFE–White Farm Equipment.

In 1982, WFE informed its dealers that two new four-wheel drive models were on the way.

Seen on the side of this model is the new White logo. WFE stood for White Farm Equipment and this is the 2-180.

This is the rocker cover of the 181 hp, V8 engine fitted to the White 4-150.

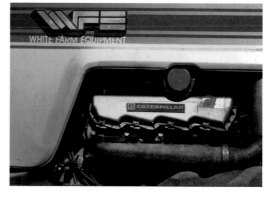

One of the new tractors included the 225hp 4-225, which replaced the 4-175 and 4-210, but its styling and configuration were very similar. The wheel tread was adjustable and the machine could be used for row crop work. The other machine, the 4-270, had bigger tyres and a larger articulated frame, which included a wider bonnet and larger grille. These still used the Caterpillar V8 engine and whilst the 4-225 used the same transmission as the past Field Boss models, the 4-270 used a new 4x4 power

This is the WFE 4-225, introduced in 1984. By then the company was under the Texas Investment ownership.

transmission. The WFE products were made between 1982 through to 1988, when once again the line found itself in financial problems. TIC off-loaded the division to Allied Products, who already owned the New Idea Equipment line, and the company became known as White-New Idea. Big changes took place with five tractors being introduced, engine power ranging from 94-188hp. The power units were CDC diesel, a joint venture between Case and Cummins.

Of the two new 'American' models the 60 was the smallest, and it was the smallest tractor being made in the USA.

The 'American' models came in during 1989 and consisted of the 60hp 60 and the 80hp 80.

AGCO was a fast-growing company that had been developed by the ex-executives of the former Allis Chalmers company. They had taken over the US division of Deutz-Allis and had now purchased the White and Hesston brands before also taking over the Massey-Ferguson concern in 1993. What they lacked was a good four-wheel drive machine for their large tractor line. The McConnell-Marc, originally a Massey-Ferguson design, was a good starter and so it was moved to the AGCO/White Cold Water, Ohio tractor plant for production. Once

Although the biggest tractors were being made in the USA, smaller ones, like this Lamborghini based 6105 was not.

Z

Zetor

1945-present

Unlike many Eastern European tractors, the Zetor is in fact a well-made, reliable and low cost machine. The company was founded in the town of Brno, in the Czech Republic, just after World War II. Prior to the war it had been owned by the Brno Arms Company, and during the war was required to manufacture vast amounts of munitions for the German military. The factory was hit by Allied bombing in 1944 and completely destroyed.

As the war came to a close, the staff got together and planned a tractor that could be built as soon as hostilities had ceased. The prototype was completed and by 1946 they started the production of the Zetor model 25 tractor. Zetor were well ahead of the game and the workers had gained experience with diesel engines during the war. They had built a diesel engine for aircraft and now they transferred that knowledge to tractor engine production. The model 25hp used a twin-cylinder, diesel engine and had a six forward and two reverse-speed transmission, also well advanced for the time. The successful 25hp model was followed by yet another success, the 30hp model, and this time there was a four-cylinder engine. The company continued to produce well constructed modern machines and in the 1960s presented a model range with two-, three- and four-cylinder diesel engines with ten-speed transmission.

This White model 6065 is also a Lamborghini in disguise, with the last two numbers relating to the power output.

installed it was fine-tuned and kitted-out with the latest gadgetry, given the name AGCO-Star and introduced in 1994. There was a choice of engines–Detroit Diesel or Cummins–so the 425hp 8425 and 360hp 8360 machines were sold during 1995 through the AGCO-White and AGCO-Allis dealerships. To keep everybody happy, the machines were painted in the White colours, white and silver, and carried an orange Allis badge. In 2001 AGCO acquired the Caterpillar Challenger tracked vehicle line and the large four-wheel drive AGCO-Star models were soon pensioned off.

During the early 1960s, Zetor presented a new range of engines. The is a 1968 diesel engine of the 3045.

Zetor tractors were simple and rugged and gained a good reputation. This is a 1960s 3546 model.

A typical British scene. This is a Zetor 7540 transporting manure on a farm in Cornwall.

The 2005 Forterra models have 24 x 18, three-speed Powershift transmission, with forward synchro-shuttle.

They had factory-built cabs from early on, and mechanical front-wheel drive (MFWD) also. Due to their low cost, Zetor tractors were exported through out the world, being licensed for production in India and Iraq in the 1950s and 1960s.

The 1970s continued well for the company until, like so many others that got caught up with the collapse of the Eastern Bloc in 1990, the future seemed suddenly uncertain. It reached an agreement with John Deere to produce some low-cost machinery after this and has survived to today, when it is truly a major player, not just in the Czech Republic but around the world.

Zetor is the leading tractor producer within the new EU member countries and one of the leading employers in the Brno region. The decision to adopt the concept of

'Zetor New' was only taken in September 2004 and its implementation has taken just nine months. Investment over this period totals 75 million Czech crowns (over $3 million) and Zetor expects a return on this within a short time frame. The Brno site has been changed substantially and some production facilities have been relocated as part of the program. The manufacturing site is more compact with straightforward logistics, ideal for the production of 10,000-15,000 tractors a year. Current machines include the Standard 4WD, 25 mph (40 kph) specification Proxima, a four-cylinder, turbo engine model with a ten forward and two reverse gear transmission, or optional 12x12 mechanical shuttle. The Forterra, four-wheel drive models–99, 109 and 116hp, four-cylinder Turbo, and 126hp six-cylinder Turbo.

The Zetor 2005 Proxima range have four- and two-wheel drive models, ranging from 68 to 88hp.

The Forterra models have a choice of four and six-cylinder turbo engines, with intercooling.

Acknowledgements

The Author would like to thank the following people and organizations for their help and contribution:

Andrew Morland Collection – without this extraordinary collection of tractor pictures, this book would never have been completed.

Wisconsin Historical Society, Wisconsin, USA. – for supplying the International Harvester historical pictures.

Paul Sharp (sharpo@sharpos-world.co.uk) photo collection.

North Dakota State University, Fargo, ND, USA.

Pictures on pages 46 and 54 are reprinted courtesy of Caterpillar Inc.

Rich Adams – www.SilverKingTractors.com

Rick Guy for his help with Gray Dort.

K R Hough – for providing his Huber pictures.

John Deere for providing the pictures on pages: 140, 141, 142 and 143 (top).

JCA, Suffolk, England, for providing the latest Steyr pictures.

AGCO; Case IH; Caterpillar Inc; Claas UK; Fendt; Ford Photographic Library, Warley, UK; J C Bamford Excavators Ltd., Rocester, UK; Kubota UK; Landini SpA; Massey-Ferguson UK; SAME; Terex, Coventry, UK; McCormick Tractors Int. Ltd., Doncaster, UK; Daimler-Chrysler, Stuttgart, Germany; New Holland UK; Ursus tractors UK; Valtra; Zetor, Norfolk,